Call to Worship

LITURGY, MUSIC, PREACHING & THE ARTS

Continuing the tradition of
Reformed Liturgy & Music

Published by the Office of Theology and Worship,
Presbyterian Church (U.S.A.), in Association with Geneva Press.
The official journal of the Presbyterian Association of Musicians.

Call to Worship

VOLUME 36.1
2002–2003

LITURGY, MUSIC, PREACHING & THE ARTS

Call to Worship

LITURGY, MUSIC, PREACHING & THE ARTS

Continuing the tradition of *Reformed Liturgy & Music* (1971–2000) and *Reformed Liturgics* (1963–69), *Call to Worship* seeks to further the church's commitment to theological integrity, corporate worship, and excellence in music, preaching, and other liturgical art forms.

Editor: Theodore A. Gill Jr.
Interior design by Rohani Design
Cover design by Night & Day Design

Congregational Ministries Division,
Presbyterian Church (U.S.A.)
Lynn E. Shurley, Chair
Donald G. Campbell, Director

Office of Theology and Worship
Joseph D. Small III, Coordinator

Presbyterian Association of Musicians
PAM National Office,
100 Witherspoon Street
Louisville, KY 40202-1396
Phone: 502-569-5288
Fax: 502-569-8465
Web: http://www.pam.pcusa.org
Alan Barthel, Executive Director,
abarthel@ctr.pcusa.org
Creston Parker, Administrative Assistant,
pam@ctr.pcusa.org

PAM Board, 2002
David Eicher, President
Craig Dobbins, President-elect
Mary Jane Cooper, Secretary
Kenneth Carter, Treasurer
Mary Ann Glover
John Horman
Mary Beth Jones
David VanderMeer
Linda Loving
Sally Gant
Brock Downward, CCM

© 2002 Office of Theology and Worship,
Presbyterian Church (U.S.A.) and Geneva Press

ISBN 0-664-50243-1
ISSN 1534-8318

Supplemental lectionary aids and prayers may be reproduced in church bulletins for one-time use without written permission.

Scripture quotations from the New Revised Standard Version of the Bible are copyright © 1989 by the Division of Christian Education of the National Council of the Churches of Christ in the U.S.A. and are used by permission.

Indexed with abstract in Religion Index One: Periodicals, American Theological Library Association; available online through BRS (Bibliographic Retrieval Services) and DIALOG; by Music Article Guide and by Religious and Theological Abstracts. This publication is available in microfilm from ProQuest.

Address editorial correspondence, materials for review, and unsolicited manuscripts to
Editor, *Call to Worship*
100 Witherspoon Street, Room 2616
Louisville, KY 40202-1396
Phone: 502-569-5311
Fax: 502-569-5501

Address advertising correspondence to
Bill Falvey
100 Witherspoon Street
Louisville, KY 40202-1396
Phone: 502-569-5085
E-mail: Bfalvey@presbypub.com

Send change of address and subscription requests to
Presbyterian Publishing Corp.
Attn: *Call to Worship* Customer Service
100 Witherspoon Street
Louisville, KY 40202-1396
Phone: 1-800-227-2872

Introduction

C ome, *Let Us Worship* is a new and exciting resource for congregations, published just as this issue of *Call to Worship* was being completed. It is unfortunate that its appearance came too late to allow systematic application of its resources to the lectionary aids later in this volume, but this will doubtless be remedied in future sets of hymn suggestions and other liturgical help.

The purpose of *Come, Let Us Worship* is summarized in its subtitle: *The Korean-English Presbyterian Hymnal and Service Book*. Produced in late 2001 by Geneva Press in Louisville, Kentucky, this hymnal was a joint project undertaken in close cooperation with the United Methodist Publishing House in Nashville. While the Methodist edition bears the same title, its subtitle is *The Korean-English United Methodist Hymnal*. The selection of hymns is identical in both versions.

The difference between the Presbyterian and Methodist editions lies in the service books that appear before the hymns and in the addition of a new Korean-English psalter at the close of the Presbyterian volume. These worship materials reflect years of intelligent and energetic work by a series of committees that have brought this project to fruition; the Presbyterian Church (U.S.A.) is especially grateful for the leadership of Paul Huh, Seung Nam Kim, Sun Bai Kim, and Boston University professor Horace T. Allen Jr.

Horace Allen explains the layout of the service book and psalter, and its significance for bilingual congregations, in this passage from his introduction:

The format of this new book uses two printing devices to make possible bilingual worship which is simultaneous rather than alternate, sequential, or translated. These devices have been tested at the "Korean Conferences on Worship & Music." The first device is to print the liturgical texts on facing pages, Korean and English in parallel columns. [This is not the practice, unfortunately, in the Methodist edition. *Ed.*] The second is to print these texts in what have come to be known as "sense lines" rather than "run-on lines," left to right margins. This allows the unison or responsive portions to be said simultaneously, and provides the texts being spoken by a leader of worship with an immediate, printed translation across the page. All that is required of the congregation is that the two linguistic groups pay attention to the pace and phrasing for each other (perhaps a novel interpretation of St. Paul's injunction to "wait for one another"—1 Cor. 11:33).

In those congregations where the new hymnal has been tried, it has been received with enthusiasm. Although much of the music is from Korean and Western sources, there is a good representation of music from countries and cultures around the world, often referred to as "global music."

Churches with multiple generations of Korean-American or a multicultural mix of Korean-speaking and English-speaking worshipers will be enriched by an acquaintance with *Come, Let Us Worship: The Korean-English Presbyterian Hymnal and Service Book* (Louisville, Ky.: Geneva Press, 2001).

THEODORE A. GILL JR.

Part One

Worship in the Life of the Church Today

Undivided Energies

Encountering the Trinity in Thought, Prayer, and Praise

BY BRIAN A. WREN

This article is based on Brian Wren's inaugural address as the John and Miriam Conant Professor of Worship at Columbia Theological Seminary, Decatur, Georgia, on Tuesday, March 27, 2001.

A funny thing happened to the doctrine of the Trinity on the way to the twenty-first century. For four hundred years, it was a developing, radically new understanding of God.

Then, in succeeding centuries, it became more and more abstruse and abstract: important, but less and less connected to piety, liturgy, and life.

Since the middle of the twentieth century, however, this neglected doctrine has become increasingly important, at least among theologians.

The doctrine of the Trinity has become a focus of encounter between Eastern and Western theology; a focus of conflict between white, male, Western theology and its feminist, womanist, mujerista, Asian, African, African American, and Latin American critics; and a focus of theological exploration worldwide—at least among theologians.

Amid all the controversies, there is wide agreement that to speak of the Trinity does not mean adding another topic to our understanding of creation, redemption, sin, salvation, and eschatology. Instead, "Trinity discourse relates to the shape and structure of the whole framework of Christian doctrine and therefore cannot be presented as one doctrine within that framework."[1]

Trinitarian doctrine, then, is central to the meaning of Christian faith. However, the energetic explorations of theologians have had little effect on the way churches worship, witness, organize their polities, think, and speak about God.

The doctrine of the Trinity is still widely perceived as unnecessary and unintelligible. At an abstract level it may be true, but so what? At the everyday level, it is nonfunctional. It is central to the meaning of Christian faith, but marginal to the practice of Christian faith.

In the liturgical year, the Trinity gets one Sunday, at the beginning of the holiday season. For most congregations, celebrating the One in Three means, at most, one Sunday, one sermon, and one doxology.

I believe that the doctrine of the Trinity has practical consequences for Christian living. To make my case, I must summarize why it matters. Then, because worship is my particular interest, I shall try to show how Trinitarian faith might affect the practice of public worship, especially Reformed worship.[2] Because we are speaking of the Trinity, I hope we may praise that of which we speak. In worship, we could do so with drama, instrumental music, the visual environment, and song. In a written presentation, poems and hymn lyrics must suffice.

"NEVER DISTANT OR ALONE"

Imagine a spaceship from Earth approaching a newly discovered planet. As it goes into orbit, its crew members are excited to find that their scanners are picking up a vast array of data showing that the planet teems with sentient, intelligent life.

Descending to the surface, they find oceans and continents, and colorful shapes that grow and change with every passing day. There are three-dimensional mathematical equations, and what look like artistic works of great beauty, but no sign of the species their scanners have detected. Yet strange events occur. They sleep, and wake to find rock formations in replicas of themselves, and fragments of bridges, highways, and buildings, in a parody of their memories of home.

Eventually, back on board their ship, the crew members stumble on the truth. All the signals of intelligence and creativity are coming not from intelligent species but from the planet itself. Somehow, over eons of time, the entire planet has become one sentient, creative being.

In a nutshell, this is the plot of Stanislaw Lem's novel, *Solaris*.

Imagine a mind whose neurons form a web spanning seas and continents. Its intelligence is astounding. Its creativity is immense.

But something is missing.

Over many earth days and weeks, the crew of the spaceship tries to communicate with this unique, planetary mind, this "Solaris." They send mathematical formulas on radio waves of all frequencies. They build molecular structures on the

Trinitarian doctrine, then, is central to the meaning of Christian faith.

surface. They use laser beams, electromagnetic pulses, and a hundred other methods of communication.

Nothing succeeds. The planet is simply not aware of them. It has never known anything other than itself. It cannot recognize another form of intelligent life.

Compared with any human being, Solaris is a godlike intelligence. Within itself, on its surface, it creates shapes and forms of beauty and complexity. But it is a unique, enclosed, and isolated being. It has never known anything like itself, or anything other than itself. So it cogitates and ponders and creates, within itself. It knows no other. It can conceive of no other. It needs no other. It will never know that we exist.

If I may use Stanislaw Lem's story as a negative parable, several of the world's religious faiths have always known that God is *not* Solaris. Christians, Jews, and Muslims do not worship a Solarian God, even though some Christian thinking gets dangerously close to such a conception.

For all the differences between Muslim, Christian, and Jew, our common experience of the Divine is that God creates beyond God's own interiority, that God wishes to have a relationship with creation, and that God creates sentient, self-aware beings who can be in a relationship with God and who, themselves, on a smaller scale, can create.

PRIMAL EXPERIENCE

Trinitarian theology is the Christian map of that awareness. It springs, not from speculation, but from history. To summarize things already well known, the earliest Christians had three distinct experiences of the Divine, which they narrated, praised, and remembered.

For many, perhaps, the first distinct experience was of the Spirit of God, the Spirit of the risen Christ: in baptism, ecstatic worship, barrier-breaking experiences of community, and the discovery of unexpected gifts. The Spirit of the Living God, who in the past came only on leaders and prophets, was now being poured out on all flesh: old and young, women and men, slaves and free citizens.

Closely associated with the experience of the Spirit, yet distinct from it, was the collective memory of Jesus of Nazareth, who had announced God's new world order, demonstrated it in his life, trusted God through betrayal and crucifixion to the point of death, had been raised from the dead, and was (is) alive among his disciples.

And all this came from the original experience of the God of Israel, who had freed Pharaoh's slaves, kept covenant with the chosen people, defended the outcast and oppressed, and created the universe by speaking a word.

New Testament voices habitually speak in terms of three experiences of one God. Here are some examples (emphasis mine):

"I bow my knees before *the Father*," says the writer of Ephesians. "I pray that . . . you may be strengthened in your inner being with power through *his Spirit*, and that *Christ* may dwell in your hearts through faith" (Eph. 3:14–19).

"As *the Father* has sent me, so I send you," says the *risen Christ* to the disciples. "When he had said this he breathed on them and said, 'Receive the *Holy Spirit*'" (John 20:21–22).

At Pentecost, Peter proclaims the message: "This *Jesus* God raised up, and of that all of us are witnesses. Being therefore exalted *at the right hand of God*, and having received *from the Father* the promise of the *Holy Spirit*, he has poured out this that you both see and hear" (Acts 2:32–33).

And Paul says to the Christians in Corinth: "The grace of the *Lord Jesus Christ*, the love of *God*, and the communion of *the Holy Spirit* be with all of you" (2 Cor. 13:13).

The biblical record does not discuss how the three experiences of divinity are related. In post-biblical times, obvious questions arose. Is one in authority over another? Is one lesser and another greater? Is one truly God, and the others, as it were, secondary expressions of God?

Such questions matter to us. Not only because we thirst to know God, but because the way God is, is the way we are called to be and become. To take one example, if God has an internal monarchy, then perhaps our churches and societies ought to be hierarchically organized, to reflect the nature of God. And if not, not!

FOUNDING METAPHORS

From early times, Trinitarian thinking focused around three "labels," Father, Son, and Holy Spirit (capitalized when they refer to the persons of the Triune God). We can summarize the discoveries of early Trinitarian thought if we look briefly at the two linguistically inseparable labels that received most attention: *father* and *son*.

I use the word *label* because, as Gail Ramshaw puts it, "Early theologians speak as if Father, Son, and Holy spirit are labels rather than images, claiming that God comes with the biblical name Father . . . not that God acts like a father." [3]

Ramshaw's point is important, but needs to be qualified. Though the best early thinkers knew what some later theologians forgot, that God as *father* is beyond gender, not a male or masculine deity who vindicates patriarchal authority, when these same thinkers use the words *father* and *son* they unavoidably do so with reference, even if only a negative reference, to their common social meanings.

Thus, a linguist who looks at these words will describe them as metaphor. By *metaphor* I do not mean ornamental speech that can be discarded, nor do I mean pictorial illustrations to help the ignorant get the benefit of higher thought. I mean by "metaphor" a particular use (or *trope*) of language, not disposable, and not easily exchangeable, that appeals to both intellect and imagination, and can sometimes gain

The biblical record does not discuss how the three experiences of divinity are related. In post-biblical times, obvious questions arose.

knowledge not otherwise obtainable.

Whatever you may think of its revelatory status, the metaphor of *father and son* is drawn partly from ancient Mediterranean society, where a good son is one who learns his father's trade and does his father's bidding. We find that thought echoed in Trinitarian discussions of the Father and the Son.

Another important source for early Trinitarian thinking was biological. Because Aristotelian biology erroneously believed that the entire being of a child was contained in the father's sperm, the woman's womb being only its incubator, it could be said that a father was biologically the sole and only origin of his offspring. This is the meaning of words like *beget, begat,* and *begotten* in older English translations of the Bible. Since a father was believed to be the sole origin of his children, the word *father* could also mean, in a more abstract sense, *origin.* We find that thought echoed in Trinitarian discussions of God as creator, and of the Father and the Son.

Finally, the words *Father* and *Son* in Christian theology reflect the New Testament title of Jesus Christ as "Son of God," and the character of God whom Jesus called Abba, Father. In the gospel record we meet a Father whose first word to and about Jesus is, "this is my beloved Son"; who sends Jesus to announce that God is reaching out to the whole people of Israel (and beyond) with generous, forgiving love, and in whose name Jesus says and shows that God does

not stand on ceremony or defend divine dignity, but reaches out to seek and save human beings who have gone, or been pushed, beyond the bounds of purity and righteousness. We find those thoughts also echoed in Trinitarian discussions of the Father and the Son.

ACHIEVEMENTS

In thinking about the primal Christian experiences of God, the value of the *father-son* metaphor is that it portrays an intimate relationship in which there is unity of purpose. This made it possible to imagine both distinction and oneness in God. As controversy followed controversy, the metaphor was radically reinterpreted. For example:

- Unlike human relationships of parent and child, this *father* is not older than this *son*: they have always been what they are, and always will be: they are *co-eternal.*

- Unlike human relationships, where parent and child are biologically connected but have different personalities and different bodies, this *father* and *son* are one; they share the "stuff" or substance of divinity: they are *consubstantial.*

- Unlike human relationships between parents and young children, this *father* does not rule over this *son* (because God cannot rule over God); and unlike ancient patriarchal relationships, where the son has no standing till he comes of age, the relationship between this *father* and this *son* is not a relationship of greater to lesser: they are "co-equal."

- Finally, because God is beyond human gender, the relationship between this *father* and this *son* is not male or sexual. A paradoxical expression of this insight comes from the year 675, at the Council of Toledo, where it was said that God the Father both "begets" and "gives birth to" God the Son *de utero patris* ("out of the Father's womb").

IMPLICATIONS

Why does this matter to Christian faith today?

First of all, if the Living God who created all things has reached out to human beings in three distinct yet inseparably interrelated ways, then, because God never deceives us but reveals to us who God truly is, it follows that the distinctions, the oneness, and the relatedness revealed to us are showing us something truthful about distinction, oneness, and relatedness in God.

To put it in the jargon of Trinitarian doctrine, the economic (or outgoing) Trinity gives us a truthful glimpse—a glimpse surely, but a truthful glimpse—of the immanent (or interior) Trinity.

Second, what God shows us about God has a bearing on how we are meant to behave with one another.

Putting these principles together, here is something of what the doctrine of the Trinity shows us:

1. God is reaching out to creation, and to humankind, in three distinct ways, so distinct that they can never be collapsed into singleness, and so unified that they can never be split into separateness.

2. God is not a *mon*ad (a "Solarian" being in splendid isolation). Instead, God knows what we call "otherness" within God's own self, as well as in God's creation. God's being is what we know as *relationship*. Relationality is within God, as well as in God's outreaching and outflowing love. The Three are not separate entities who have relation: they *are* relation.

3. God is not a *mon*arch (one who rules alone), nor is there an internal monarchy or hierarchy within God. The relationship between the Three is not one of commanding and obeying but of order without subordination, in dynamic communion, eternal agreement, and mutual love. It immediately follows that visual and verbal images of God as an all-commanding ruler are out of step with Trinitarian faith, and become idolatrous if they are presented as the normative or overruling image of God.

4. God is not a society, much less a mutual admiration society. The relationality, dynamic communion, and outreaching love of the Holy Trinity are closer than any relationship between human beings can ever be. These Three are One as they draw life from one another, share life with one another, and exist in one another, in a relationship of permeation without confusion.

Metaphorically, the communion of the Three is aptly described as a cooperative, moving, flowing, dance—provided we understand that the dance is open, not closed, and that all humankind, and all creation, are invited to join in.[4]

SHAPING TRINITARIAN WORSHIP

In the space of one article, I can note some issues only in passing.

On preaching, let me state my conviction that Trinitarian preaching springs, not from intellectual assent to the doctrine, but from a faith and prayer life that are at the deepest level, Trinitarian: in conviction as well as concept, intuitively as well as intellectually, spontaneously as well as intentionally.

As regards baptism, I am unconvinced by the ecumenical weight loaded on to the phrase, "Father, Son, and Holy Spirit," either as a test of the validity of Christian baptism or as an adequate way of baptizing in the name of the Trinity. Part of my concern has to do with the language issues I shall speak about in a moment. Partly, also, to quote two recent writers, "compact formulae are not always the best way to express Trinitarian praise. Constantly using the same short phrase reinforces the idea that the Trinity is a logical puzzle or a mathematical formula, not a loving and multifaceted reality to which we witness."[5] Amen!

As regards Holy Communion, the whole service ought powerfully to show, not merely our communion with Christ, but the divine communion that makes our communings possible. Within the service, the Great Prayer of Thanksgiving is an opportunity to honor the distinctiveness of the Three, and meet the manifold oneness of the One. From this viewpoint it is questionable whether the long-standing custom of having the prayer spoken by one, and only one voice, is adequately Trinitarian.

If I had time to look at creeds, I would agree with Ruth Duck and Patricia Wilson-Kastner that "creeds that best serve worship are testimonies: they seek to express the faith of the churches in a concise yet comprehensive way, in a mode of thanksgiving and praise."[6] I would argue that, though the occasional use of ancient creeds may connect us, at least poetically, with the communion of saints, it is doubtful whether they can express today's Trinitarian faith in a concise yet comprehensive way.

Finally, I would worry considerably about the Trinitarian lopsidedness of the liturgical year. If we allow the liturgical year to shape Trinitarian worship, we find ourselves attending quite adequately to the source and origin of all things, and the wonders of creation, between September and November, when a high proportion of worshipers are in church; then giving high-energy attention to the Word from Advent through to Ascensiontide with Christmas and Easter as the highest points of the year; then relegating the Spirit to a rush of pentecostal wind followed by months of "ordinary time," much of which is vacation time. I suggest the following:

- In fully Trinitarian worship, we meet all Three all year round, in prayer, praise, thanksgiving, and song—and of course in preaching.
- Trinitarian worship, all year round, tries to speak, pray, sing about, and visualize the Trinity in a way that expresses the co-equality of the Three, and leaves no room for the notion that one is more important than another.
- Trinitarian worship, all year round, tries to speak, pray, sing about, and visualize the Trinity in a way that expresses the complete, joyful, loving unity of the Three who are One, and the richness of Trinitarian relationships calls for a faith deeper and richer than "just me and Jesus."[7]
- Trinitarian worship, all year round, tries to do justice to the distinctiveness of each of the Three who are One. For example, though Trinitarian faith holds that the Eternal Word and the Living Spirit were intimately present with the Origin of All who met Moses on the mountaintop, Trinitarian faith, all year round, will highlight, sing about, and give thanks for God's covenantal story with ancient Israel, and with believing Judaism today.

In the space available, I focus on two issues: Trinitarian worship speech and our need to know and trust the presence of the Holy Spirit.

TRINITY TALK

One unavoidable issue is the language we use to speak to, and about, God as Trinity. On this controversial issue there is a wide range of opinion. From one end of the spectrum come arguments that the traditional language is hopelessly patriarchal, serves the powers of domination, and must therefore be dismantled and replaced.

From the other end of the spectrum come claims that traditional terminology, especially "Father, Son, and Holy Spirit," is mandatory, irreplaceable, and hegemonic: mandatory, meaning that God insists we speak in these terms, which thus become irreplaceable; and hegemonic, meaning that the traditional language overrules all other forms of Trinitarian speech.

INTENT AND EFFECT

In any attempt at communication, what is actually communicated from one person to another depends partly on what the sender intends to say, and partly also on what the hearer hears. Intent and effect may, or may not, coincide.

For theologians who uphold the traditional terminology, their main emphasis is usually on what they intend it to communicate. Though a minority intend to communicate a view of the Divine as in some sense masculine, most do not. Theologians like Jürgen Moltmann, Ted Peters, Leonardo Boff, and Colin Gunton use "Father, Son, and Holy Spirit," fully intending to convey the relationality, order without subordination, dynamic communion, and outflowing love that Trinitarian theology discovered as it relentlessly reinterpreted these terms. From the "traditional" end of the spectrum, the argument tends to be something like this: These are the terms that have come down to us; it is better to reinterpret than replace them; and in any case, you can't substitute one metaphor for another— to do so is a change of theology, not merely of terminology.

There is some weight to this view, especially the point that metaphors are not easily changed; if you take an unwanted metaphor back to the theology store and ask for a new one, you'll get a replacement that does something different.

At the other end of the spectrum, people who question traditional Trinitarian terminology do so partly because they believe that, whatever the intent, its effects have become irreversibly problematic. As a linguist, I give weight to the *effects* of linguistic communication, because overwhelmingly, usage determines meaning. Speaking of God's compassion in the mid-eighteenth century, Charles Wesley wrote, "To me, to all, thy bowels move." Nowadays, you can—if you wish—explain to a congregation that we should keep saying "bowels" because it *really* means "compassion," or you can change the line (as hymnals have long since done) to something like, "to me, to all, thy mercies move." The way people use the word *bowels* has changed so much that it is irreversibly (and laughably) misleading to go on using it. I suspect that traditional Trinitarian terminology is equally close to irreversible misdirection.

DOCTRINE AND DEVOTION

One good reason for changing Wesley's words is that they are written for the devotional mode of theological discourse, not the doctrinal mode.

In the doctrinal mode, our purpose is thought and reflection. We try to stand back from our subject matter, and even from the language we are using, so that we can think about it and question it.

The doctrinal mode is perfectly suited for the lecture hall, the classroom, the symposium, the careful reading of a book, the critical viewing of a movie, and some aspects of hearing a sermon.

In the doctrinal mode, we can achieve some degree of detachment even from the words we are using, to the extent of redefining them away from popular, everyday meanings.

In the devotional mode, however, our purpose is not detachment, but commitment; not reflection, but immersion. The language of prayer, praise, petition, lament, and thanksgiving is a vehicle for a hoped-for encounter with the Holy. The logic of the devotional mode is not to

People who question traditional Trinitarian terminology do so partly because they believe that, whatever the intent, its effects have become irreversibly problematic.

stand back but to plunge in. What counts in the devotional mode is not the theologian's intent, but the meaning his or her words immediately and commonly convey.

Thus, when we use "Father-Son" God-talk in the devotional mode, there is minimal room for redefinition. In worship, the qualifications and explanations of theologians have limited effect, because what counts is the discourse's immediate impact and common-speech meanings and associations.

PROBLEMS COMPOUNDED

The problem of Father-Son terminology in the devotional mode is compounded by the male-centered use that theologians, church authorities, and artists have persistently made of it. In theology, "God as Father" language has frequently been used, not with the carefulness of early Trinitarian thought, but to present an image of God as analogous to a male authority figure.

Thus, Martin Luther wrote that God the Father is the model of all father figures. Karl Barth spoke movingly of God as the merciful Father. The social gospel movement talked about the Fatherhood of God and the brotherhood of man. In worship, writes Gail Ramshaw, "the faithful have sought to be connected to God, and the names of God recurring in the church's prayer life provide this primary connection. Father came to mean not Abba, not resistance to emperor worship, not the philosoph-

ical Unoriginate Origin, not the key to Christology, but a personalized masculine authority figure."[8]

Moreover, God-as-Father language cannot be confined to what goes in churches or seminaries. It has cultural ramifications. "The use of predominantly masculine language (for God) is one significant way in which patriarchal culture is passed from one generation to another. Using many masculine images and no feminine images for God sends the message that women are not made in the image of God and thus are less valuable than men."[9]

Religious art has had an equally powerful impact. By repeatedly picturing the Trinity as "an old man, a young man, and a third thing"[10] artists have filled the imagination of generations of worshipers, sermons, and Sunday school lessons with the indelible misconceptions that "God the Father" is like an old man; that the man Jesus embodies a male, or male-like, divinity; and that the technical phrase, "three Persons," implies that God is three separate, and male, beings. Hollywood movies follow suit, whether God is the cute old man played by George Burns in *Oh, God!,* or the deep male voice that thunders from mountaintops and storm clouds.

Against this background, the repeated use in worship of the traditional Trinitarian formula may have effects not foreseen by theologians. For example, if we say over and over again, "Father, Son, and Holy Spirit," "Father, Son, and Holy Spirit," "Father, Son, and Holy Spirit," and never speak of the Three in a different sequence, we are embedding in our imagination a sequence that suggests—because "Father" always comes first—that God the Father is more important than God the Son—in technical language a *mon*archy of the First Person of the Trinity.

Or, at the very least, we are inviting worshipers to meet the mystery of God as an all-male one-parent family with either a resident phantom (if we say Ghost) or a whiff of bourbon (if we say Spirit).

To make one final comparison, in the doctrinal mode we can take terms like *Father, Son,* and *Holy Spirit,* and keep using them while explaining them with secondary, nongendered, nonhierarchical speech. In language of praise and devotion, it is only partially possible to "translate," and continuous translation is unworkable and unworshipful; for example:

> *Our Father* [but by this we mean not a male parent figure, whether abusing or caring, authoritarian or egalitarian, but God beyond sexuality, beyond male and female, beyond masculine and feminine, infinitely gracious and utterly reliable, who has graciously decided that a name associated with male authority is the only name that he—but of course we don't mean "he"—will permit us to use about him—but of course we don't mean "him"], *who art in heaven* (Hmmm . . . how shall we translate "Heaven"?) . . . *In the Name of the Father* [pause for translation], *and of the Son* [pause for explanation]

and of the Holy Spirit [pause for exhaustion], *Amen.*

PRAISING A MYSTERY

In the devotional mode, many worshipers still find meaning and assurance in traditional Trinitarian speech; and its use in baptism cements a valuable—though partial—ecumenical consensus.[11] Because of this, it is important to emphasize the fact that I do not wish to erase it, but rather to end its monarchic rule by setting it in a constellation of more varied prayer and praise.

It is also important to emphasize that, whatever language we use—including the language of Spirit, Father, and Son—we use it hoping to encounter divine mystery.[12]

The Trinity is a mystery, not a secret. Secrets puzzle us, but lose their fascination as soon as they are revealed. A mystery deepens the more it is pondered and known. The mystery of human personality is a good example: the better we know someone we love, the more we wonder at the mystery of who and what they are. So it is with the mystery of God.[13] My poem *The Song of Three Children* (see p. 19) is one attempt to evoke, and be encountered by, God's revealed mystery.

REFORMED STRENGTH AND WEAKNESS

If I were asked to pinpoint some of the strengths of Reformed worship today, I would point to the value we

The Song of Three Children

I met three children in the street.
They did not give me trick or treat
but whispered, laughed, and called my name.
I nearly walked away,
but something made me stay
and join them in their game.

"Now let's pretend that we are God,"
they said, and ran to where I stood.
They danced around me in a ring
and sang, "You must agree
to give us questions three,
so ask us anything."

They waited, sitting on the ground,
and did not move or make a sound.
I thought and puzzled long that day,
and then, to my surprise,
I looked into their eyes,
and knew what I would say:

"Now listen to my questions three,"
I said," and you must answer me:
What is your name, and Are you real,
and Can you see and know
how humans think and grow,
and fathom how we feel?"

The first child stood up tall,
and suddenly I felt quite small
as solemnly she said:
"We never give our name away,
but listen hard to what I say:
God is not a she, God is not a he,
God is not an it or a maybe.
God is a moving, loving,
knowing, growing mystery."

The second child moved so fast
I hardly saw her spinning past
as all around she sang:
"I'll dance my dance of destiny
till you are all as real as me:
I made you. We know you. I love you."

The third child took my hand
and whispered, "Yes, we understand.
I know what children think and do,
for I have been a child like you.
I know how it feels to walk and run,
to sing and shout, and play in the sun,
or cry in the night, or fall to the ground,
or tremble with fright, or be lost and found.
I know how it feels to look at the sky
and keep on asking why and why."

I met three children on my way,
and never knew, in all our play,
their age or name or why they came,
yet all the world is new,
and everything I do
will never be the same.

God is not a she, God is not a he,
God is not an it or a maybe.
God is a moving, loving,
knowing, growing mystery.

How Wonderful the Three-in-One*

How wonderful the Three-in-One,
    whose energies of dancing light
are undivided, pure and good,
    communing love in shared delight.

Before the flow of dawn and dark,
    Creation's Lover dreamed of earth,
and with a caring deep and wise,
    all things conceived and brought to birth.

The Lover's own Belov'd, in time,
    between a cradle and a cross,
at home in flesh, gave love and life
    to heal our brokenness and loss.

Their Equal Friend all life sustains
    with greening power and loving care,
and calls us, born again by grace,
    in Love's communing life to share.

How wonderful the Living God:
    Divine Beloved, Empow'ring Friend,
Eternal Lover, Three-in-One,
    our hope's beginning, way and end.

---

*This poem develops a metaphor coined by St. Augustine of Hippo, who suggested that the Trinity can be understood in terms of One who Loves, One who is loved, and the bond of love between them. Augustine's metaphor allows us to draw on a variety of human love-relationships to glimpse the mystery of God, and is here strengthened by describing the Spirit in personal terms ("Equal Friend"), rather than a sub-personal "bond."

place on thoughtful, committed, impassioned preaching that digs deep into tradition, experience, and the biblical text; to our emphasis, at best, on offering people space to explore Christian faith and make a mature decision about it; and our ability, at best, to trust the grace of God and be ever suspicious of our own feelings, motivations and the machinations of the powers that be.

If I were asked to pinpoint the main weakness in Reformed worship, I would say that, though our theology is formally Trinitarian, we have a radically defective practical theology of one Third of the Three, such that we do not know how to allow for and trust the power of the Holy Spirit in our worship—and perhaps elsewhere.

One of my faculty colleagues pinpoints this problem by speaking with gentle irony about "Presbyterian Pentecost."

Presbyterian Pentecost is not the unseemly disorder described in the Acts of the Apostles, with tongues of fire, the appearance of intoxication, ecstatic utterance, and a rushing mighty wind.

Presbyterian Pentecost occurs in the Gospel of John, where Jesus quietly breathes on his disciples and says, "Receive the Holy Spirit." Not a gale, not a breeze, not a wind, but a breath. Just enough Spirit to feel a gentle movement of air on your face; nowhere near enough to blow you along, or sweep you off your feet. Obviously, when Jesus did not blow upon his disciples, but breathed on them, he was anticipating Paul's instruction to do all things decently and in order.

There is humor, but also sadness, in that picture. Reformed worship desperately needs an infusion of Spirit.

EMBODIMENT

First, our worship needs to be more embodied. Paradoxically, when the Spirit is present, the body moves, and is moved. And when the body moves, we more readily recognize the Spirit's power and presence.

I do not mean by this that Reformed congregations should dance down the road and join the hand-clapping, body swaying, enthusiastic singing of the nearest pentecostal church—though I would have nothing against that if their theology remained Reformed: Reformed theology and pentecostal enthusiasm would be a powerful combination. And at the very least, it would be wonderful if Reformed congregations could give themselves permission to move when they sing, and learn to clap on the correct beat, or off-beat.

Whether or not we go as far as that, I am convinced that, in order more fully to know the presence of the Spirit, we must do more with our bodies than park them in the pew. The passing of the peace in some Reformed congregations seems to take longer than it once did: perhaps because, whether or not we verbalize it, many of us long for an opportunity to get up, move, and meet people.

This is not the place to give a recipe for movement, or a list of actions that make worship embodied. I simply suggest that when planning worship, we ask the following: What will the congregation be invited to *do*, physically, today? Or, what movement—in dance, drama, dramatized Scripture reading, or choral singing—will communicate something of the gospel, bodily and nonverbally, to the whole congregation? Will we, perhaps, stand, turn and face one another, and form small circles for guided or spontaneous prayer? Will we invite people, on All Saints' Sunday, to write the name of someone now in the communion of saints, come forward, and attach it to a banner? Will there be, today, something that we do, and in doing it, remember?

ARTISTRY

My second suggestion is that we shall know the power of the Spirit more fully as we learn how to trust, and use, all the arts in worship. When I speak of "worship arts" I do not limit my meaning to "high art": I mean all the art and craft skills in a given congregation— from opera singing, jazz guitar, classical cello, drama, painting and drawing, to quilting, basket-weaving, baking, home improvement skills, and cabinet making. For example, it is good if someone in the congregation has the artistry to make a large, evocative, and beautiful banner. But it is essential to find someone who knows how to climb a ladder and string a wire across the chancel to hold the banner safely in place.

We need the arts and crafts in worship, because though there is order in the work of the Spirit, there is also Holy disorder. The Spirit sparks creativity, appeals through all the senses, makes unexpected connections, and touches us in ways that cannot be verbalized or explained.

When I speak of "creativity," I do not mean only creativity in art. It is a great mistake to limit our concept of creativity either to "the arts" or to the Holy Spirit. Though we may experience the gift of creativity, of making unexpected connections, as the work of the Spirit, creativity is a creation-gift of the whole Trinity, given to all humankind, in all kinds of human work: not just in "art" but in accounting, welding, legal argument, town planning, business management, scientific research, and everyday problem-solving.

All I am suggesting, within this larger framework of human creativity, is that in Trinitarian worship, the imaginative use of craft and art are among the most powerful ways the Spirit can touch us in the depths of our being.

It is time for Reformed Christians—the people of the Word—to renounce our distrust of the nonverbal and nonrational dimensions of worship and put more trust in the Third dimension of the Three who are One.

It is time for Reformed Christians—the people of the Word—to renounce our distrust of the nonverbal and nonrational dimensions of worship and put more trust in the Third dimension of the Three who are One.

SPACES FOR SPIRIT

To quote the title of a book by Nancy Chinn, a superbly gifted visual artist with strong Presbyterian connections, our worship needs to make "Spaces for Spirit."[14] I could draw much from her book, but have space for just one quotation. It sums up perfectly what I mean by trusting the Spirit in our worship:

> Most artists have a secret: We never end up making what we intended to create. Always along the way the art asserts itself. The materials create new tensions, new ways of seeing, new possibilities. The act of working it out uncovers what the artist could not fully have predicted.
>
> Art making is like that. We leave behind the marks of that conversation with the materials that is evidence of that same Spirit, that Holy one, stirring in the unconfined space of our imagination.
>
> The church needs us (artists) precisely because our work cannot be explained. We say to the church. "You are invited to come into our work, invited to enter it, to be taken up for a moment, for a passage of time that is your life, for time away from time. You are invited to enter into a relationship. Here you are asked to encounter, to listen, to hear the other. And in the hearing, the pause, the silence, what will come?
>
> "You will hear what you cannot hear alone. You will hear your new self, the self you will become. You will hear yourself, your holy self unfolding in a new response, a new thought, a new idea.
>
> "What we invite you to hear cannot be controlled. It cannot be defined. It is not a gentle flow of small breezes from nowhere on a hot steamy day. No. What we unleash is the stuff of a gale, of a hurricane, of a mighty wind, of a Pentecost wind. It is the wind of freedom, the breath of revolution, the glimpse of what might yet be."[15]

Here, in conclusion, is a song of praise. I invite you to speak, sing, and in your heart give praise and adoration to the Three who are One, the Holy and Undivided Trinity:

Praise the Lover of Creation
Praise the Spirit, Friend of Friends,
Praise the true Beloved, our Savior,
Praise the God who makes and mends,
strong, surrendered, many-splendored,
Three whose Oneness never ends.

BRIAN A. WREN is the Conant Professor of Worship at Columbia Theological Seminary, Decatur, Georgia; a minister of the United Reformed Church in the United Kingdom; and the author of more than two hundred hymns.

NOTES

1. Christoph Schwöbel, "Introduction—The Renaissance of Trinitarian Theology: Reasons, Problems and Tasks," in *Trinitarian Theology*

Today: Essays on Divine Being and Act, ed. Christoph Schwöbel (Edinburgh: T. & T. Clark, 1995), 2.

2. For a wide-ranging exploration of the practice of Trinitarian faith, not only in worship, but in the church's structure and mission, see David S. Cunningham, *These Three Are One: The Practice of Trinitarian Doctrine* (Malden, Mass., and Oxford: Blackwell Publishers, 1998).

3. Gail Ramshaw, *God Beyond Gender: Feminist Christian God-Language* (Minneapolis: Fortress Press, 1995), 80.

4. "Each divine person is irresistibly drawn to the other, taking his/her existence from the other, containing the other in him/her-self, while at the same time pouring self out into the other," Catherine Mowry LaCugna, *God for Us: The Trinity and Christian Life* (San Francisco: Harper, 1991), 271. She points out that the Greek term for this relationship, *perichoresis*, comes from the verb *perichoreo*, to encompass, not from *perichoreuo* (to dance around): thus, though cooperative dance is an apt metaphor for *perichoresis*, it does not translate it (footnote 94, p. 312).

5. Ruth C. Duck and Patricia Wilson-Kastner, *Praising God: The Trinity in Christian Worship* (Louisville, Ky.: Westminster John Knox Press, 1999), 32. On baptism see Ruth C. Duck, *Gender and the Name of God: The Trinitarian Baptismal Formula* (New York: Pilgrim Press, 1991).

6. Duck and Wilson-Kastner, *Praising God*, 47.

7. These three guidelines, supplemented by my own examples, are drawn from Duck and Wilson-Kastner, *Praising God*, 28. By Israel I mean, of course, ancient Israel as God's chosen people, and their successors, not the modern-day State of Israel.

8. Ramshaw, *God Beyond Gender*, 81.

9. Duck and Wilson-Kastner, *Praising God*, 6.

10. Ibid., 77.

11. The "ecumenical consensus" on this issue is not universal and excludes significant Christian groupings and denominations.

12. When I say "mystery" I mean the Trinity, not the doctrine of the Trinity. The Trinity is mysterious, but the doctrine of the Trinity is a human exploration and should be articulated as clearly as possible. See Ted Peters, *God as Trinity: Relationality and Temporality in Divine Life* (Louisville, Ky.: Westminster John Knox Press, 1993), 16–17.

13. The distinction between mystery and secret is drawn from lectures by George B. Caird of Mansfield College Oxford (1917–1984).

14. Nancy Chinn, *Spaces for Spirit: Adorning the Church* (Chicago: Liturgy Training Publications, 1998), chap. 2.

15. Ibid., 9–10.

Calvin, Sacraments, and Ecclesiology

What Makes a Church a Church?

BY MARTHA L. MOORE-KEISH

INTRODUCTION: SACRAMENTS AS MARKS OF THE CHURCH

It is commonplace for people to observe today that the church is in a very different position than it was forty or fifty years ago. Gone are the days when the church was the center of every community, when the biggest choice people had to make on a Sunday morning was whether to go to the Baptist, Methodist, Presbyterian, or Catholic service. Gone are the days when everyone knew what a church building looked like and had a pretty good idea of what went on inside. Churches—or at least mainline churches—are moving to the margins of society, and fewer and fewer people have a clear picture of who we are and what we do.

This changed position gives us a good opportunity to take a step back and ask some basic questions about who we are and what we do. What is a church, anyway? What makes a church a church?

In the sixteenth century, John Calvin wrestled with this very question in another situation of social and religious change. Up until that point, in the West, the church meant pretty much one thing: the Great Church, whose head was the pope. There was plenty of variation within the Roman church, but everyone assumed they knew what a church was and what it did. But then Luther and Zwingli came along with their serious challenges to sacramental practice and papal authority, and suddenly there

> *Churches—or at least mainline churches—are moving to the margins of society.*

was a question about what really con- stituted a legitimate church. Calvin, in the next generation, modified a statement of Luther to give the Reformed tradition our definitive statement on how to recognize a church: "Wherever we see the Word of God purely preached and heard, and the sacraments administered according to Christ's institution, there, it is not to be doubted, a church of God exists."[1] Note that this is not a formal definition, but a "hermeneutical key," a way of dis- cerning where a church is. There may be a lot of other stuff going on, says Calvin, but as long as there is faith- ful preaching and hearing of the Word of God and administration of the sacraments, that's a church. He might have said, conversely, that there may be a lot of other stuff going on, but if either Word or sacraments are absent, then that's not a church.

A more recent writer, Lutheran theologian Gordon Lathrop, says that at its most basic level, the church is the gathered people, the congrega- tion, or what some folks call the assembly, doing certain things: read- ing and hearing the Word and cele- brating the sacraments. That's what the church is. When you start talking about the church, in this view, you have to begin with the gathered peo- ple and their central actions of pro- claiming, hearing, washing, and breaking bread. This is a contempo- rary formulation of Luther's and Calvin's statement, but it challenges much of what we say when we describe a church today.

How do we describe the func- tional marks of the church today? What do we in fact look for when we try to discern where a faithful church is present? Word and sacraments? Number of programs, size of budget, number of people in the pew?

For instance, is the communal life of a church defined by baptism or the ongoing life of the church? That is, do we define a church by who is bap- tized, or by who is there week after week? *Baptism and the Unity of the Church*, an ecumenical study docu- ment from the Faith and Order Commission of the World Council of Churches, says,

> the communion realized in the daily life of the church often is constituted by a different set of people than the communion con- stituted by the bond of baptism. When this difference is simply a function of the fact that some will always fall away, fundamental questions are not raised. When, however, the difference between the communion defined by bap- tism and the communion defined by the regular life of the church comes to be a difference in prin- ciple or a difference of large pro- portions, the status of baptism as a fundamental bond of commu- nion is placed in question.

In other words, if there is a big dif- ference between those who regularly participate in church life and those who are baptized, this raises ques- tions about what baptism is really all about. This problem can arise in at least three ways: 1. regarding baptized children as less than full members of the church (as, for instance, with a practice of downplaying baptism and emphasizing confirmation as the point of "joining the church"), 2. massive nonparticipation of the baptized (as when children are baptized as a rite of passage without continuing participation in the life of the church), or 3. large-scale participation of the nonbaptized (as in places where active congregations include many who are not baptized or being prepared for baptism). All of these jeopardize the status of baptism as a bond of Communion.[2]

Do we define the church by who is baptized, or by who is an "active member"? In the Presbyterian Church (U.S.A.), per capita giving is tied to "active membership" rather than baptized membership. Churches contribute to the General Assembly according to the number of people who are active members, not according to the number of baptized members. This is different from some other churches, such as the Evangelical Lutheran Church in Ameica (ELCA), and it undermines the notion that baptism, not age or cognitive ability or financial status, is what makes us members of the body of Christ. Our budgetary structure suggests that we discern a church where people are active attenders, serving on committees, engaged in evangelism and outreach. Such active participation is to be encouraged, but when it is made the criterion of true membership, the status of baptism is undermined.

So: do we really look to Word and sacraments as marks of the church? Or do we count as the marks of the church: profession of faith in Jesus Christ, authority of Scripture, and holiness of life, as in the recent Confessing Church movement in the PC(USA)? Don't get me wrong; I am not going to argue against any of these things. Calvin certainly called for faithfulness to the Word of God as embodied in Jesus Christ and revealed in Scripture, and he understood holiness of life to follow from faithfulness to God's Word. But I do want to point out that there is a difference between judging the authenticity of a church by the presence of Word and sacrament and judging it by its assent to a set of theological principles. In several ways, then, though the Reformed tradition affirms that Word and sacrament are the marks by which we know where the church is, our practice does not reflect this affirmation.

We Reformed have usually been pretty good about insisting on the centrality of the Word in our churches. Biblical scholarship, strong preaching, regular Bible study—historically, these have been strong suits for us. The centrality of the Word was clearly demonstrated to me during the year my husband, Chris, and I served as seminary interns in East Kilbride, on the west coast of Scotland. Each and every Sunday, worship began with a procession into the church: the pastor, Mr. Gilfillan, Chris, and I would march solemnly

Do we really look to Word and sacraments as marks of the church?

behind Archie the beadle, who carried the enormous pulpit Bible. Archie staggered up the ten steps into the pulpit, set down the Bible and opened it, then made his way back down to ground level. Worship had begun. Yes, we Reformed have done well at proclaiming in word and ritual the centrality of the Word in our churches.

But what about sacraments? Have we always focused as much time and energy in our consideration of baptism and the Lord's Supper as marks of the church? What difference does it make to insist that celebration of the sacraments "according to Christ's institution" is a fundamental way of describing the church? That is the question I wish to lift up. I will begin by considering Calvin and his understanding of the sacraments. I will then reflect on how his understanding of sacraments shaped his understanding of the church, and how our own ecclesiology might be affected if we take seriously sacraments as marks of the church.

CALVIN

We began with Calvin's words on the sacraments as marks of the church: "Wherever we see the Word of God purely preached and heard, and the sacraments administered according to Christ's institution, there . . . a church of God exists."[3] This statement came out of the Reformation problem of distinguishing the true church, once the Roman Catholic Church no longer seemed to hold that status. The church had long had

four "creedal marks": one, holy, catholic, and apostolic. This language comes from the Nicene Creed, and when medieval theologians talked about the "marks of the church," this is what they meant. But at the Reformation, these creedal marks no longer worked as visible signs of where the true church was. Reformers might have argued that there continued to be "one true church," but it was not easily recognizable once that one true church was no longer identified with Rome. So, beginning with Martin Luther, Word and sacraments were held up as visible marks of the church.[4] Calvin later amended Luther's formulation to say that the Word of God purely preached *and heard*, and the sacraments administered according to Christ's institution constituted the marks of the church. The change was to emphasize the importance of people actually hearing what was preached; it was not enough for the Word to be preached if it was not heard by someone. But the two marks of Word and sacrament remained in place.

At another point, Calvin said that we cannot know "God's secret predestination," but we have been given certain ways to recognize members of the church: "those who, by confession of faith, by example of life, and by partaking of the sacraments, profess the same God and Christ with us."[5] What an odd statement this sounds today! Imagine a church leader claiming today that sacramental participation is a marker by which we can discern members of Christ's body.

If either Word or sacrament was removed, according to Calvin, the church is compromised: "For there is nothing that Satan plots more than to remove and do away with one or both of these. Sometimes he tries by effacing and destroying the marks to remove the true and genuine distinction of the church. Sometimes he tries by heaping contempt upon them to drag us away from the church in open rebellion."[6] Listen to the force of that statement: if Word or sacraments are effaced, destroyed, held in contempt, then this is Satan's work! Surely we would agree that if the Word of God were removed from the life of the church, that would no longer be a church. If the Bible or the pulpit were set aside or covered in extraneous objects, no one would stand for it. But if there are no baptisms, if the font is kept in a back closet because there is no need for it on a regular basis, if Communion is not a regular part of the worship of the people and they think of the table as more of a place for flowers and offering plates than for food and drink, do we think this undermines the life of the church? Would Calvin call this Satan's work?

Word and sacraments are equally marks of the church, claimed Calvin. In one section of the *Institutes*, he chided those who insisted on holiness of life as a primary mark of the church, since the church is always composed of good and bad. He said,

There have always been those who, imbued with a false conviction of their own perfect sanctity,

as if they had already become a sort of airy spirits, spurned association with all men in whom they discern any remnant of human nature. . . . There are others who sin more out of ill-advised zeal for righteousness than out of that insane pride. When they do not see a quality of life corresponding to the doctrine of the gospel among those to whom it is announced, they immediately judge that no church exists in that place.

Calvin went on to acknowledge the problem and the importance of holy living to follow from the gospel. But, he argued, no one should leave a church because it does not have "perfect purity and integrity of life." The true church is marked by the Word of God and the sacraments; holiness of life is the proper human response to these gifts, but such holiness is not itself a mark of the church.[7] The point for Calvin was that Christ really does work through the Word and sacraments, and so even if we ourselves cannot see the effect of this working, as long as the gifts are there, we should regard the assembly as a true church.

According to Calvin, the main point of the sacraments was to unite Christians with Jesus Christ. As Ronald Wallace put it, "Calvin looks on both sacraments as having the same end—to testify, and to assist in

Word and sacraments are equally marks of the church, claimed Calvin.

effecting our union with the body of Christ. Baptism, however, mainly bears witness to our initiation into this union, while the Lord's Supper is a sign of our continuation in this union."[8] Calvin talked about being received into the church and being engrafted into Christ interchangeably in his description of baptism. It is the same for Eucharist. Both sacraments, when administered in the context of ordered ministry, were for Calvin real means of grace, accomplishing union with Christ's body, the church.

CALVIN'S VIEW OF BAPTISM

Before addressing directly the question of how Calvin's understanding of the sacraments shaped his understanding of the church, we will briefly explore his baptismal theology and his eucharistic theology. First, baptism. According to Calvin, baptism accomplishes four things:

1. *Forgiveness*: Baptism is "token and proof of our cleansing, confirming forgiveness of sins."[9] In baptism, our sins are "so abolished, remitted, and effaced that they can never come to [God's] sight, be recalled, or charged against us." This is always corporate, not individual. Calvin emphasized that it is the church that is sanctified, cleansed, saved by Christ. In support of this, he cited Ephesians 5:26, which says that Christ gave himself up for the church "in order to make her holy by cleansing her with the washing of water by the word." The symbolism of

water makes it clear that baptism is about washing, cleansing, and by extension, forgiving sins.

2. *Regeneration*: In baptism, we die and are reborn in Christ. Calvin called this "mortification and renewal in Christ."[10] This was not only a call to die to our desires by Christ's example, but a call to participate in Christ's death and resurrection. "Baptism is a sign that we enter into life in Christ only through death, that there is a gulf between the realm of nature and the realm of grace, that what is new in Christ is indeed a new creation, and not simply a reshaping and improving and heightening of the old."[11] Baptism is the death, or mortification, of the old, and the birth of the new Christian.

3. *Union with Christ*: According to Calvin, "[w]e are not only engrafted into the death and life of Christ, but so united to Christ himself that we become sharers in all his blessings."[12] This is the basic meaning of both sacraments that we mentioned already. In baptism, we "put on Christ," receiving new life and new identity in him.

4. *Covenant theology*: Calvin presented these three "meanings of baptism" at the beginning of his baptismal discussion in the *Institutes*. But later, in his discussion of infant baptism, covenant theology came to the fore. In this context, birth into a Christian family is continuous with new birth in baptism. Baptism is adoption into the covenant by God's free grace. Children of believers are wel-

comed into the covenant because of their parents' faith. If the children of believers are born into the covenant, why withhold the sign? asked Calvin.[13] The church is a covenant community established by God. Just as circumcision was the sign of the old covenant, so baptism is the sign of the new covenant, and it has the added bonus that girl babies as well as boy babies are visibly included in that covenant.

Although covenant theology has continued to be a strong theme in Reformed baptismal theology and practice, we should recognize that there is some tension between the understanding of baptism as repentance or regeneration and baptism as incorporation into covenant community. In talking about baptism as act of repentance and token of mortification and renewal in Christ, Calvin implied that coming to baptism is a conscious act; yet discussion of baptism as engrafting into the covenant implies that new birth is continuous with natural birth in the Christian community. Although Calvin himself did not resolve this tension, we may be able to hold these together with the observation that in our practice, adults are to be baptized as children, and children as adults. In adult baptism, we must always remember that the conscious decision to come to baptism is not a work, but a response to God's free gift of grace. Adults become infants again in the waters of baptism. And, on the other hand, infant baptism

marks a new beginning, a death and new birth just as much as it would for one coming to baptism as an adult.

Throughout Calvin's discussions of baptism, the reformer described baptism as both an unmerited gift of grace and a call to ever-increasing holiness of life. In talking about forgiveness, regeneration, union, and covenant, he focused on both the event-character of God's gift in baptism and the ongoing claim that such a gift places on human life. So on the one hand, we can do nothing to earn God's grace; as Calvin explained in the *Institutes*, "We are initiated into the society of the church by the sign of baptism, which teaches us that entrance into God's family is not open to us unless we first are cleansed of our filth by his goodness."[14] On the other hand, we do respond to the gift of baptism. Holiness of life is our response of gratitude for God's goodness. This is something the baptized continue to seek throughout their lives. Baptism does not mean that we are reborn to pure angelic life (argued Calvin against the Anabaptists), because we continue to pray "forgive us our debts" all our days. This is one unifying theme throughout Calvin's baptismal theology.

Finally, as I have repeated several times, baptism for Calvin had a corporate, not an individual, focus. The language of repentance, regeneration, union, and covenant all focus on the community of faith, not individual salvation. When he drew parallels between baptism and the Old Testament images of crossing the Red Sea and being baptized in the cloud, he was describing the salvation of the community of faith, not salvation of discrete individuals. "One baptism" for Calvin meant that baptism is "common to all: so that by means of it we begin to form one body and soul."[15] Though Calvin's baptismal theology had some unresolved tensions, then, recurring themes bound it together: baptism as gift and call, and baptism as corporate reality.

CALVIN'S VIEW OF EUCHARIST

Now we turn briefly to Calvin's eucharistic theology. The movement of "grace and gratitude" was Calvin's basic eucharistic pattern, which also described the shape of the Christian life. In Communion, God provides everything that we need for life, even though we have done nothing to earn this gift. We respond to God's grace with lives of grateful praise.

Although this is the basic movement of the Eucharist, more can be said about Calvin's understanding of what the Eucharist is and does. In the "Short Treatise on the Lord's Supper," he listed three purposes of the Eucharist:

1. *Spiritual nourishment*, in which we are united with Christ. In the Lord's Supper, God lifts us up and feeds us with the body and blood of Christ, engrafting us into Christ's very body.
2. *Incitement to gratitude* for all God's goodness to us. The Eucharist displays God's bountiful goodness to us, evoking our response of gratitude for all of God's grace.
3. *Exhortation to holy living and mutual love*. As we break bread

and share the cup together, we are united and nourished for lives of faithfulness.

In other words, considering all three of these purposes together, the Lord's Supper establishes right relations among participants and between participants and God.

As with his baptismal theology, so also in his eucharistic theology Calvin focused on the communal dimension of the sacrament. In discussing the way in which Christ is present in the Eucharist, Calvin focused on the presence of Christ in the gathered community, not in the material elements alone. Rather than arguing for transubstantiation of the elements, Calvin asserted a kind of transubstantiation of the community: through participation in the holy Supper, we are gathered into the presence of Christ and transformed into his body for the world. Again, this is no individual act of piety, but a communal event.[16]

How does this transformation, this "transubstantiation of the community," happen? Two things are necessary, according to Calvin: first, God's grace, and second, our faith. Of primary importance is God's action in promising to act in and through the Lord's Supper, through the juxtaposition of words and symbols, to bring us to Christ. But Calvin acknowledged that in order for the Supper to unite us with Christ, we must have faith. We must have the vision to perceive what is going on around the table, that this is no ordinary meal, but the wedding feast of the Lamb. Both objective gift and our faith are necessary for this action, and Calvin argued strongly for both, depending on which misunderstanding he was addressing at the moment. Always remember, however, that for Calvin, faith itself was a gift and not our own work. So even though he argued that the sacraments are ineffective without faith, we cannot regard our own faith as something that we summoned up out of our own willpower. God alone gives us the power to believe, the ability to perceive Jesus Christ as the host of the heavenly banquet. Faith is as much of a gift of grace as the presence of Jesus Christ in Communion.

When both grace and faith are present, the Lord's Supper feeds us with and engrafts us into the body of Christ, and by that engrafting, binds us together into one. As with baptism, Eucharist in Calvin's theology is both gift and call. As first and foremost God's gracious gift, the Supper nourishes us with Christ's body and blood. As call, this same Supper "exhorts" us to holy living, calling us to increased faithfulness. Both baptism and Eucharist, then, come to us from beyond ourselves and draw us beyond our own narrow boundaries, toward the reign of God.

SEVEN WAYS SACRAMENTAL THEOLOGY SHAPES ECCLESIOLOGY

So how does Calvin's sacramental theology influence his understanding of the church? And how might we gain a new perspective on ecclesi-

ology by starting with an examination of sacraments? Calvin did not talk about the church without talking about the sacraments. What he said about the sacraments, therefore, is intimately linked with what he said about the church. To push this just a little further, we might say that when Calvin described what sacraments are and what they do, he was describing what the church is and does. Assuming this inextricable link between church and sacrament in Calvin's thought, then, I propose that Calvin's sacramental theology shapes his ecclesiology in seven ways. In what follows, I take Calvin's theology as my beginning point, but at times I push beyond Calvin to some logical outworkings of his thought. In this way, I hope to present a new perspective on what makes a church in our present situation.

1. *Sacraments present and join us to Christ.* Both Communion and baptism for Calvin signified and accomplished the union of the faithful with Christ. "Union with Christ" was both the content of the sacraments and a description of the Christian life. If the sacraments unite the faithful with Christ, then the church, the gathering of the faithful, is the body of Christ, called to be a witness of God's love for the world. And indeed Calvin often described the church as "body of Christ." This means that our identity is grounded outside ourselves, in the person of Jesus Christ.

This may all sound a bit abstract, a bit disconnected from the real practice of sacraments in our churches, so let us think for a moment about baptism and Communion as we know them. At baptism, we remember that Jesus was baptized in the Jordan by John, and we also remember that he talked about his death as a baptism. When we ourselves hear these words and then are washed (or at least moistened) with water, we identify ourselves with the baptism and the death of Christ. Likewise, when we come to the table, we hear or recite the words "Take, eat. This is my body, broken for you. This is my blood shed for the forgiveness of sins." And we take the bread and beverage, and we eat and drink. And whatever we think is going on there, when we are gathered together around those words and symbols, we are inserting ourselves into the story of Jesus Christ. It is like the Passover narrative, in which our Jewish friends and neighbors recite the story of Israel's salvation as their own story. We gather with Christ around the Communion table. We meet Christ in the washing at the font. That is how we learn who we are.

Sacraments, along with the Word, present Christ. By facing them regularly and in their fullness, we learn who we are. Gordon Lathrop says, "the church begins to know itself not by contemplating its own identity, but by beholding the face of Christ in that word, bath and table that manifest God's identity."[17] The Swiss Reformed theologian Jean-Jacques von Allmen similarly said, "It is not by looking at itself, even washed clean, that the Church learns what it is. What makes the Church first glimpse, and then see clearly, its true face is meeting with Christ. . . . It is on Christ's face that the Church learns who it is."[18] Sacraments join us with Christ, and therefore the church receives its identity from meeting Christ in the Word, at the font, and around the table.

2. *Sacraments draw us into community.* In uniting us with Christ, the sacraments also unite us with one another. Calvin consistently portrayed baptism in communal terms: the community as a whole is forgiven and washed, the community is regenerated, the community is engrafted into the body of Christ, the community is welcomed into one covenant. Through baptism, a people is chosen to be in relationship to God in the same way that the people of Israel were chosen. It is not that individuals are chosen, but a people is chosen. In his eucharistic theology, too, he stressed the corporate dimension of the sacrament: union with the body of Christ at Communion is not individual, but corporate. At this point it is particularly difficult to talk about the sacraments and the church separately, for the sacraments constitute the church, and the church nourishes its members through the sacraments. As Calvin put it, the church conceives and gives us birth and then nourishes us at her breast; the actions of the church are the sacraments.

The twentieth-century Scottish theologian Donald Baillie observed that one of the great gifts of the Reformed practice of serving Communion was the passing of the bread and wine down the pews, because this emphasizes the priesthood of all believers and the communal nature of the meal. This may not always be true in practice today (much of the time, pew Communion can be an exercise in individual piety) but the impulse is right: this is a communal meal, not an individual snack.[19]

Going beyond Calvin for a moment, we can also say not only that the sacraments draw us into community, but that the sacraments presuppose community. It is the community of faith that allows for baptism, and it is this community that shares the Lord's Supper. Without the context of the faithful community, baptism would be just an odd ritual of dripping water on someone's head, and the Supper would be a poor excuse for a meal. The church provides the frame for the sacraments, and the sacraments provide the life-giving symbols for the church. This view of sacraments and of church criticizes any understanding of sacraments as individual experiences and any understanding of the church as a random collection of individuals.

3. *Sacraments call us to acknowledgment of sin.* When Calvin described baptism in terms of forgiveness and regeneration, he was acknowledging that we humans are corrupted and in need of cleansing and rebirth. Though our sins are forgiven at baptism, we are not utterly converted to the "angelic life," affirmed Calvin, and so we pray "forgive us our sins" throughout our lives. In this way, Calvin connected the sacrament of baptism with ongoing acknowledgment of sin.

We can also see the acknowledgment of sin in our baptismal liturgy, which calls us to turn from sin and turn to Jesus Christ. Even if one does not use this classic language of the baptismal renunciations, each service of baptism includes some reference to our need for forgiveness and cleansing as well as our need for the ongoing "nurture and admonition" of the church. Each time we celebrate a baptism, and each time we remember our own baptism, we remember the ways in which we are new creations in Christ and yet still sinful people.

So also we acknowledge human sinfulness at the Lord's Supper. Each celebration of Communion confronts us with the meal that Jesus shared with his disciples on the night before he was arrested and put to death. While it is, on one level, a joyful feast, it is also a reminder of the fact that it was for our sins that our Lord suffered torture and death. In coming to the table, we are reminded of the reality of human sin—individual and corporate—and the need for forgiveness.

This point criticizes the view that sacraments and church are either occasions for pure happiness *or* affirmations of the status quo. Baptism is a joyful welcoming of a new life into the life of Christ, but it is also a kind of death, and the first step into a new life of demanding discipleship. Baptism sets us apart from the old life and turns us to the new life. Communion, too, is an occasion of joy but also reminds us of the effects of sin and the source of our forgiveness.

If the sacraments call us to acknowledgment of sin, then so also the church is called to a frank admission of its own corruption. This point balances the preceding one; even as the church is the body of Christ, it is also a sinful human institution, and so it is always called to confess its chronically narrow and self-serving tendencies.

4. *Sacraments remind us of our dependence.* In his sacramental discussions, Calvin described the church as mother of believers and the sacraments as the nourishment a mother gives her children: "For there is no other way to enter into life unless this mother conceive us in her womb, give us birth, nourish us at her breast, and lastly, unless she keep us under her care and guidance until, putting off mortal flesh, we become like the angels."[20] This image recalls for us the way in which the church is not merely a human institution, but a divine gift— a "means of grace" which God has given to lead us to more faithful living.

Sacraments are gifts from God that point out our radical dependence. We do not give birth to ourselves or feed ourselves. In the Reformed tradition of infant baptism, the act of bathing the infant in (or sprinkling the infant with) the waters of the font reminds us that God claims us before we ever know who or what God is. Even in the baptism of adults or older children, baptism is a new birth, an act that you cannot do to yourself. Baptism is something done to you by another person, mirroring, of course, the action of God.

Communion, likewise, is not an act we do of our own accord. It is an act given to us by Jesus Christ, and he is the one who welcomes us to his table. Brian Gerrish points out that in Calvin's theology, this gift of Christ at Communion, this act of utter grace, leads to our gratitude out of the realization that everything we have and everything we are we owe to God. This is the movement of the entire Christian life.

To put it another way, sacraments give us something outside ourselves to believe in. Gerhard Forde, in a 1993 article on baptism in *Interpretation*, says, "Baptism is the revelation of the will of God, something that comes to us from without, an 'external' thing. Without the external thing, faith has nothing to believe except, perchance, some ancient religious history. Faith then simply collapses inward upon itself. . . . Because of its irreducible externality, baptism is a preeminent sign of the priority and therefore the offense of pure grace."[21] Even our act of believing does not come first. God's acts of choosing, washing, feeding, precede us, come to us from outside ourselves, prompting a response of gratitude and faith.

The sacraments point to our dependence as individuals, but if we take the sacraments as a starting point for understanding the church, we realize that the church, too, is a dependent reality, not self-generated. The church is, to be sure, always a human institution, but it is also a gift of God. *Baptism and the Unity of the Church* says, "the church is not self-constituting. Its fundamental character is given to it by God. The church is thus a dependent reality, dependent upon the institution of its essential actions by Christ and upon the activity of the Spirit within these actions. We receive the communion which the church is."[22] The community of faith is founded outside itself, in the gifts and actions of God. Gordon Lathrop says that the church is "genuine community not by immediate access to each other's souls but by shared participation in the signs of God's great mercy."[23] It is the external things that show us who God is, and therefore who we are. Only by shared participation in these gifts of God will our cultures and our lives be transformed.

5. *Sacraments acknowledge our full humanity and Christ's full humanity.* Not only do sacraments remind us of our dependence, but they remind us of our humanity, with all of its blessings and limitations. In his discussion of sacraments, Calvin frequently employed the notion of accommodation: in the sacraments, God accommodates God's very self to our limitations. For instance, he said at one point, "Shut up as we are in the prison house of our flesh, we have not yet attained angelic rank. God, therefore, in his wonderful providence accommodating himself to our capacity, has prescribed a way for us, though still far off, to draw near to him."[24] We need not embrace Calvin's negative view of embodied humanity as a "prison house of flesh" to affirm with him that God's action of using physical means to commu-

nicate with us is a gracious acknowledgment of our particular creaturely capacities. In the sacraments, God works through physical means to unite us with Christ.

In both sacraments, we are dealing with physical realities that involve our bodies: in baptism, we are washed in water; in Communion, we are fed with bread and wine/juice. These symbols remind us that Jesus Christ was incarnate, that he too was washed and fed. And they remind us that we as human beings require food and drink, and that we are cleansed by water. Symbols like these communicate with our embodied selves in a way that words alone cannot do.

If we disregard or downplay the physical realities of the sacraments, we imply that the physical dimension of our being and of Christ's being is less important than some disembodied "spiritual" dimension of who we are. And this verges on the popular heresy of Docetism, which turns up its nose at the real embodied humanity of Jesus. We are bodies, and we participate in Christ's body.

The church as the body of Christ has to do with our bodies, our concrete physical selves, and this has implications both for moral life and for political involvement. Christ did not stand apart from the world in an otherworldly realm, and neither is the church called to separate itself from the embodied world. The church as body of Christ criticizes both those who would restrict religious life to private morality *and* those who restrict it to public political activism. If we have been engrafted into the body of Christ, then all of our lives are claimed and changed—inner and outer, public and private, body, mind, and will.

6. *Sacraments are ethical acts.* If the sacraments have to do with our whole selves, then clearly full sacramental participation requires—even constitutes—ethical living. In Calvin's terms, sacraments precede and nourish holiness of life. Baptism and the Lord's Supper are at once utterly unmerited gifts of grace and calls to increasing sanctification. In baptism, we are forgiven and made new so that we can live as God's faithful covenant people in the world. At Communion, we are nourished, and we respond with gratitude through our holy living.

When we are baptized, we become part of a community in which "there is no longer Jew or Greek, there is no longer slave or free, there is no longer male and female"(Gal. 3:28). We have a new identity in Christ, and this new identity is not for our individual gratification. It sets us apart from some of the values and practices of this world. Baptismal identity criticizes all other identity markers. The "politics of baptism" establishes identity in a way that critiques all other ways of establishing identity.[25] In talking about the "politics of baptism," Gordon Lathrop points out that baptism makes us unclean, not ritually pure. It unites us to the unclean death of Jesus, and it unites us with the unclean and profane ones of the world.[26] When we become one with Jesus in baptism, we throw out all of our old ways of discerning purity and class distinction.

Likewise, the eucharistic table recalls Jesus' practice of feeding the multitudes, providing for all who did not have enough to eat. It also recalls his practice of dining with those who were regarded as inappropriate dinner guests in his society: tax collectors and other sinners. Communion is not just a private meal for the comfort of Jesus' chosen few. The "economy of the Eucharist" is in critical dialogue with all other means of distributing food.

In his groundbreaking book *Torture and Eucharist*, William Cavanaugh examines the church in Chile under the brutal Pinochet regime. At the beginning of the Pinochet years, the church was paralyzed, both by fear and by its old perception that it was responsible for people's souls while the state was responsible for their bodies. As the years went on and the numbers of the "disappeared" grew, the church gradually changed course, and through its vibrant practice of celebrating the Eucharist, it forged communities of the faithful who were eventually able to voice their opposition to the torture of the state. It was through the celebration of Communion that Christians in Chile were able to form strong communities of resistance to the oppression of the government. This is a flesh and blood example of the way sacraments themselves can constitute communities of ethical action.[27]

7. *Sacraments point toward God's coming reign.* According to Calvin, not only do the sacraments fit us for holy living or ethical action in this world, but they also anticipate the

world to come. They are eschatological signs. In the *Institutes*, he stated that the church cares for us through the sacraments until we put off mortal flesh and become like the angels.[28] They are provisional means that point beyond themselves to our ultimate union with Christ. With regard to baptism, Calvin made it clear that baptism does not immediately grant us entrance to pure angelic life, but it does anticipate that angelic life. The waters give us new birth, anticipating the final resurrection of our bodies. In talking about the flood as a type of baptism, Calvin suggested the eschatological significance of that sacrament: just as the flood in the time of Noah washed away the sin of the world, so our baptism washes away our sin, and so also will God eventually wash away all sin and make the world new. In his eucharistic theology, Calvin also struck an eschatological note: at Communion, if both God's grace and our faith are present, we are caught up and united with the risen Christ in a way that anticipates the final wedding feast of the Lamb.

The main point is that the sacraments are the church being itself—rehearsing the reign of God. In an essay on the Eucharist as a mark of the body of Christ, historical theologian Richard Norris says,

> The eucharist, then, is God's taking us on in Christ, assigning us a participation in his body as our destiny and calling. . . . [I]t is the real thing, but in the form, if you please, of a preliminary rehearsal, like a tentative performance of the

last act of *Hamlet*. Yet it is no small thing to stage, in liturgy and in life: a sign, a dress rehearsal, of the reign of God. Everyone knows it is only a rehearsal. The full reality is yet to come. Such a rehearsal, however, is more than a "mark" of the church. It is what the church is.[29]

The church is an eschatological community, a community of those who look for Christ's reign and who try to embody that reign here and now.

CONCLUSION

Calvin has given us a sacramental theology that is thoroughly integrated with his ecclesiology. He could not talk about one without talking about the other. In Book 4 of the *Institutes*, the section dealing with the church, Calvin discussed the following: Word, sacraments, and the structures required to uphold these things (ministry and discipline). These are the vital aspects of the church, in his estimation. At the outset of his discussion of the visible church, he talked about sacraments: "By baptism we are initiated into faith in [Christ]; by partaking in the Lord's Supper we attest our unity in true doctrine and love; in the Word of the Lord we have agreement, and in the preaching of the Word the ministry instituted by Christ is preserved."[30] When he described the functions of ministers, he said that we are "to proclaim the gospel and to administer the sacraments."[31] That's it. And the second function is not in fine print somewhere, but held equally alongside the first.

Beginning with his integration of ecclesiology and sacramental theology, I have suggested seven ways in which our understanding of the church might be enriched by beginning with the sacraments:

1. Sacraments present and join us to Christ, and therefore the church is the body of Christ.
2. Sacraments draw us into community, and the church is this community, this covenant people, this new creation.
3. Sacraments call us to acknowledgment of sin, and so also the church is called to confess its sinfulness and shortcomings.
4. Sacraments remind us of our dependence, and so too we remember that the church is a dependent reality, founded on the gifts and actions of God.
5. Sacraments acknowledge our full humanity and Christ's full humanity, and so the church too is a fully human institution with responsibilities for the bodies as well as the souls of its members.
6. Sacraments are ethical acts, and so the church is a community of holy living, both in the private and in the public arena.
7. Sacraments point toward God's coming reign, and likewise the church is an eschatological community, a living dress rehearsal for the reign of God.

According to Calvin, sacraments consist of divine gift and human

reception: Jesus Christ comes to us in and through the bread and wine and water, but we must have faith to receive that gift. In parallel fashion, the church is both divine and human: God's means of grace combined with our human faults and failings. Calvin attended to the divine and the human dimensions of both sacraments and church, but his emphasis was squarely on God's initiative. God works in and through the sacraments to unite us to Christ, and God gives us the faith to receive Christ. Likewise, God works in and through the church, the body of Christ, and draws us into the church even when we do not deserve such grace. This may be the most valuable and the most challenging thing we can learn from Calvin's ecclesiology today: that the church is not something that we form of our own accord. It is not a product of our reaching out to God, but a gift of God reaching out to us. ∎

MARTHA MOORE-KEISH serves as an associate for worship in the Office of Theology and Worship, Presbyterian Church (U.S.A.). This article is based on a paper she presented at the North American Academy of Liturgy in January 2002.

NOTES

1.   John Calvin, *Institutes of the Christian Religion* 4.1.9; Library of Christian Classics, ed. John T. McNeill, trans. Ford Lewis Battles (Philadelphia: Westminster Press, 1960).

2.   See Michael Root and Risto Saarinen, eds., *Baptism and the Unity of the Church* (Grand

Rapids: Wm. B. Eerdmans Publishing Co.; Geneva: WCC Publications, 1998), 28ff.

3. Calvin, *Institutes* 4.1.9.

4. See Charles Wiley, unpublished dissertation, excerpt on Calvin and the marks of the church.

5. Calvin, *Institutes* 4.1.8.

6. Ibid., 4.1.11.

7. Ibid., 4.1.13.

8. Ronald S. Wallace, *Calvin's Doctrine of the Word and Sacrament* (Edinburgh: Oliver and Boyd, 1953), 150; cf. Calvin, *Institutes* 4.18.19.

9. Calvin, *Institutes* 4.15.1.

10. Ibid., 4.15.5.

11. Wallace, 177.

12. Calvin, *Institutes* 4.15.6.

13. Ibid., 4.16.5.

14. Ibid., 4.1.20.

15. Commentary on Eph. 4:5, *CR* 51:191. Cited in Wallace, 176.

16. See Alasdair I. C. Heron, *Table and Tradition* (Philadelphia: Westminster Press, 1983), 127.

17. Gordon W. Lathrop, *Holy People: A Liturgical Ecclesiology* (Minneapolis: Augsburg- Fortress, 1999), 9.

18. "The Theological Frame of a Liturgical Renewal," in *Church Quarterly* 2 (1969–70): 8–23. Cited in Lathrop, 9, and in Geoffrey Wainwright, *Doxology: The Praise of God in Worship, Doctrine, and Life* (New York: Oxford University Press, 1980), 122.

19. See Donald Baillie, *The Theology of the Sacraments, and Other Papers* (New York: Charles Scribner's Sons, 1957).

20. Calvin, *Institutes* 4.1.4.

21. Gerhard O. Forde, "Something to Believe: A Theological Perspective on Infant Baptism." *Interpretation* vol. 47, no. 3 (July 1993): 233f.

22. *Baptism and the Unity of the Church*, 17f.

23. Lathrop, *Holy People,* 47.

24. Calvin, *Institutes* 4.1.1.

25. Lathrop, *Holy People*, 165.

26. Ibid., 182.

27. William Cavanaugh, *Torture and Eucharist: Theology, Politics, and the Body of Christ* (Oxford: Blackwell Publishers, 1998).

28. Calvin, *Institutes* 4.1.4.

29. Richard A. Norris Jr., "The Eucharist in the Church," in *Marks of the Body of Christ*, ed. Carl E. Braaten and Robert W. Jenson (Grand Rapids: Wm. B. Eerdmans, 1999), 94.

30. Calvin, *Institutes* 4.1.7.

31. Ibid., 4.3.6.

The Baptism of Our Lord

One Model for a Sunday Liturgy

BY ALAN BARTHEL

BACKGROUND TO THE SUNDAY

By mid-January, we have come from the heights of the festivals of the incarnation, Christmas and Epiphany, which proclaim boldly the manifestation of God in human flesh. Beginning with the Baptism of the Lord, we are invited for the next weeks to consider what it means for us to have God's child Jesus live among us as one of us. On this festival day, we consider the beginnings of his ministry, his baptism, and the relationship between his baptism and our own. In the words of Harold Daniels,

> As in Jesus' baptism, Word and Spirit make our baptism and send us out in ministry. In the waters of baptism we are buried with Christ, cleansed of our sins, and raised with him in resurrection. We are reborn by the power of the Spirit and are declared the children of God. We are joined to Christ and his church, and with all the baptized we are called to share in Jesus' ministry.[1]

Along with our ecumenical partners, we are just beginning to reclaim the New Testament and early church understanding of baptism, which is radically different from the understanding that is manifest in the liturgies of most of our churches. Today is a great day to act ourselves into all that baptism means.

The basic order for worship will follow the fourfold pattern (ordo) of Gathering, Word, Table, and Sending. With its focus on Scripture and sacrament, the main body of the service moves broadly from hearing to doing, from proclamation to thanksgiving, and from Word to table.

Gathering—The people gather in response to God's call, offering praise in words of Scripture, prayer, and song. The people acknowledge their sinfulness and receive the declaration of God's forgiveness.

The Word—Scriptures are read and their message is proclaimed. Psalms, hymns, spiritual songs, or anthems may be sung between the readings. Responses to the proclamation of God's Word include expressions of faith and commitment, and the offering of prayers for worldwide, national, and local needs.

The Eucharist—As hearing becomes doing, the tithes and offerings of the people are gathered, and the table is set with bread and wine. The people are invited to the table of the Lord. Prayer is offered in which God is praised for creation and providence, Christ's work of redemption is remembered with thanksgiving, and the Holy Spirit is invoked upon and in the church. The bread is broken, and the bread and wine are served to the people.

Sending—The people are sent forth with God's blessing to serve.[2]

THE MODEL SERVICE FOR THE BAPTISM OF OUR LORD

GATHERING RITE

This is a festival Sunday, white is the dominant color, and our attention should be drawn to the baptismal font and an abundance of water. Symbols of the Trinity and images of the Holy Spirit, or a voice from heaven saying "This Is My Beloved Son . . . ," may also enrich this liturgy. Plumb the Scriptures for other images.

PRELUDE

One of the things that distinguishes gathering for worship from, say, going to a movie, lecture, or a concert is that in worship those gathered are the ones doing the action instead of being the ones acted upon. One church I know in its Sunday bulletin prints the biblical (lectionary) texts for the following week with the admonition, "The act of reading and praying the Scriptures in advance of worship is a spiritual discipline all Christians should engage in daily." Opening one's mind and heart to God's Word is one way we can prepare for worship. We expect the pastor, the organist and choir director, the readers and the choirs to prepare, but all too often we do not expect the congregation to prepare for worship. Indeed, congregations should make preparation for worship an expectation. Spiritual, prayerful preparation for worship gives us a new perspective when considering what to do for the prelude. How are we to help God's people gather and prepare to meet Christ in the Word, at the table, and in one another?

Along with our ecumenical partners, we are just beginning to reclaim the New Testament and early church understanding of baptism.

One suggestion for this particular Sunday, which can be appropriated in any size congregation, is to plan a prelude that focuses on the hymns particular to the Baptism of Our Lord. The texts of these hymns can provide material for meditation while the tunes are realized in one of several ways.

A musical meditation, which involves the congregation and choirs in singing a few of these hymns, is one way to engage the people's imagination. Another might be to use Luther's hymn "When Jesus to the Jordan Came." One of the choirs might sing the stanzas of this hymn *in alternatum* with the organ (with other instruments) playing chorale preludes based on this tune. This is the kind of hymn that the children should be taught, and the children's choir might provide the choral melody between the instruments' preludes. Someone said, "If we really care about the faith of our children, we will only teach them hymns that will sustain them till life's end." This is one such hymn. A contemporary text by Carl Daw, "Mark How the Lamb of God's Self-Offering," would make another wonderful setting for a prelude set to the tune of Rendez à Dieu. "What King Would Wade" by Thomas H. Troeger, set to Carol Doran's tune in *New Hymns for the Lectionary*, provides a visual and aural picture of being washed in the river.

Others include:

We may also plan a processional of a different kind! Today our processional will involve the cross, the Christ Candle (Christ, the Light of the World), and the presiding party, clergy and readers. They enter the worship space during the silence (the congregation stands at their entrance) and gather on the chancel steps, remaining there in silent prayer for a few moments.

*GREETING AND OPENING PRAYER

The presider says:
The Grace of our Lord Jesus Christ,
    the love of God and the communion
    of the Holy Spirit be with you.
And also with you.

A voice came out of the cloud, saying:
This is my Son, my Chosen; listen to
    him!

Let us pray:
Eternal God,
at the Baptism of Jesus in the River
    Jordan
you proclaimed him your beloved Son,
and anointed him with the Holy Spirit.

Grant that all who are baptized into his
    name
may keep the covenant they have
    made,
and boldly confess him as Lord and
    Savior;
who with you and the Holy Spirit lives
    and reigns,
one God, in glory everlasting.
    Amen.

"Christ, When for Us You Were Baptized,"   *Presbyterian Hymnal,* 70
"Lord, When You Came to Jordan,"   *Presbyterian Hymnal,* 71
"When Jesus Came to Jordan,"   *Presbyterian Hymnal,* 72

*Processional Hymn

"Holy God, We Praise Your Name"

Those churches with the necessary resources might use John Ferguson's arrangement of this hymn, which includes bells, choirs, brass, and congregation. The focus is on the praise of God the Three in One, as should always be the case for the opening hymn.

The procession proceeds to the font, where there is a pause in the hymn (after stanza two or three), and the Litany for the Baptism of the Lord is prayed. (See BCW, 200.) The procession and hymn continue to the appropriate places. Ferguson's arrangement of the hymn can end either on a powerful full verse or a mystical reprise of the Te Deum and the equally powerful, quiet words, "and the song goes on."

The people are now ready to hear the word of God!

Service of the Word

Old Testament
Isa. 42:1–9
The Word of the Lord
Thanks be to God

Psalm 29

"The God of Heaven" *Presbyterian Hymnal*, 180

Set this up as an antiphonal psalm, with the choir or cantor singing the verses and the congregation singing in full voice the refrain that occurs at the end of each stanza, "Glory, glory, glory!" The cantor sings the refrain; all repeat it and all sing it at the direction of the cantor. Children's voices can also provide leadership of this psalm. The random ringing of bells together with a sound track of storms, crashing water, and thunder over which the people cry "Glory!" should heighten the drama and add a sense of mystery to this text and tune.

Epistle
Acts 10:34–43
The Word of the Lord
Thanks be to God

*Hymn of the Day
"Down Galilee's Slow Roadway"
(Stanzas 1 and 2)

Down Galilee's slow roadways
a stranger traveled on
from Nazareth to Jordan
to be baptized by John.
He went down to the waters
like soldier, scribe and slave,
but there within the river
the sign was birth and grave.

Arising from the river
he saw the heavens torn;
it seemed the sky so open
revealed the Spirit's form.
The holy dove descended
amid a glorious voice:
"You are my own beloved—
my child, my heart, my choice."

During the hymn, you might consider processing the Bible into the midst of the congregation for the reading of the gospel.

* Gospel
Matt. 3:13–17
The Word of the Lord
Thanks be to God

* HYMN OF THE DAY
Down Galilee's Slow Roadway
(Stanza 3)

We too have found a roadway;
it led us to this place
We all have had to travel
in search of hope and grace.
But now beside this water
again a voice is heard.
"You are my own, my chosen,
beloved of your Lord."

SERMON

BAPTISM AND RENEWAL OF BAPTISMAL VOWS
The Baptism of the Lord is one of the four or five days most appropriate for the celebration of baptism (see *Call to Worship* 35, no. 3 [2001]: 31). If there are no baptisms on this day, it is most appropriate, as suggested in the hymn of the day, to bring our own baptisms to mind with a renewal of our baptismal vows.

REAFFIRMATION OF THE BAPTISMAL COVENANT

The reaffirmation rite is led from the font. (See the article "From Liturgical Text to Transformation" in *Call to Worship* 35, no. 3 [2001]: 31–44.)

* PROCESSIONAL HYMN
Crashing Waters at Creation

SCRIPTURE SENTENCES
Just as the body is one
and has many members,
and all the members of the body,
    though many,
are one body,
so it is with Christ.

For in the one Spirit
we were all baptized into one body—
Jews or Greeks, slaves or free—
and we were all made to drink of one
    Spirit.
Now you are the body of Christ
and individually members of it.

God has told you what is good;
and what does the Lord require of you
but to do justice, and to love kindness,
and to walk humbly with your God?

The minister continues, using one of the following:

Trusting in the gracious mercy of God,
do you turn from the ways of sin
and renounce evil and its power in the
    world?
I do.
Do you turn to Jesus Christ
and accept him as your Lord and
    Savior,
trusting in his grace and love?
I do.
Will you be Christ's faithful disciple,
obeying his Word and showing his love?
I will, with God's help.

(From this point, see the article "From Liturgical Text to Transformation," *Call to Worship* 35, no. 3 [2001]: 31–44.)

PROFESSION OF FAITH: APOSTLES' CREED

THANKSGIVING OVER WATER
Following the prayer of thanksgiving, the minister may place his or her hand into the water of the font, lift up some water, let it fall back into the font, and then make the sign of the cross over the people, while saying:

Remember your baptism and be
    thankful.

In the name of the Father and of the Son and of the Holy Spirit.
Amen.

One of several actions is possible here:

- "Asperges," the presider sprinkles the congregation with water using a pine branch that is dipped in water from the font.
- The congregation members are invited to the font to put their hand in the water and mark their foreheads remembering their baptisms.
- The congregation is invited to the font for the laying on of hands. *The minister lays both hands on the head of each of the candidates in turn, while offering one of the following prayers. The sign of the cross may be traced on the forehead of each person. Oil prepared for this purpose may be used.*

> O Lord, uphold N by your
>   Holy Spirit.
> Daily increase in him/her your
>   gifts of grace:
> the spirit of wisdom and
>   understanding,
> the spirit of counsel and
>   might,
> the spirit of knowledge and
>   the fear of the Lord,
> the spirit of joy in your
>   presence,
> both now and forever

The candidate answers:

> **Amen.**

or

Defend, O Lord, your servant N, with your heavenly grace, that he/she may continue yours forever, and daily increase in your Holy Spirit more and more, until he/she comes to your everlasting kingdom.

The candidate answers:

> **Amen.**

During any of these actions,
- the congregation might sing appropriate baptismal hymns
- the choir might perform an anthem such as those suggested in *Call to Worship* 35, no. 1 (2001): 109.

PRAYERS OF THE PEOPLE
A good source for prayers that need to be worked to fit your local circumstance is found in *Intercession for the Christian People*, edited by Gail Ramshaw, published by Pueblo Publishing. The people's responses may be sung. Include a prayer of confession in the prayers.

SERVICE OF THE TABLE

THE PEACE

OFFERTORY
The ideal anthem or hymn at this point will relate baptism and Eucharist. One such hymn is Sylvia Dunstan's "Servants of the Savior." Other fine suggestions can be found in *Call to Worship* 35, no. 1 (2001): 108–109.

INVITATION

THE GREAT THANKSGIVING PRAYER

A fine eucharistic prayer for the Baptism of the Lord will be found in the BCW. A festival setting of the people's responses, Holy, Holy, Holy; Memorial Acclamation; and Great Amen is fitting for this day.

COMMUNION

POST COMMUNION PRAYER

SENDING FORTH

HYMN

"Today We All Are Called to Be Disciples" *Presbyterian Hymnal,* 434

The hymn reminds us of our baptismal calling.

Or: "We Know That Christ Is Raised" *Presbyterian Hymnal,* 495

BLESSING AND COMMISSIONING

POSTLUDE

A postlude on "Engleberg" is appropriate, or change the position of the last hymn with the blessing and commissioning and use a Concertato setting of "We Know That Christ Is Raised" that includes brass and handbells. ■

ALAN BARTHEL is the executive director of the Presbyterian Association of Musicians.

NOTES

1. Harold Daniels, "The Extraordinary Festivals of Ordinary Time," *Reformed Liturgy & Music* 33.1 (1999), 40.

2. *Book of Common Worship,* 34.

Book Review

Hymns for the Gospels

REVIEWED BY ALAN BARTHEL

This wonderful new hymnal supplement is for Roman Catholics, Lutherans, Presbyterians, Episcopalians, Methodists, and others. It is truly a gift that contains a hymn based on the gospel reading for each Sunday of Years A, B, and C, intended for all Christians who use either the Roman or the Revised Common lectionary.

Robert Batistini, past president of the Hymn Society in the United States and Canada, and Thomas Smith, former executive director of the Society, collaborated on this project, collecting some of the best hymn texts of the late twentieth and early twenty-first centuries. Such writers as Thomas Troeger, Sylvia Dunstan, Herman Stuempfle, Fred Pratt Green, Margaret Clarkson, Timothy Dudley-Smith, Carl Daw, and Brian Wren are among those names many Presbyterian Association of Musicians (PAM) members and other readers will recognize.

In many ways, these hymns are meant to function as Bach's cantatas did in the Lutheran liturgies of his day. They are, in a sense, mini-homilies or proclamations of the Word that break open the gospel, exposing its core and holding our lives up to it.

The cover is the first example we see of the care GIA took to produce a quality work. Its gold lettering shines out above the rich deep plum color cover into which is embossed a cross with the symbols of the four evangelists at its intersection. In the book's preface, the two editors tell us that "In this volume [they] have endeavored to give a new dimension to the 'hymn of the day' concept. We began by identifying all of the gospel passages read on the Sunday of the three-year cycle of readings, *accommodating the variants among different versions of the Lectionary*" (italics mine). A real gift!

There is no "table of contents" as such, but rather an "Index of Gospel Passages and Related Hymns." This index begins with Matthew, the Gospel for Year A, and lists the passages as they occur numerically, not as they flow from the lectionary, which

Hymns for the Gospel,
2001
240 pp., $6.95
(Paperback)

> *It is truly a gift that contains a hymn based on the gospel reading for each Sunday of Years A, B, and C.*

makes the book usable by those who, for whatever peculiar reason, do not follow the lectionary.

Turning to the hymns themselves, which follow this index, try as I might, I was not able to crack the logic of the ordering of the hymns. They do not follow the lectionary order, they are not alphabetical, nor do the editors seem to have revealed their thinking on the ordering. Realizing this may reveal more about my limitations, I will leave it to you to figure out.

The page layout is clean and easy to read. Texts are interlined, making the hymns easier to sing by those who read music. The downside of interlining, of course, is that the sense of poetry and theology is less readily apparent. If one of the poetic devices is visual, it is totally lost. Also included on the page is text and tune information. It would have been helpful to have the Scripture reference on the page as well, because if you start with the hymn itself, finding its Scripture reference will be a tedious process.

"Finally," write the authors, "lest the whole exercise become academic by requiring congregations to navigate a new and unfamiliar tune each week, most of the texts in this collection have been set to familiar tunes to accommodate instant accessibility." Of course, such a goal, while laudable, also brings its own set of limitations. A number of tunes are overused; PICARDY, for one. A few of

the tunes do not do justice to the text they carry; for example, number 54, *From the River to the Desert*, by Sylvia Dunstan. She wrote this text to the Welsh tune RHUDDLAN because it fit the scene she was trying to paint, the conversation between Jesus and the evil one in the desert. The first half of the tune is somewhat somber and matches the tone of the evil one as he tempts Jesus. The second half, when Jesus speaks words recorded in the gospel, lifts us clearly and surely into a major mode. PICARDY, while a wonderful tune, just does not capture the tension and conflict between Jesus and the evil one. My wish would have been for the editors to provide the best tune for the words and let the individual church worry about finding a familiar tune if they were nervous about using an unfamiliar one. It is far easier to move to a familiar tune than it is to try to introduce a new tune to a text that is already set to a familiar tune. Nevertheless, all this does not change the fact that "Hymns for the Gospels" is an excellent resource.

At the back of the book there are three indices: 1) Acknowledgment and Copyright information; 2) Subject; and 3) Title (first line).

This is a wonderful, wonderful resource and should be on the shelf of every church musician and pastor. Batistini and Smith are to be congratulated! Highly recommended! ◼

ALAN BARTHEL is the executive director of the Presbyterian Association of Musicians.

Part Two

The Historical Record

Past Commentaries with Future Implications

Preaching the Lectionary: Two Cheers and Some Questions

BY DAVID G. BUTTRICK

[This article originally appeared in *Reformed Liturgy & Music*, vol. 28, Spring 1994.]

A by-product of mid-century liturgical renewal has been a turn to lectionary preaching. Ever since Protestant prayer books in the 1970s grabbed, revised, and published the Catholic lectionary from Vatican II, we have witnessed a revival of preaching from assigned lectionary passages. With the publication of the Common Lectionary and the Revised Common Lectionary, the custom of preaching prescribed passages has become almost de rigueur. So now we have groups of clergy studying the same assigned texts together. And we have exegetical/homiletic aids pumped out to match lectionary readings, everything from the Proclamation series to in-the-mail *Word and Witness* or *Biblical Preaching Journal*.[1] We even have magazines such as *Lectionary Homiletics* providing a full package of exegesis, historical research, and homiletic wisdom by subscription.[2] Nowadays lectionary preaching has taken hold.

COUNTING UP GAINS

QUESTION: HAS PREACHING FROM A LECTIONARY BEEN BENEFICIAL?

Presumably the lectionary has built into congregations some sense of the church year. Though lectionaries are always slanted and are seldom completely satisfactory,[3] at least they form an annual pattern, a theological pattern recalling the constitutive event of the church, namely, the life, death, and resurrection of Jesus Christ as well as the giving of his Spirit. Lectionaries do not exist for the sake of the Bible, but rather to help the church remember the Christ-event. Thus, with the turn to lectionary preaching, many churches have been swept into a recognition of the church year and, through the church year, to a liturgical acknowledgment of Jesus Christ. A gain indeed!

Ecumenical study groups have sprung up and, though they have been disappearing lately, they have been a pleasant lectionary by-product. Often such groups have packaged Catholic priests and mainline Protestant types together. Though most Catholic seminaries require their students to be acquainted with contemporary Protestant theology, unfortunately the converse is seldom true. Protestant clergy are woefully ignorant of the theological changes that have taken place in Catholicism since Vatican II. But in lectionary study groups, clergy of all faiths discover that, more often than not, they read Scripture in much the same way. So the lectionary has provided an occasion for ecumenical friendship and discussion. The bad old days when Protestants, to prove themselves to themselves, would castigate Rome—"The Whore of Babylon"—can happily be swept behind us.

Is the multiplication of lectionary study aids a benefit? Lectionary guides are, I think, a mixed blessing. Do Protestant clergy still study Scripture systematically, or are they reaching for a lectionary aid every week and doing a quick fix on some disparate passage? More, are preachers doing the tough, skilled work of homiletics, or have lectionary aids moved beyond scriptural commentary, so that ministers are picking up sermon sketches or, sometimes, whole sermons? Some years ago there were about three dozen major "Homily Services" providing for Catholic clergy.[4] Inasmuch as the ratio of priests to people these days is about one to three thousand, there is some justification for homily services—priests need all the shortcuts they can get simply to survive! But the current Protestant ratio is only about two hundred people per pastor. As a result, there used to be few sermon services for Protestants, and the few were viewed with a degree of suspicion. Ministers were enriched by having to "roll their own" sermons and do their own theological and biblical study. No wonder that ministers' libraries were large. But now, with the lectionary, there are many, many sermon services for Protestants, most of which are making money. So though lectionary study guides are providing occasions for

Though lectionaries are always slanted and are seldom completely satisfactory, at least they form an annual pattern, a theological pattern recalling the constitutive event of the church.

Lectionary guides are, I think, a mixed blessing.

study per se, they may also be undercutting the creative, thoughtful work of research and preaching. Maybe Protestant ministers are too busy for study, spending most of their time in counseling and/or institutional management, a sure sign of the Protestant *fin de siècle* ("end of an era") pathology. Are lectionary aids a benefit? We can give no more than a hesitant half-cheer.

What about a general gain in biblical literacy? Has not pericope preaching formed a knowledge of Scripture among congregational members? Not really. One of the oddities of the Biblical Theology Movement during the twentieth century is that, in spite of all the high-powered biblical emphasis, the laity do not seem to know more Bible than did their parents or their grandparents in faith. The Biblical Theology Movement, particularly in its Barthian "Word of God" form, has triumphed in many American parishes. There have been gains: commentaries have been published—the ICC, *IB,* AB, NIC, Interpretation, Hermeneia, and so forth. In the twentieth century, neo-orthodoxy turned back to the Bible. As a result, most Protestant parishes have multiple Bible study circles that, like lectionary preaching, seem to study Scripture a little chunk at a time. But biblical literacy does not seem to have risen dramatically. People fling around Bible verses, particulary over such hot issues as homo-

Preaching from pericopes has changed homiletic method, generally for the good.

sexuality, but in terms of any real theological comprehension of Scripture, preaching from the lectionary seems strangely ineffective. Once upon a time, you could scratch a Presbyterian and find an amateur theologian every time. Nowadays, a scratched Presbyterian sounds like management seminars or back copies of *Psychology Today.* Few are preaching pericopes week by week and are proud of being "Word of God" biblical, but oddly enough our churches have become theologically illiterate. So, what about lectionary preaching? We can offer no more than a tentative cheer.

LEARNING TO PREACH—AGAIN

Preaching from pericopes has changed homiletic method, generally for the good. Many of the "how-to" homiletic books published in the early half of the twentieth century presumed preaching from single-verse texts, which, of course, were seldom more than pretexts for topical sermons. So Andrew Blackwood advised preachers to select very short texts—for example, "Choose life . . ." or "I will fear no evil: for thou art with me . . ."—because ministers could repeat brief texts often during their sermons and laity would recall such phrases easily.[5] Ilion Jones was even more emphatic:

Use "textual" sermons sparingly . . . in a textual sermon, the points of the discussion are found in the text itself . . . Micah 6:8, "He has told you, O man, what is good; and what does the LORD require of you but to do justice, and to love kindness, and to walk humbly with your God?" is an example of a text that lends itself naturally to the "textual" treatment. It states clearly three things that may become the three points of the outline. . . . Someone has estimated that it would be difficult, however, to find in the whole Bible a hundred texts suitable for textual treatment.[6]

So preachers pumped out sermons on short Bible verses—"Be still and know that I am God" "Who do men say that I am?" "When he came to himself . . ." and even single-word sermons, as for example on the well-known Pauline, "therefore." So the lectionary has certainly urged a more substantial exposition of Scripture than was possible with single-verse sermons. We should probably rejoice in the change.

But the practice of preaching lections did more; it forced preachers to glance at the interrelating of homiletic and scriptural form. Texts were not simply "shells" containing some kernel to be labeled "original meaning"; no, they were intentional, designed to *do* as much as *mean*. Thus, the problem for preachers was not merely translating an "original meaning" (if such could ever be recovered) for twentieth-century people, but trying to design sermons so that the performative purpose of particular passages might be fulfilled.

A few books were unusually influential. Amos Wilder, under the sway of the "new hermeneutic," wrote *The Language of the Gospel: Early Christian Rhetoric* suggesting that forms—dialogue, story, parable, and poem—were not dispensable "shells" but were crucial to meaning.[7] Wilder's work seemed to inaugurate a flood of "literary critical" approaches—structuralist, reader-response, phenomenological, and so forth. Then, a decade later, Hans Frei's *The Eclipse of Biblical Narrative* came along, triggering a turn toward narrative preaching that is still much in vogue.[8] We might add recent parable study to the list. In 1975, the Society for Biblical Literature formed a parables seminar. Out of the seminar came works by Robert Fund, Dan Via Jr., and John Dominic Crossan.[9] Later, Bernard Brandon Scott issued his substantial *Hear Then the Parable*, a book that many preachers found opened their eyes to parable preaching in a new way.[10] Parables were surely performative and, therefore, demanded a sophisticated homiletic approach.

No wonder that homileticians have been busy trying to find new ways to preach from the Bible;[11] the Bible itself is presented quite differently through multiplying studies of literary and/or rhetorical form.[12] So, pericope preaching has responded to an explosion in literary critical studies of scriptural passages. As a result, we are beginning to catch sight of a new homiletic forming in the mind of the church. And, a new homiletic is certainly worth cheering. So, perhaps we can give another cheer for lectionary preaching.

THE LECTIONARY SHAPE

What exactly is our lectionary? Though Episcopalian, Catholic, and Lutheran lectionaries do not entirely coordinate with Common Lectionary texts, nevertheless the several Christian traditions do share many of the same readings much of the time. In addition to a selection of Psalms, lectionaries provide readings from the Hebrew Bible, from the Epistles, and from the four Gospels. In some traditions, people participate in a Prayer for Illumination prior to the readings,[13] and in other traditions they stand for the gospel, a leftover from the celebration of Christ's incarnation that still brightens Byzantine worship. The chosen readings are scheduled in a three-year cycle. Some Epistle lessons are arranged as *lectio continua* ("continuous readings"), thus providing for sustained study of particular letters. Coordination (sometimes tenuous) is usual between the reading of the Hebrew Scriptures and the Gospels. But, except on special feast days, all three readings seldom relate to one another—even though there are compulsive clergy who suppose they should preach a three-part sermon featuring all the lessons every week, a form of homiletic insanity.

Although Christian lectionaries celebrate Christ, they provide readings from the Hebrew Bible. From the beginning, Christians searched the Hebrew Scriptures to understand who Christ was and why he was crucified. But we should not suppose that we read the Hebrew Bible only because of Christ, an unpleasantly imperialistic position. No, the Hebrew Scriptures provide Christian communities with the structure of their faith, a structure they share with temple and synagogue. For the Hebrew Scriptures begin with myths of creation and the fall; and all along, they project toward God's future, building up an eschatological vision of Zion, a vision incorporated in the final chapters of Revelation. So, the Hebrew Bible forms creation and eschaton, a pattern of meaning within which the event of Jesus Christ occurs.

The Hebrew Scriptures also offer a context for faith that enables us to grasp the significance of Christ, namely the notion of covenant. God's convent *hesed* defines law, prompts prophecy, undergirds wisdom, and enlivens the singing of psalms. Such a context fills Christian liturgy: We sing psalms, we reaffirm God's covenant law, and, even if reluctantly, we hear the hard voice of the prophets. The Hebrew Scriptures shape the profundity of our faith. Without the Hebrew Bible, Christianity could turn into a glib "Jesus People" cult, which in fact has happened in some whirling Protestant circles. But the Hebrew Scriptures offer not only a searching of the depths of our common humanity but a questioning of religion itself, our religion, with a kind of cheerful if sometimes disarming honesty. Of late, homileticians have noticed that ministers are mostly preaching from the Gospel lessons—some informal surveys calculate about 70 percent of the time! No wonder that Christianity today tends toward thinness; we have neglected our faith, namely, the faith of the Hebrew Scriptures that we share with Israel.

Epistle readings may be even more neglected. But they are our primary witness to the forming of the Christian enterprise. Does not 1 Corinthians 15:3–11 offer the earliest recital of resurrection testimony? And 1 Corinthians 11:23–26 surely gives us a first call to Eucharist.[14] More, the Pauline letters hand us the gospel message, good news that prompts both our preaching and liturgical praise. Though the Gospels tell us stories of Jesus, the Epistles hand out early Christian theology with which we can understand the Gospels. If Epistle lessons are seldom preached, the church will suffer. For Pauline letters are apocalyptic;[15] they are based on two-aeon thinking. Thus, with eschatology, they counter the church's perennial tendency to celebrate itself in liturgy; after all, the church does not have forever. Of course, with the Epistles, the problem we face is that brief lectionary aids cannot provide preachers with an adequate grasp of Pauline theology, or dish out smart hermeneutic strategies to "demythologize" passages for proclamation. So, these days, out of a kind of copelessness, preachers seem to be running scared from Epistle lessons.

Now a key to the lectionary is, as we have said, the church year. And the church year in turn exists to help the church recall a constitutive Christ-event. Lectionaries do not exist to serve the Bible per se, or to promote biblical authority. No, the lectionary is a way of remembering Christ through major festivals. Some readings, of course, are prompted by elaborations of the church year; for example, Ember Days. Liturgy has always had a way of stitching in ornamentation between clear, clean lines. But minor festivals are not crucial to the structure of the Christ-event and, therefore, cannot be considered compulsory. If lectionaries become "law," they can destroy the free proclamation of the gospel. Preachers must have liberty *not* to preach the lectionary (or *not* the Bible either!). For, obviously, the gospel can be preached and a patterned church year observed without direct recourse to a lectionary.

ASKING SOME QUESTIONS

Can we now venture some brief, sharp questions?[16]

1. Is lectionary preaching theologically sane?

Whether we admit it or not, we lectionary preachers seem to assume that every designated swatch of Scripture has some sort of God-message tucked inside—after all, do we not name Bible readings "Word of God"? But many of the lections are not defined literary units, and some may not even be terribly significant. A doughty grandmother of ours had a box divided into thirty-one sections. In each section there was a small rolled-up scroll with a verse from Scripture. Every day in the month you could tweezer up a message from God. Dare we ask in what way lectionary preaching is much different? How can an isolated passage, clipped out of context, be packed with ultimate God-meaning?

2. Does lectionary preaching suppress prophecy?

If preaching must always begin with an assigned passage, how can the pulpit speak to the "nowness" of human event? A graduate student in the Midwest has been studying pulpit response to the so-called "Gulf War" of 1991. He picked three sample cities and phoned the two dozen largest Protestant parishes to see how they addressed that solemn January Sunday when war was decided. He discovered that almost none of the churches mentioned the war in sermons. The usual explanation: "We follow the lectionary." (Consider what might have happened to the civil rights movement had Martin Luther King Jr. felt bound by a lectionary!) Now we can argue that the Bible is prophetic, and no doubt we are correct. But separate pericopes can scarcely provide a basis for the Bible's prophetic witness. What the lectionary can do is to give timid preachers a "biblical" excuse for silence.

3. Does lectionary preaching rivet sermons to past-tense revelations?

James Barr[17] has labeled the twentieth century the "revelation through history" era. No doubt the label is appropriate. For dialectical theology, stressing the Otherness of God, tended to deny any "natural theology" as well as the presentments of what used to be termed "religious affection"—thus, effectively deleting God-consciousness from the contemporary world! Of course, dialec-

tical theology may have been crowded into such a narrowed position by the rise of descriptive sciences as well as the delineations of Freud. "Mighty acts of God" history seemed a safe alternative, particularly when you could argue that such history has been written down in a book, the Holy Bible, which happily we Christians possess. So wielding historical-critical method, ministers preached from a revelation-in-history Bible, often filling their sermons with discussions of the biblical past. Gradually our message seemed to turn into nostalgia—"once upon a time God acted." The apostle Paul shouted, "Now is the day of salvation," but, subtly, our sermons slipped into an odd preoccupation with past-tense religion. Most modern theologians have scuttled the notion of God as an "actor" in revelation history, but we preachers may still read lections within a historicist model.

4. Is there an emerging tension between preaching the Bible and preaching the gospel?

Many sermons nowadays seem to be short talks about the Bible. Now the Bible is surely a good gift of God, and preachers should be grateful for the gift ("gift" is, of course, a more biblical word than "authority"). But, as we all know, the Bible can be sexist, anti-Semitic, and even unpleasantly smug. After all, the human authors of Scripture were as worldly, prejudiced, self-righteous, and sinful as we. Nonetheless, these days, there is some tendency to embrace all Scripture without reservation under the rubric "Word of God."

Some months ago we welcomed a smart speaker to the Vanderbilt campus. The speaker spoke on how to preach Psalm 137:9: "Happy shall they be who take your little ones and dash them against the rock!" The talk was brilliant, witty, and full of insight. But, after the speech, a first question from the audience was devastating: "Why bother?" In other words, why would preachers want to preach a baby-bashing text when they could declare the good news? Theologically the church reveres Scripture because it contains the gospel message and not because it is, without reduction, some sort of "Word of God."

SO WHY DO WE PREACH?

Why do we preach? In church, our preaching falls under the Anselmian notion of "Faith Seeking Understanding." Presumably, people in church are believers, albeit secular-in-style believers. Thus, preaching to the faithful is theological activity; we are seeking some knowledge of God to fill our faith. As we explore the mystery of God, we draw on our theological heritage, a tradition going all the way back to early centuries. Do not PC(USA) types clutch (sometimes unread) a *Book of Confessions*? We will also turn to Scripture. But notice the object of our concern is the mystery of God, a mystery in which we live and serve *right now*. The in-church preaching agenda is theological. Thus the Bible is something that we *turn to* and not necessarily something with which we *must* always begin.

Not surprisingly, neo-orthodox "Word of God" theology began to form about the same time as declared fundamentalism. They are both part of a reactionary tide that, in our frightened age, seems to have swept over the church. In the 1960s, Word of God theology armed the civil rights movement. Today, the political right wing seems to be toting most of the Bibles, and right-wing Word of God theology will use Scripture to put down women's rights, to undercut the peace movement, to oppose abortion, and to bash gay-lesbian persons. So "biblical preaching" is no safeguard against cultural agendas. The Bible cannot be labeled Word of God if it is used oppressively.

Lectionary preaching can serve the memory work of the church year. But lectionaries can turn demonic if taken captive by dominating notions of biblical authority. A lectionary, like the Bible, can be a gift, but only if received as given, in freedom—liturgical and homiletic freedom. ■

DAVID G. BUTTRICK, a noted author and speaker, served at the time he wrote this article as professor of homiletics and worship at the Divinity School of Vanderbilt University in Nashville.

NOTES

1. The Proclamation series is published by Fortress Press (Minneapolis); *Word and Witness,* edited by Paul Scott Wilson, is published by Liturgical Publications (New Berlin, Wis.); *Biblical Preaching Journal,* edited by Gary W. Kidwell, is published by the Biblical Preaching Institute (Versailles, Ky.).

2. *Lectionary Homiletics,* edited by David B. Howell, is published by Lectionary Homiletics (Midlothian, Va.).

3. See John Reumann, "A History of Lectionaries: From the Synagogue at Nazareth to Post-Vatican II," *Interpretation*, vol. 31, no. 2 (April 1977), 116–30; also, Shelly E. Cochran, "The Church Year and Its Influence on Preaching," *The Academy of Homiletics: Papers of the Annual Meeting* (December 4–8, 1990), 33–42. Cochran spots "inherent biases and hermeneutic tendencies" in a very savvy fashion.

4. See Robert P. Waznak, "A Descriptive and Evaluative Study of Contemporary Catholic Homiletic Services in the Light of the Philosophy of the Second Vatican Council," Ph.D. dissertation. Temple University, 1973.

5. Andrew W. Blackwood, *The Preparation of Sermons* (Nashville: Abingdon, 1948), 50.

6. Ilion T. Jones, *Principles and Practice of Preaching: A Comprehensive Study of the Art of Sermon Construction* (Nashville: Abingdon, 1956), 82–83.

7. Amos Wilder, *The Language of the Gospel: Early Christian Rhetoric* (New York: Harper & Row, 1964).

8. Hans W. Frei, *The Eclipse of Biblical Narrative: A Study in Eighteenth and Nineteenth Century Hermeneutics* (New Haven, Conn.: Yale University Press, 1974).

9. For a brief history of the parable seminar and its impact, see Norman Perrin, *Jesus and the Language of the Kingdom: Symbol and Metaphor in New Testament Interpretation* (Philadelphia: Fortress Press, 1976), part 3.

10. Bernard Brandon Scott, *Hear Then the Parable: A Commentary on the Parables of Jesus* (Minneapolis: Fortress Press, 1989).

11. See Richard Eslinger, *A New Hearing: Living Options in Homiletic Method* (Nashville: Abingdon, 1987).

12. Edgar V. McKnight has been a chronicler of new critical methodologies; see his *The Bible and the Common Reader: An Introduction to Literary Criticism* (Philadelphia: Fortress Press, 1985).

13. American pietism often moved the prayer immediately before the sermon as if preaching alone needed prayer. But Calvin prayed before the reading of Scripture, for Scripture also was insufficient without the Holy Spirit.

14. Contra Joachim Jeremias, *The Eucharistic Words of Jesus* (New York: Charles Scribner's Sons, 1966), chap. 4.

15. J. Christiaan Beker, *Paul the Apostle: The Triumph of God in Life and Thought* (Philadelphia: Fortress Press, 1980).

16. The questions echo material in my *A Captive Voice: The Liberation of Preaching* (Louisville, Ky.: Westminster John Knox Press, 1994).

17. See James Barr, "Revelation through History in the Old Testament and in Modern Theology," *New Theology*, no. 1, ed. Martin E. Martin and Dean G. Peerman (New York: Macmillan, 1964), 60–74.

Scriptural Index to the Lectionary

Scripture Texts as They Appear in the Revised Common Lectionary *for Years A, B, and C*

Scripture Lesson	Liturgical Date	Lectionary Year
Gen. 1:1–2:4a	Trinity Sunday	A
Gen. 1:1–2:4a	Easter Vigil	ABC
Gen. 1:1–5	Baptism of the Lord	B
Gen. 2:15–17; 3:1–7	Lent 1	A
Gen. 2:18–24	Ordinary 27	B
Gen. 3:8–15	Ordinary 10	B
Gen. 6:9–22; 7:24; 8:14–19	Ordinary 9	A
Gen. 7:1–5, 11–18; 8:6–18; 9:8–13	Easter Vigil	ABC
Gen. 9:8–17	Lent 1	B
Gen. 11:1–9	Pentecost	C
Gen. 12:1–4a	Lent 2	A
Gen. 12:1–9	Ordinary 10	A
Gen. 15:1–6	Ordinary 19	C
Gen. 15:1–12, 17–18	Lent 2	C
Gen. 17:1–7, 15–16	Lent 2	B
Gen. 18:1–15, (21:1–17)	Ordinary 11	A
Gen. 18:1–10a	Ordinary 16	C
Gen. 18:20–32	Ordinary 17	C
Gen. 21:8–21	Ordinary 12	A
Gen. 22:1–14	Ordinary 13	A
Gen. 22:1–18	Easter Vigil	ABC
Gen. 24:34–38, 42–49, 58–67	Ordinary 14	A
Gen. 25:19–34	Ordinary 15	A
Gen. 28:10–19a	Ordinary 16	A
Gen. 29:15–28	Ordinary 17	A

Scripture Lesson	Liturgical Date	Lectionary Year
Gen. 32:22–31	Ordinary 18	A
Gen. 32:22–31	Ordinary 29	C
Gen. 37:1–4, 12–28	Ordinary 19	A
Gen. 45:1-15	Ordinary 20	A
Gen. 45:3–11, 15	Ordinary 7	C
Gen. 50:15–21	Ordinary 24	A
Exod. 1:8–2:10	Ordinary 21	A
Exod. 3:1–15	Ordinary 22	A
Exod. 12:1–14	Ordinary 23	A
Exod. 12:1–4, (5–10), 11–14	Holy Thursday	ABC
Exod. 14:10–31; 15:20–21	Easter Vigil	ABC
Exod. 14:19–31	Ordinary 24	A
Exod. 15:1b–11, 20–21	Ordinary 24	A
Exod. 15:1b–13, 17–18	Easter Vigil	ABC
Exod. 16:2–4, 9–15	Ordinary 18	B
Exod. 16:2–15	Ordinary 25	A
Exod. 17:1–7	Lent 3	A
Exod. 17:1–7	Ordinary 26	A
Exod. 19:2–8a	Ordinary 11	A
Exod. 20:1–4, 7–9, 12–20	Ordinary 27	A
Exod. 20:1–17	Lent 3	B
Exod. 24:12–18	Transfig.	A
Exod. 32:1–14	Ordinary 28	A
Exod. 32:7–14	Ordinary 24	C
Exod. 33:12–23	Ordinary 29	A
Exod. 34:29–35	Transfig.	C
Lev. 19:1–2, 9–18	Ordinary 7	A
Lev. 19:1–2, 15–18	Ordinary 30	B
Num. 11:4–6, 10–16, 24–29	Ordinary 26	A
Num. 11:24–30	Pentecost	B
Num. 21:4–9	Lent 4	B
Deut. 4:1–2, 6–9	Ordinary 22	B
Deut. 5:12–15	Ordinary 9	B
Deut. 6:1–9	Ordinary 31	A
Deut. 8:7–18	Thanksgiving	A
Deut. 11:18–21, 26–28	Ordinary 9	A
Deut. 11:18–21, 26–28	Ordinary 9	B
Deut. 18:15–20	Ordinary 4	C
Deut. 26:1–11	Thanksgiving	C
Deut. 26:1–11	Lent 1	C
Deut. 30:9–14	Ordinary 15	A
Deut. 30:15–20	Ordinary 6	C
Deut. 30:15–20	Ordinary 23	A
Deut. 34:1–12	Ordinary 30	A

Scripture Lesson	Liturgical Date	Lectionary Year
Josh. 3:7–17	Ordinary 31	C
Josh. 5:9–12	Lent 4	B
Josh. 24:1–2a, 14–18	Ordinary 21	A
Josh. 24:1–3a, 14–25	Ordinary 32	A
Judg. 4:1–7	Ordinary 33	B
Ruth 1:1–18	Ordinary 31	B
Ruth 3:1–5; 4:13–17	Ordinary 32	B
1 Sam. 1:4–20	Ordinary 33	B
1 Sam. 2:1–10	Ordinary 33	C
1 Sam. 2:18–20, 26	Christmas 1	B
1 Sam. 3:1–10, (11–20)	Ordinary 2	B
1 Sam. 3:1–10, (11–20)	Ordinary 9	B
1 Sam. 8:4–11, (12–15), 16–20, (11:14–15)	Ordinary 10	B
1 Sam. 15:34–16:13	Ordinary 11	B
1 Sam. 16:1–3	Lent 4	A
1 Sam. 17:(1a, 4–11, 19–23), 32–49	Ordinary 12	B
1 Sam. 17:57–18:5, (10–16)	Ordinary 12	B
2 Sam. 1:1,17–27	Ordinary 13	B
2 Sam. 5:1–5, 9–10	Ordinary 14	B
2 Sam. 6:1–5, 12b–19	Ordinary 15	B
2 Sam. 7:1–11, 16	Advent 4	B
2 Sam. 7:1–14a	Ordinary 16	B
2 Sam. 11:1–15	Ordinary 17	B
2 Sam. 11:26–12:13a	Ordinary 18	B
2 Sam. 11:26–12:10, 13–15	Ordinary 11	C
2 Sam. 18:5–9, 15, 31–33	Ordinary 19	B
2 Sam. 23:1–7	Reign of Christ 34	B
1 Kgs. 2:10–12; 3:3–14	Ordinary 20	B
1 Kgs. 3:5–12	Ordinary 17	A
1 Kgs. 8:(1, 6, 10–11), 22–30, 41–43	Ordinary 21	B
1 Kgs. 8:22–23, 41–43	Ordinary 9	C
1 Kgs. 17:8–16	Ordinary 32	B
1 Kgs. 17:8–16, (17–24)	Ordinary 10	C
1 Kgs. 17:17–24	Ordinary 10	C
1 Kgs. 18:20–21, (22–29), 30–39	Ordinary 9	C
1 Kgs. 19:1–4, (5–7), 8–15a	Ordinary 12	C
1 Kgs. 19:4–8	Ordinary 19	B
1 Kgs. 19:9–18	Ordinary 19	A
1 Kgs. 19:15–16, 19–21	Ordinary 13	C
1 Kgs. 21:1–10, (11–14), 15–21a	Ordinary 11	C
2 Kgs. 2:1–12	Transfig.	B
2 Kgs. 2:1–2, 6–14	Ordinary 13	C

Scripture Lesson	Liturgical Date	Lectionary Year
2 Kgs. 4:42–44	Ordinary 17	B
2 Kgs. 5:1–3, 7–15c	Ordinary 28	C
2 Kgs. 5:1–14	Ordinary 6	B
2 Kgs. 5:1–14	Ordinary 14	C
Neh. 8:1–3, 5–6, 8–10	Ordinary 3	C
Esth. 7:1–6, 9–10; 9:20–22	Ordinary 26	B
Job 1:1; 2:1–10	Ordinary 27	B
Job 19:23–27a	Ordinary 32	C
Job 23:1–9, 16–17	Ordinary 28	B
Job 38:1–7, (34–41)	Ordinary 29	B
Job 38:1–11	Ordinary 12	B
Job 42:1–6, 10–17	Ordinary 30	B
Ps. 1	Ordinary 6	C
Ps. 1	Easter 7	B
Ps. 1	Ordinary 25	B
Ps. 1	Ordinary 23	C
Ps. 1	Ordinary 30	A
Ps. 2	Transfig.	A
Ps. 4	Easter 3	B
Ps. 5:1–8	Ordinary 11	C
Ps. 8	Trinity Sunday	AC
Ps. 8	New Year	ABC
Ps. 8	Ordinary 27	B
Ps. 9:9–20	Ordinary 12	B
Ps. 13	Ordinary 13	A
Ps. 14	Ordinary 17	B
Ps. 14	Ordinary 24	C
Ps. 15	Ordinary 4	A
Ps. 15	Ordinary 22	B
Ps. 15	Ordinary 16	C
Ps. 16	Easter 2	A
Ps. 16	Easter Vigil	ABC
Ps. 16	Ordinary 33	B
Ps. 16	Ordinary 13	C
Ps. 17:1–7, 15	Ordinary 18	A
Ps. 17:1–9	Ordinary 32	C
Ps. 19	Easter Vigil	ABC
Ps. 19	Lent 3	B
Ps. 19	Ordinary 3	C
Ps. 19	Ordinary 27	A
Ps. 19	Ordinary 24	B
Ps. 19:7–14	Ordinary 26	B
Ps. 20	Ordinary 11	B
Ps. 22	Good Friday	ABC
Ps. 22:1–15	Ordinary 28	B

Scripture Lesson	Liturgical Date	Lectionary Year
Ps. 22:19–28	Ordinary 12	C
Ps. 22:23–31	Lent 2	B
Ps. 22:25–31	Easter 5	B
Ps. 23	Easter 4	ABC
Ps. 23	Lent 4	A
Ps. 23	Ordinary 28	A
Ps. 23	Ordinary 16	B
Ps. 24	All Saints	B
Ps. 24	Ordinary 15	B
Ps. 25:1–9	Ordinary 26	A
Ps. 25:1–10	Lent 1	B
Ps. 25:1–10	Advent 1	C
Ps. 25:1–10	Ordinary 15	C
Ps. 26	Ordinary 27	B
Ps. 26:1–8	Ordinary 22	A
Ps. 27	Lent 2	C
Ps. 27:1, 4–9	Ordinary 3	A
Ps. 29	Baptism of the Lord 1	ABC
Ps. 29	Trinity Sunday	B
Ps. 30	Ordinary 6	B
Ps. 30	Easter 3	C
Ps. 30	Ordinary 14	C
Ps. 30	Ordinary 10	C
Ps. 30	Ordinary 13	B
Ps. 31:1–5, 19–24	Ordinary 9	A
Ps. 31:9–16	Palm/Passion Sunday	ABC
Ps. 31:1–5, 15–16	Easter 5	A
Ps. 32	Lent 1	A
Ps. 32	Lent 4	C
Ps. 32	Ordinary 11	C
Ps. 32:1–7	Ordinary 31	C
Ps. 33:1–12	Ordinary 10	A
Ps. 33:12–22	Ordinary 19	C
Ps. 34:1–8, (19–22)	Ordinary 30	B
Ps. 34:1–8	Ordinary 19	B
Ps. 34:1–10, 22	All Saints	A
Ps. 34:9–14	Ordinary 20	B
Ps. 34:15–22	Ordinary 21	B
Ps. 36:5–10	Ordinary 2	C
Ps. 37:1–9	Ordinary 27	C
Ps. 37:1–11, 39–40	Ordinary 7	C
Ps. 40:1–11	Ordinary 2	A
Ps. 41	Ordinary 7	B
Pss. 42 and 43	Ordinary 12	C
Pss. 42 and 43	Easter Vigil	ABC

Scripture Lesson	Liturgical Date	Lectionary Year
Ps. 43	Ordinary 31	A
Ps. 45:10–17	Ordinary 14	A
Ps. 45:1–2, 6–9	Ordinary 22	B
Ps. 46	Easter Vigil	ABC
Ps. 46	Ordinary 9	A
Ps. 46	Ordinary 34	C
Ps. 47	Ascension	ABC
Ps. 48	Ordinary 14	B
Ps. 49:1–12	Ordinary 18	C
Ps. 50:1–6	Transfig.	B
Ps. 50:7–15	Ordinary 10	A
Ps. 50:1–8, 22–23	Ordinary 19	C
Ps. 51:1–10	Ordinary 24	C
Ps. 51:1–12	Ordinary 18	B
Ps. 51:1–12	Lent 5	B
Ps. 51:1–17	Ash Wednesday	ABC
Ps. 52	Ordinary 16	C
Ps. 54	Ordinary 25	B
Ps. 62:5–12	Ordinary 3	B
Ps. 63:1–8	Lent 3	C
Ps. 65	Thanksgiving	A
Ps. 65	Ordinary 30	C
Ps. 65:(1–8), 9–13	Ordinary 15	A
Ps. 66:1–9	Ordinary 14	C
Ps. 66:1–12	Ordinary 28	C
Ps. 66:8–20	Easter 6	A
Ps. 67	Ordinary 20	A
Ps. 67	Easter 6	C
Ps. 68:1–10, 32–35	Easter 7	A
Ps. 69:7–10, (11–15), 16–18	Ordinary 12	A
Ps. 70	Ordinary 32	A
Ps. 71:1–6	Ordinary 4	C
Ps. 71:1–6	Ordinary 21	C
Ps. 72:1–7, 10–14	Epiphany	ABC
Ps. 72:1–7, 18–19	Advent 2	A
Ps. 77:1–2, 11–20	Ordinary 13	C
Ps. 78:1–7	Ordinary 32	A
Ps. 78:1–4, 12–16	Ordinary 26	A
Ps. 78:23–29	Ordinary 18	B
Ps. 79:1–9	Ordinary 25	C
Ps. 80:1–7, 17–19	Advent 4	A
Ps. 80:1–7, 17–19	Advent 1	B
Ps. 80:1–7	Advent 4	C
Ps. 80:1–2, 8–19	Ordinary 20	C
Ps. 80:7–15	Ordinary 27	A

Scripture Lesson	Liturgical Date	Lectionary Year
Ps. 81:1–10	Ordinary 9	B
Ps. 81:1–10	Ordinary 9	B
Ps. 81:1, 10–16	Ordinary 22	C
Ps. 82	Ordinary 20	C
Ps. 82	Ordinary 15	C
Ps. 84	Ordinary 21	B
Ps. 84:1–7	Ordinary 30	C
Ps. 85	Ordinary 17	C
Ps. 85:1–2, 8–13	Advent 2	B
Ps. 85:8–13	Ordinary 19	A
Ps. 85:8–13	Ordinary 15	B
Ps. 86:1–10, 16–17	Ordinary 12	A
Ps. 86:11–17	Ordinary 16	A
Ps. 89:1–4, 15–18	Ordinary 13	A
Ps. 89:1–4, 19–26	Advent 4	B
Ps. 89:20–37	Ordinary 16	B
Ps. 90:1–8, (9–11), 12	Ordinary 33	A
Ps. 90:1–6, 13–17	Ordinary 30	A
Ps. 90:12–17	Ordinary 28	B
Ps. 91:1–2, 9–16	Lent 1	C
Ps. 91:1–6, 14–16	Ordinary 26	C
Ps. 91:9–16	Ordinary 29	B
Ps. 92:1–4, 12–15	Ordinary 11	B
Ps. 92:1–4, 12–15	Ordinary 8	C
Ps. 93	Ordinary 34	B
Ps. 93	Ascension	B
Ps. 95	Lent 3	A
Ps. 95:1–7a	Ordinary 34	A
Ps. 96	Christmas Day 1	ABC
Ps. 96	Ordinary 9	C
Ps. 96:1–9, (10–13)	Ordinary 29	A
Ps. 96:1–9	Ordinary 9	C
Ps. 96:1–9	Ordinary 9	C
Ps. 97	Christmas Day 2	ABC
Ps. 97	Easter 7	C
Ps. 98	Christmas Day 3	ABC
Ps. 98	Easter Vigil	ABC
Ps. 98	Easter 6	B
Ps. 98	Ordinary 32	C
Ps. 98	Ordinary 33	C
Ps. 99	Ordinary 29	A
Ps. 99	Transfig.	AC
Ps. 100	Ordinary 11	A
Ps. 100	Reign of Christ 34	A
Ps. 100	Thanksgiving	C

Scripture Lesson	Liturgical Date	Lectionary Year
Ps. 103:(1–7), 8–13	Ordinary 24	A
Ps. 103:1–8	Ordinary 21	C
Ps. 103:1–13, 22	Ordinary 8	B
Ps. 104:1–9, 24, 35c	Ordinary 29	B
Ps. 104:24–34, 35b	Pentecost	ABC
Ps. 105:1–6, 16–22, 45b	Ordinary 19	A
Ps. 105:1–6, 37–45	Ordinary 25	A
Ps. 105:1–6, 23–26, 45c	Ordinary 22	A
Ps. 105:1–11, 45b	Ordinary 17	A
Ps. 106:1–6, 19–23	Ordinary 28	A
Ps. 107:1–3, 17–22	Lent 4	B
Ps. 107:1–3, 23–32	Ordinary 12	B
Ps. 107:1–7, 33–37	Ordinary 31	A
Ps. 107:1–9, 43	Ordinary 18	C
Ps. 110	Ascension	C
Ps. 111	Epiphany 4	B
Ps. 111	Ordinary 20	B
Ps. 111	Ordinary 28	C
Ps. 112	Ordinary 22	C
Ps. 112:1–9 (10)	Ordinary 5	A
Ps. 113	Ordinary 25	C
Ps. 114	Easter Vigil	ABC
Ps. 114	Easter Evening	ABC
Ps. 114	Ordinary 24	A
Ps. 116:1–4, 12–19	Easter 3	A
Ps. 116:1–2, 12–19	Ordinary 11	A
Ps. 116:1–2, 12–19	Maundy Thursday	ABC
Ps. 116:1–9	Ordinary 24	B
Ps. 118:1–2, 14–24	Easter	ABC
Ps. 118:1–2, 19–29	Palm/Passion Sunday	ABC
Ps. 118:14–29	Easter 2	C
Ps. 119:1–8	Ordinary 6	A
Ps. 119:1–8	Ordinary 31	B
Ps. 119:9–16	Lent 5	B
Ps. 119:33–40	Ordinary 7	A
Ps. 119:33–40	Ordinary 23	A
Ps. 119:97–104	Ordinary 29	C
Ps. 119:105–112	Ordinary 15	A
Ps. 119:129–136	Ordinary 17	A
Ps. 119:137–144	Ordinary 31	C
Ps. 121	Lent 2	A
Ps. 121	Ordinary 29	C
Ps. 122	Advent 1	A
Ps. 123	Ordinary 23	A
Ps. 123	Ordinary 14	B

Scripture Lesson	Liturgical Date	Lectionary Year
Ps. 124	Ordinary 21	A
Ps. 124	Ordinary 26	B
Ps. 125	Ordinary 23	B
Ps. 126	Advent 3	B
Ps. 126	Ordinary 30	B
Ps. 126	Thanksgiving	B
Ps. 126	Lent 5	C
Ps. 127	Ordinary 32	B
Ps. 128	Ordinary 17	A
Ps. 130	Lent 5	A
Ps. 130	Ordinary 13	B
Ps. 130	Ordinary 19	B
Ps. 130	Ordinary 10	B
Ps. 131	Ordinary 8	A
Ps. 132:1–2, (13–18)	Reign of Christ 34	B
Ps. 133	Ordinary 20	A
Ps. 122	Ordinary 12	B
Ps. 133	Easter 2	B
Ps. 136:1–9, 23–26	Easter Vigil	ABC
Ps. 137	Ordinary 27	C
Ps. 138	Ordinary 21	A
Ps. 138	Ordinary 10	B
Ps. 138	Ordinary 17	C
Ps. 138	Ordinary 5	C
Ps. 139:1–6, 13–18	Ordinary 2	B
Ps. 139:1–6, 13–18	Ordinary 9	B
Ps. 139:1–6, 13–18	Ordinary 23	C
Ps. 139:1–12, 23–24	Ordinary 16	A
Ps. 143	Easter Vigil	ABC
Ps. 145:1–8	Ordinary 25	A
Ps. 145:8–9, 14–21	Ordinary 18	A
Ps. 145:8–14	Ordinary 14	A
Ps. 145:10–18	Ordinary 17	B
Ps. 145:1–5, 17–21	Ordinary 32	C
Ps. 146:5–10	Advent 3	A
Ps. 146	Ordinary 32	B
Ps. 146	Ordinary 23	B
Ps. 146	Ordinary 26	C
Ps. 146	Ordinary 31	B
Ps. 146	Ordinary 10	C
Ps. 147:1–11, 20c	Ordinary 5	B
Ps. 147:12–20	Christmas 2	ABC
Ps. 148	Christmas 1	ABC
Ps. 148	Easter 5	C
Ps. 149	Ordinary 23	A

Scripture Lesson	Liturgical Date	Lectionary Year
Ps. 149	All Saints	C
Ps. 150	Easter 2	C
Prov. 1:20–33	Ordinary 24	B
Prov. 8:1–8, 19–21; 9:4b–6	Easter Vigil	ABC
Prov. 8:1–4, 22–31	Trinity Sunday	C
Prov. 9:1–6	Ordinary 20	B
Prov. 22:1–2, 8–9, 22–23	Ordinary 23	B
Prov. 25:6–7	Ordinary 22	C
Prov. 31:10–31	Ordinary 25	B
Eccl. 1:2, 12–14; 2:18–23	Ordinary 18	C
Song 2:8–13	Ordinary 9	B
Song 2:8–13	Ordinary 22	B
Isa. 1:1, 10–20	Ordinary 19	C
Isa. 1:10–18	Ordinary 31	C
Isa. 2:1–5	Advent 1	A
Isa. 5:1–7	Ordinary 27	A
Isa. 5:1–7	Ordinary 20	C
Isa. 6:1–8	Trinity Sunday	B
Isa. 6:1–8, (9–13)	Ordinary 5	C
Isa. 7:10–14	Annunciation	ABC
Isa. 7:10–16	Advent 4	A
Isa. 9:1–4	Ordinary 3	A
Isa. 9:2–7	Christmas Day 1	ABC
Isa. 11:1–10	Advent 2	A
Isa. 12	Ordinary 33	C
Isa. 12:2–6	Easter Vigil	ABC
Isa. 12:2–6	Advent 3	C
Isa. 25:1–9	Ordinary 28	A
Isa. 25:6–9	Easter Evening	ABC
Isa. 25:6–9	Easter	B
Isa. 25:6–9	All Saints	B
Isa. 35:1–10	Advent 3	A
Isa. 35:4–7a	Ordinary 23	B
Isa. 40:1–11	Advent 2	B
Isa. 40:21–31	Ordinary 5	B
Isa. 42:1–9	Baptism of the Lord 1	A
Isa. 43:1–7	Baptism of the Lord 1	C
Isa. 43:16–21	Lent 5	C
Isa. 43:18–25	Ordinary 7	B
Isa. 44:6–8	Ordinary 16	A
Isa. 45:1–7	Ordinary 29	A
Isa. 49:1–7	Ordinary 2	A
Isa. 49:8–16a	Ordinary 8	A
Isa. 50:4–9	Palm/Passion Sunday	ABC
Isa. 50:4–9a	Ordinary 24	B

Scripture Lesson	Liturgical Date	Lectionary Year
Isa. 51:1–6	Ordinary 21	A
Isa. 52:7–10	Christmas Day 3	ABC
Isa. 52:13–53:12	Good Friday	ABC
Isa. 53:4–12	Ordinary 29	B
Isa. 55:1–5	Ordinary 18	A
Isa. 55:1–9	Lent 3	C
Isa. 55:1–11	Easter Vigil	ABC
Isa. 55:10–13	Ordinary 8	C
Isa. 55:10–13	Ordinary 15	A
Isa. 56:1, 6–8	Ordinary 20	A
Isa. 58:1–9a (9b–12)	Ordinary 5	A
Isa. 58:1–12	Ash Wednesday	ABC
Isa. 58:9b–14	Ordinary 21	C
Isa. 60:1–6	Epiphany	ABC
Isa. 61:1–4, 8–11	Advent 3	B
Isa. 61:10–62:3	Christmas 1	B
Isa. 62:1–5	Ordinary 2	C
Isa. 62:6–12	Christmas Day 2	ABC
Isa. 63:7–9	Christmas 1	A
Isa. 64:1–9	Advent 1	B
Isa. 65:1–9	Ordinary 12	C
Isa. 65:17–25	Ordinary 33	C
Isa. 65:17–25	Easter	C
Isa. 66:10–14	Ordinary 14	C
Jer. 1:4–10	Ordinary 4	C
Jer. 1:4–10	Ordinary 21	C
Jer. 2:4–13	Ordinary 22	C
Jer. 4:11–12, 22–28	Ordinary 24	C
Jer. 8:1–9:1	Ordinary 25	C
Jer. 11:18–20	Ordinary 25	B
Jer. 14:7–10, 19–22	Ordinary 25	C
Jer. 15:15–21	Ordinary 22	A
Jer. 17:5–10	Ordinary 6	C
Jer. 18:1–11	Ordinary 23	C
Jer. 20:7–13	Ordinary 12	A
Jer. 23:1–6	Reign of Christ 34	C
Jer. 23:1–6	Ordinary 16	B
Jer. 23:1–6	Ordinary 34	C
Jer. 23:23–29	Ordinary 20	C
Jer. 28:5–9	Ordinary 13	A
Jer. 29:1, 4–7	Ordinary 28	C
Jer. 31:1–6	Easter	A
Jer. 31:7–9	Ordinary 30	B
Jer. 31:7–14	Christmas 2	ABC
Jer. 31:27–34	Ordinary 29	C

Scripture Lesson	Liturgical Date	Lectionary Year
Jer. 31:31–34	Lent 5	B
Jer. 32:1–3a, 6–15	Ordinary 26	C
Jer. 33:14–16	Advent 1	C
Lam. 1:1–6	Ordinary 27	C
Lam. 3:19–26	Ordinary 27	C
Lam. 3:23–33	Ordinary 13	B
Ezek. 2:1–5	Ordinary 14	B
Ezek. 17:22–24	Ordinary 11	B
Ezek. 18:1–4, 25–32	Ordinary 26	A
Ezek. 33:7–11	Ordinary 23	A
Ezek. 34:11–16, 20–24	Ordinary 33	A
Ezek. 34:11–16, 20–24	Reign of Christ	A
Ezek. 36:24–28	Easter Vigil	ABC
Ezek. 37:1–14	Lent 5	A
Ezek. 37:1–14	Easter Vigil	ABC
Ezek. 37:1–14	Pentecost	B
Dan. 7:1–3, 15–18	All Saints	C
Dan. 7:9–10, 13–14	Ordinary 34	B
Dan. 12:1–3	Ordinary 33	B
Hos. 1:2–10	Ordinary 17	C
Hos. 2:14–20	Epiphany 8	B
Hos. 5:15–6:6	Ordinary 10	A
Hos. 11:1–11	Ordinary 18	C
Joel 2:1–2, 12–17	Ash Wednesday	ABC
Joel 2:21–27	Thanksgiving	B
Joel 2:23–32	Ordinary 30	C
Amos 5:6–7, 10–15	Ordinary 28	B
Amos 5:18–24	Ordinary 32	A
Amos 6:1a, 4–7	Ordinary 26	C
Amos 7:7–15	Ordinary 15	B
Amos 7:7–17	Ordinary 15	C
Amos 8:1–12	Ordinary 16	C
Amos 8:4–7	Ordinary 25	C
Jonah 3:1–5, 10	Epiphany 3	B
Jonah 3:10–4:11	Ordinary 25	A
Mic. 3:5–12	Ordinary 31	A
Mic. 5:2–5a	Advent 4	C
Mic. 6:1–8	Ordinary 4	A
Hab. 1:1–4; 2:1–4	Ordinary 27	C
Hab. 1:1–4; 2:1–4	Ordinary 31	C
Zeph. 1:7, 12–18	Ordinary 33	A
Zeph. 3:14–20	Easter Vigil	ABC
Zeph. 3:14–20	Advent 3	C
Hag. 1:15b–2:9	Ordinary 32	C
Zech. 9:9–12	Ordinary 14	A

Scripture Lesson	Liturgical Date	Lectionary Year
Mal. 3:1–4	Presentation	ABC
Mal. 3:1–4	Advent 2	C
Mal. 4:1–2a	Ordinary 33	C
Matt. 1:18–25	Advent 4	A
Matt. 2:1–12	Epiphany	ABC
Matt. 2:13–23	Christmas 1	A
Matt. 3:1–12	Advent 2	A
Matt. 3:13–17	Baptism of the Lord 1	A
Matt. 4:1–11	Lent 1	A
Matt. 4:12–23	Ordinary 3	A
Matt. 5:1–12	Ordinary 4	A
Matt. 5:1–12	All Saints	A
Matt. 5:13–20	Ordinary 5	A
Matt. 5:21–37	Ordinary 6	A
Matt. 5:38–48	Ordinary 7	A
Matt. 6:1–6, 16–21	Ash Wednesday	ABC
Matt. 6:24–34	Ordinary 8	A
Matt. 6:25–33	Thanksgiving	B
Matt. 7:21–29	Ordinary 9	A
Matt. 7:21–29	Ordinary 9	A
Matt. 9:9–13, 18–26	Ordinary 10	A
Matt. 9:35–10:8, (9:23)	Ordinary 11	A
Matt. 10:24–39	Ordinary 12	A
Matt. 10:40–42	Ordinary 13	A
Matt. 11:2–11	Advent 3	A
Matt. 11:16–19, 25–30	Ordinary 14	A
Matt. 13:1–9, 18–23	Ordinary 15	A
Matt. 13:24–30, 36–43	Ordinary 16	A
Matt. 13:31–33, 44–52	Ordinary 17	A
Matt. 14:13–21	Ordinary 18	A
Matt. 14:22–33	Ordinary 19	A
Matt. 15:(10–20), 21–28	Ordinary 20	A
Matt. 16:13–20	Ordinary 21	A
Matt. 16:21–28	Ordinary 22	A
Matt. 17:1–9	Transfig.	A
Matt. 17:1–9	Lent 2	A
Matt. 18:15–20	Ordinary 23	A
Matt. 18:21–35	Ordinary 24	A
Matt. 20:1–16	Ordinary 25	A
Matt. 21:1–11	Palm/Passion Sunday	A
Matt. 21:23–32	Ordinary 26	A
Matt. 21:33–46	Ordinary 27	A
Matt. 22:1–14	Ordinary 28	A
Matt. 22:15–22	Ordinary 29	A
Matt. 22:34–46	Ordinary 30	A

Scripture Lesson	Liturgical Date	Lectionary Year
Matt. 23:1–12	Ordinary 31	A
Matt. 24:36–44	Advent 1	A
Matt. 25:1–13	Ordinary 32	A
Matt. 25:14–30	Ordinary 33	A
Matt. 25:31–46	New Year	ABC
Matt. 25:31–46	Reign of Christ 34	A
Matt. 26:14–27:66	Palm/Passion Sunday	A
Matt. 27:11–54	Palm/Passion Sunday	A
Matt. 27:57–66	Holy Saturday	ABC
Matt. 28:1–10	Easter	A
Matt. 28:1–10	Easter Vigil	A
Matt. 28:16–20	Trinity Sunday	A
Mark 1:1–8	Advent 2	B
Mark 1:4–11	Baptism of the Lord 1	B
Mark 1:9–15	Lent 1	B
Mark 1:14–20	Ordinary 3	B
Mark 1:21–28	Ordinary 4	B
Mark 1:29–39	Ordinary 5	B
Mark 1:40–45	Ordinary 6	B
Mark 2:1–12	Ordinary 7	B
Mark 2:13–22	Ordinary 8	B
Mark 2:23–3:6	Ordinary 9	B
Mark 3:20–35	Ordinary 10	B
Mark 4:26–34	Ordinary 11	B
Mark 4:35–41	Ordinary 12	B
Mark 5:21–43	Ordinary 13	B
Mark 6:1–13	Ordinary 14	B
Mark 6:14–29	Ordinary 15	B
Mark 6:30–34, 53–56	Ordinary 16	B
Mark 7:1–8, 14–15, 21–23	Ordinary 22	B
Mark 7:24–37	Ordinary 24	B
Mark 8:27–38	Lent 2	B
Mark 8:31–38	Lent 2	B
Mark 9:2–9	Transfig.	B
Mark 9:2–9	Ordinary 25	B
Mark 9:30–37	Ordinary 26	B
Mark 9:38–50	Ordinary 27	B
Mark 10:2–16	Ordinary 28	B
Mark 10:17–31	Ordinary 29	B
Mark 10:35–45	Ordinary 30	B
Mark 10:46–52	Palm/Passion Sunday	B
Mark 11:1–11	Ordinary 31	B
Mark 12:28–34	Ordinary 32	B
Mark 12:38–44	Ordinary 33	B

Scripture Lesson	Liturgical Date	Lectionary Year
Mark 13:1–8	Advent 1	B
Mark 13:24–27	Palm/Passion Sunday	B
Mark 14:1–15:47	Palm/Passion Sunday	B
Mark 15:1–39 (40–47)	Easter	B
Mark 16:1–8	Easter	B
Mark 16:1–8	Easter Vigil	B
Luke 1:26–38	Annunciation	ABC
Luke 1:26–38	Advent 4	B
Luke 1:39–45, (46–55)	Advent 4	C
Luke 1:39–57	Visitation	ABC
Luke 1:47–55	Advent 3	AB
Luke 1:47–55	Advent 4	BC
Luke 1:68–79	Advent 2	C
Luke 1:68–79	Reign of Christ 34	C
Luke 2:1–14, (15–20)	Christmas Day 1	ABC
Luke 2:(1–7), 8–20	Christmas Day 2	ABC
Luke 2:15–21	Holy Name	ABC
Luke 2:22–40	Presentation	ABC
Luke 2:22–40	Christmas 1	B
Luke 2:41–52	Christmas 1	C
Luke 3:1–6	Advent 2	C
Luke 3:7–18	Advent 3	C
Luke 3:15–17, 21–22	Baptism of the Lord 1	C
Luke 4:1–13	Lent 1	C
Luke 4:14–21	Ordinary 3	C
Luke 4:21–30	Ordinary 4	C
Luke 5:1–11	Ordinary 5	C
Luke 6:17–26	Ordinary 6	C
Luke 6:20–31	All Saints	C
Luke 6:27–38	Ordinary 7	C
Luke 6:39–49	Ordinary 8	C
Luke 7:1–10	Ordinary 9	C
Luke 7:11–17	Ordinary 10	C
Luke 7:36–8:3	Ordinary 11	C
Luke 8:26–39	Ordinary 12	C
Luke 9:28–36	Lent 2	C
Luke 9:28–36, (37–43)	Transfig.	C
Luke 9:15–62	Ordinary 13	C
Luke 10:1–11, 16–20	Ordinary 14	C
Luke 10:25–37	Ordinary 15	C
Luke 10:38–42	Ordinary 16	C
Luke 11:1–3	Ordinary 17	C
Luke 12:13–21	Ordinary 18	C
Luke 12:32–40	Ordinary 19	C

Scripture Lesson	Liturgical Date	Lectionary Year
Luke 12:49–56	Ordinary 20	C
Luke 13:1–9	Lent 3	C
Luke 13:10–17	Ordinary 21	C
Luke 13:31–35	Lent 2	C
Luke 14:1, 7–14	Ordinary 22	C
Luke 14:25–33	Ordinary 23	C
Luke 15:1–3, 11b–32	Lent 4	C
Luke 15:1–10	Ordinary 24	C
Luke 16:1–13	Ordinary 25	C
Luke 16:19–31	Ordinary 26	C
Luke 17:5–10	Ordinary 27	C
Luke 17:11–19	Thanksgiving	A
Luke 17:11–19	Ordinary 28	C
Luke 18:1–8	Ordinary 29	C
Luke 18:9–14	Ordinary 30	C
Luke 19:1–10	Ordinary 31	C
Luke 19:28–40	Palm/Passion Sunday	C
Luke 20:27–38	Ordinary 32	C
Luke 21:5–19	Ordinary 33	C
Luke 21:25–36	Advent 1	C
Luke 22:14–23:56	Palm/Passion Sunday	C
Luke 23:1–49	Palm/Passion Sunday	C
Luke 23:33–43	Reign of Christ 34	C
Luke 24:1–12	Easter Vigil	C
Luke 24:1–12	Easter	C
Luke 24:13–35	Easter 3	A
Luke 24:13–49	Easter Evening	ABC
Luke 24:36b–48	Easter 3	B
Luke 24:44–53	Ascension	ABC
John 1:(1–9), 10–18	Christmas 2	ABC
John 1:1–14	Christmas Day 3	ABC
John 1:6–8, 19–28	Advent 3	B
John 1:29–42	Ordinary 2	A
John 1:43–51	Ordinary 2	B
John 2:1–11	Ordinary 2	C
John 2:13–22	Lent 3	B
John 3:1–17	Lent 2	A
John 3:1–17	Trinity Sunday	B
John 3:13–17	Holy Cross	ABC
John 3:14–21	Lent 4	B
John 4:5–42	Lent 3	A
John 5:1–9	Easter 6	C
John 6:1–21	Ordinary 17	B
John 6:24–35	Ordinary 18	B
John 6:25–35	Thanksgiving	C

Scripture Lesson	Liturgical Date	Lectionary Year
John 6:35, 41–51	Ordinary 19	B
John 6:51–58	Ordinary 20	B
John 6:56–69	Ordinary 21	B
John 7:37–39	Pentecost	A
John 9:1–41	Lent 4	A
John 10:1–10	Easter 4	A
John 10:11–18	Easter 4	B
John 10:22–30	Easter 4	C
John 11:1–45	Lent 5	A
John 11:32–44	All Saints	B
John 12:1–8	Lent 5	C
John 12:12–16	Palm/Passion Sunday	B
John 12:20–33	Lent 5	B
John 13:1–17, 31b–35	Maundy Thursday	ABC
John 13:31–35	Easter 5	C
John 14:1–14	Easter 5	A
John 14:8–17, (25–27)	Pentecost	C
John 14:15–21	Easter 6	A
John 14:23–29	Easter 6	C
John 15:1–8	Easter 5	B
John 15:9–17	Easter 6	B
John 15:26–27; 16:4b–15	Pentecost	B
John 16:12–15	Trinity Sunday	C
John 17:1–11	Easter 7	A
John 17:6–19	Easter 7	B
John 17:20–26	Easter 7	C
John 18:1–19:42	Good Friday	ABC
John 18:33–37	Reign of Christ 34	B
John 20:1–18	Easter	ABC
John 20:19–23	Pentecost	A
John 20:19–31	Easter 2	ABC
John 21:1–19	Easter 3	C
Acts 1:1–11	Ascension	ABC
Acts 1:6–14	Easter 7	A
Acts 1:15–17, 21–26	Easter 7	B
Acts 2:1–21	Pentecost	ABC
Acts 2:14a, 22–32	Easter 2	A
Acts 2:14a, 36–41	Easter 3	A
Acts 2:42–47	Easter 4	A
Acts 3:12–19	Easter 3	B
Acts 4:5–12	Easter 4	B
Acts 4:32–35	Easter 2	B
Acts 5:27–32	Easter 2	C
Acts 7:55–60	Easter 5	A
Acts 8:14–17	Baptism of the Lord 1	C

Scripture Lesson	Liturgical Date	Lectionary Year
Acts 8:26–40	Easter 5	B
Acts 9:1–6, (7–20)	Easter 3	C
Acts 9:36–43	Easter 4	C
Acts 10:34–43	Baptism of the Lord 1	A
Acts 10:34–43	Easter	ABC
Acts 10:44–48	Easter 6	B
Acts 11:1–18	Easter 5	C
Acts 16:9–15	Easter 6	C
Acts 16:16–34	Easter 7	C
Acts 17:22–31	Easter 6	A
Acts 19:1–7	Baptism of the Lord 1	B
Rom. 1:1–7	Advent 4	A
Rom. 1:16–17; 3:22b–28, (29–31)	Ordinary 9	A
Rom. 4:1–5, 13–17	Lent 2	A
Rom. 4:13–25	Ordinary 10	A
Rom. 4:13–25	Lent 2	B
Rom. 5:1–5	Trinity Sunday	C
Rom. 5:1–8	Ordinary 11	A
Rom. 5:1–11	Lent 3	A
Rom. 5:12–19	Lent 1	A
Rom. 6:1b–11	Ordinary 12	A
Rom. 6:3–11	Easter Vigil	ABC
Rom. 6:12–23	Ordinary 13	A
Rom. 7:15–25a	Ordinary 14	A
Rom. 8:1–11	Ordinary 15	A
Rom. 8:6–11	Lent 5	A
Rom. 8:12–17	Trinity Sunday	B
Rom. 8:12–25	Ordinary 16	A
Rom. 8:14–17	Pentecost	C
Rom. 8:22–27	Pentecost	B
Rom. 8:26–39	Ordinary 17	A
Rom. 9:1–5	Ordinary 18	A
Rom. 10:5–15	Ordinary 19	A
Rom. 10:8b–13	Lent 1	C
Rom. 11:1–2a, 29–32	Ordinary 20	A
Rom. 12:1–8	Ordinary 21	A
Rom. 12:9–16b	Visitation	ABC
Rom. 12:9–21	Ordinary 22	A
Rom. 13:8–14	Ordinary 23	A
Rom. 13:11–14	Advent 1	A
Rom. 14:1–12	Ordinary 24	A
Rom. 15:4–13	Advent 2	A
Rom. 16:25–27	Advent 4	B
1 Cor. 1:1–9	Ordinary 2	A

Scripture Lesson	Liturgical Date	Lectionary Year
1 Cor. 1:3–9	Advent 1	B
1 Cor. 1:10–18	Epiphany 3	A
1 Cor. 1:18–25	Lent 3	B
1 Cor. 1:18–31	Ordinary 4	A
1 Cor. 2:1–12, (13–16)	Ordinary 5	A
1 Cor. 3:1–9	Ordinary 6	A
1 Cor. 3:10–11, 16–23	Ordinary 7	A
1 Cor. 4:1–5	Ordinary 8	A
1 Cor. 5:6b–8	Easter Evening 8	ABC
1 Cor. 6:12–20	Ordinary 2	B
1 Cor. 7:29–31	Ordinary 3	B
1 Cor. 8:1–13	Ordinary 4	B
1 Cor. 9:16–23	Ordinary 5	B
1 Cor. 9:24–27	Ordinary 6	B
1 Cor. 10:1–13	Lent 3	C
1 Cor. 11:23–26	Holy Thursday	ABC
1 Cor. 12:1–11	Ordinary 2	C
1 Cor. 12:3b–13	Pentecost	A
1 Cor. 12:12–31a	Ordinary 3	C
1 Cor. 13:1–13	Ordinary 4	C
1 Cor. 15:1–11	Easter	B
1 Cor. 15:1–11	Ordinary 5	C
1 Cor. 15:12–20	Ordinary 6	C
1 Cor. 15:19–26	Easter	C
1 Cor. 15:35–38, 42–50	Ordinary 7	C
1 Cor. 15:51–58	Ordinary 8	C
2 Cor. 1:18–22	Ordinary 7	B
2 Cor. 3:1–6	Ordinary 8	B
2 Cor. 3:12–4:2	Transfig.	C
2 Cor. 4:3–6	Transfig.	B
2 Cor. 4:5–12	Ordinary 9	B
2 Cor. 4:13–5:1	Ordinary 10	B
2 Cor. 5:6–10, (11–13), 14–17	Ordinary 11	B
2 Cor. 5:16–21	Lent 4	C
2 Cor. 5:20b–6:10	Ash Wednesday	ABC
2 Cor. 6:1–13	Ordinary 12	B
2 Cor. 8:7–15	Ordinary 13	B
2 Cor. 9:6–15	Thanksgiving	A
2 Cor. 12:2–10	Ordinary 14	B
2 Cor. 13:11–13	Trinity Sunday	A
Gal. 1:1–12	Ordinary 9	C
Gal. 1:1–12	Ordinary 9	C
Gal. 1:11–24	Ordinary 10	C
Gal. 2:15–21	Ordinary 11	C

Scripture Lesson	Liturgical Date	Lectionary Year
Gal. 3:23–29	Ordinary 12	C
Gal. 4:4–7	Christmas 1	B
Gal. 5:1, 13–25	Ordinary 23	C
Gal. 6:(1–6), 7–16	Ordinary 14	C
Eph. 1:3–14	Christmas 2	ABC
Eph. 1:3–14	Ordinary 15	B
Eph. 1:11–23	All Saints	C
Eph. 1:15–23	Ascension	ABC
Eph. 1:15–23	Reign of Christ 34	A
Eph. 2:1–10	Lent 4	B
Eph. 2:11–22	Ordinary 16	B
Eph. 3:1–12	Epiphany	ABC
Eph. 3:14–21	Ordinary 17	B
Eph. 4:1–16	Ordinary 18	B
Eph. 4:25–5:2	Ordinary 19	B
Eph. 5:8–14	Lent 4	A
Eph. 5:15–20	Ordinary 20	B
Eph. 6:10–20	Ordinary 21	B
Phil. 1:3–11	Advent 2	C
Phil. 1:21–30	Ordinary 25	A
Phil. 2:1–13	Ordinary 26	A
Phil. 2:5–11	Palm/Passion Sunday	ABC
Phil. 3:4b–14	Ordinary 27	A
Phil. 3:4b–14	Lent 5	C
Phil. 3:17–4:1	Lent 2	C
Phil. 4:1–9	Ordinary 28	A
Phil. 4:4–7	Advent 3	A
Phil. 4:4–9	Thanksgiving	C
Col. 1:1–14	Ordinary 15	C
Col. 1:11–20	Reign of Christ 34	C
Col. 1:15–28	Ordinary 16	C
Col. 2:6–15, (16–19)	Ordinary 17	C
Col. 3:1–4	Easter	A
Col. 3:1–11	Ordinary 18	C
Col. 3:12–17	Christmas 1	C
1 Thess. 1:1–10	Ordinary 29	A
1 Thess. 2:1–18	Ordinary 30	A
1 Thess. 2:9–13	Ordinary 31	A
1 Thess. 3:9–13	Advent 1	C
1 Thess. 4:13–18	Ordinary 32	A
1 Thess. 5:1–11	Ordinary 33	A
1 Thess. 5:16–24	Advent 3	B
2 Thess. 1:1–4, 11–12	Ordinary 31	C
2 Thess. 2:1–5, 13–17	Ordinary 32	C
2 Thess. 3:6–13	Ordinary 33	C

Scripture Lesson	Liturgical Date	Lectionary Year
1 Tim. 1:12–17	Ordinary 34	C
1 Tim. 2:1–7	Thanksgiving	B
1 Tim. 2:1–7	Ordinary 25	C
1 Tim. 6:6–19	Ordinary 26	C
2 Tim. 1:1–14	Ordinary 27	C
2 Tim. 2:8–15	Ordinary 28	C
2 Tim. 3:14–4:5	Ordinary 29	C
2 Tim. 4:6–8, 16–18	Ordinary 30	C
Titus 2:11–14	Christmas Day 1	ABC
Titus 3:4–7	Christmas Day 2	ABC
Phlm. 1–21	Ordinary 23	C
Heb. 1:1–4, (5–12)	Christmas Day 3	ABC
Heb. 1:1–4; 2:5–12	Ordinary 27	B
Heb. 2:10–18	Christmas 1	A
Heb. 2:14–18	Presentation	ABC
Heb. 4:12–16	Ordinary 28	B
Heb. 4:14–16; 5:7–9	Good Friday	ABC
Heb. 5:1–10	Ordinary 29	B
Heb. 5:5–10	Lent 5	B
Heb. 7:23–28	Ordinary 30	B
Heb. 9:11–14	Ordinary 31	B
Heb. 9:24–28	Ordinary 32	B
Heb. 10:4–10	Annunciation	ABC
Heb. 10:5–10	Advent 4	C
Heb. 10:11–14, (15–18), 19–25	Ordinary 33	B
Heb. 10:16–25	Good Friday	ABC
Heb. 11:1–3, 8–16	Ordinary 19	C
Heb. 11:29–12:2	Ordinary 20	C
Heb. 12:18–29	Ordinary 21	C
Heb. 13:1–8, 15–16	Ordinary 22	C
Jas. 1:17–27	Ordinary 22	B
Jas. 2:1–10, (11–13), 14–17	Ordinary 23	B
Jas. 3:1–12	Ordinary 24	B
Jas. 3:13–4:3, 7–8a	Ordinary 25	B
Jas. 5:7–10	Advent 3	A
Jas. 5:13–20	Ordinary 26	B
1 Pet. 1:3–9	Easter 2	A
1 Pet. 1:17–23	Easter 3	A
1 Pet. 2:2–10	Easter 5	A
1 Pet. 2:19–25	Easter 4	A
1 Pet. 3:13–22	Easter 6	A
1 Pet. 3:18–22	Lent 1	B
1 Pet. 4:12–14; 5:6–11	Easter 7	A
2 Pet. 1:16–21	Transfig.	A
2 Pet. 3:8–15a	Advent 2	B

Scripture Lesson	Liturgical Date	Lectionary Year
1 John 1:1–2:2	Easter 2	B
1 John 3:1–3	All Saints	A
1 John 3:1–7	Easter 3	B
1 John 3:16–24	Easter 4	B
1 John 4:7–21	Easter 5	B
1 John 5:1–6	Easter 6	B
1 John 5:9–13	Easter 7	B
Rev. 1:4b–8	Reign of Christ 34	B
Rev. 1:4–8	Easter 2	C
Rev. 5:11–14	Easter 3	C
Rev. 7:9–17	All Saints	A
Rev. 7:9–17	Easter 4	C
Rev. 21:1–6a	All Saints	B
Rev. 21:1–6	Easter 5	C
Rev. 21:10, 21:22–22:5	Easter 6	C
Rev. 22:12–14, 16–17, 20–21	Easter 7	C

Part Three

Aids for the *Revised Common Lectionary*

Year B—Advent 2002 through Reign of Christ 2003

Introduction to Lectionary Aids

BY DON ARMITAGE, DEBBIE DIERKS-WASHINGTON,
STEVE AND VICKI FEY, SALLY GANT,
THEO GILL, AND SHELDON SORGE

LECTIONARY AIDS

Call to Worship's lectionary aids are based on the *Revised Common Lectionary*, an ecumenical planning resource for the liturgical year. Hymn suggestions corresponding to the biblical texts each week are designated by the following abbreviations:

O = Old Testament reading
A = Acts of the Apostles reading
E = Epistle reading
G = Gospel reading

For additional hymn suggestions, visit www.ppcpub.com.

A KEY TO FREQUENTLY CITED RESOURCES

Once again this year, the compilers of the following lectionary aids are deeply indebted to the former editors and writers of our predecessor journal, *Reformed Liturgy & Music*, which serves as a model and mine for the resource we produce. We are especially grateful to Peter C. Bower for *Handbook for the Revised Common Lectionary* (Louisville, Ky.: Westminster John Knox, 1996).

HYMNS

HB   *The Hymnbook* (Philadelphia: Presbyterian Church in the U.S.A., 1955)
LBW   *Lutheran Book of Worship* (Minneapolis: Augsburg Publishing House, 1978)
NCH   *The New Century Hymnal* (Cleveland: Pilgrim Press, 1995)

Volume 36.1 / 2002–2003   *Introduction to Lectionary Aids*   *85*

PH	*The Presbyterian Hymnal* (Louisville, Ky.: Westminster/John Knox Press, 1990)
RL	*Rejoice in the Lord* (Grand Rapids: Wm. B. Eerdmans Publishing Co., 1985)
TFF	*This Far by Faith: An African American Resource for Worship* (Minneapolis: Augsburg-Fortress, 1999)
WOV	*With One Voice* (Minneapolis: Augsburg-Fortress, 1995)

OTHER SUGGESTED SOURCES

Come, Let Us Worship: The Korean-English Presbyterian Hymnal and Service Book (Louisville, Ky.: Geneva Press, 2001)

The Faith We Sing (Nashville: Abingdon Press, 2000) TFWS

Giving Thanks in Song and Prayer: Hymntunes of Sally Ann Morris (Chicago: GIA Publications, Inc., 2001) G-4930

Halle, Halle: We Sing the World Round: Songs from the World Church (Garland, Tex.: Choristers' Guild, 1999) CGC42

How Sweet the Sound, Service Music for Piano (St. Louis: Concordia, 1997) 97-6891

Journey to Easter: Hymn Settings for Piano for Palm Sunday, Holy Week, & Eastertide (Dayton: Lorenz, 2000)

Keys of the Kingdom: Piano Arrangements for Easter/Ascension/Pentecost (Nashville: Abingdon Press, 1999)

Lift Up Your Hearts: Songs for Creative Worship (Louisville, Ky.: Geneva Press, 1999) LUYH

Music for Manuals: Chant-Based Hymns (Fenton, Mo.: MorningStar Music Publishers, 1996) MSM-10-849

New Hymns for the Lectionary: To Glorify the Maker's Name (New York: Oxford University Press, 1986)

A New Metrical Psalter. Texts only with suggested hymn tunes. (New York: Church Hymnal Corp., 1982) ANMP

The Psalter (1993) (Louisville, Ky.: Westminster/John Knox Press, 1993)

Psalter for Christian Worship (Louisville, Ky.: Witherspoon Press, 1999) PCW

Psalter for Worship, Cycles A, B, C (Minneapolis: Augsburg-Fortress, 1999)

The Psalter Hymnal (Grand Rapids: CRC Publications, 1987). Includes metrical settings for all 150 psalms. PH87

Renew! Songs and Hymns for Blended Worship (Carol Stream, Ill.: Hope Publishing Co., 1995)

Seasonal Chorale Preludes for Manuals Only. Book Two: Easter, Whitsun, Trinity, Festivals and General (New York: Oxford University Press)

Taizé: Songs for Prayer (Chicago: GIA Publications, 1998)

Wood Works: Nine Settings of Hymns and Folk Tunes for Piano (Dayton: Sacred Music Press)

Wonder, Love, and Praise: A Supplement to the Hymnal 1982 (New York: Church Hymnal Corp., 1997) WLP

PRAYERS OF CONFESSION

Sheldon Sorge, associate for theology and worship in the Office of Theology and Worship, Presbyterian Church (U.S.A.), wrote the prayers of confession and the suggested, accompanying "hymns of assurance" that appear in the lectionary aids for each Sunday and festival day of the liturgical year. His "Guidelines for Using the Prayers of Confession" appeared in *Call to Worship* 35, no. 1 (2001): 91.

THE STUDY CATECHISM, FULL VERSION

Because the Heidelberg Catechism was featured in Year A, 2001–2002, the lectionary aids for Year B provide the Study Catechism of the Presbyterian Church (U.S.A.) in fifty-two easy installments. This catechism was approved for educational and liturgical use by the General Assembly in June 1999. Any comments on the catechism will be welcomed by the Office of Theology and Worship, 100 Witherspoon Street, Louisville, Kentucky, 40202-1396.

NOTATIONS ON SELECTED ANTHEMS

Key to notations of musical accessibility by choirs:

(A) = Accessible
(M) = Moderate
(C) = Challenging
(SC) = Small Church

December 1, 2002

Isaiah 64:1–9 — The prophet prays for God's coming, that the people may be reformed.

Psalm 80:1–7, 17–19 — A prayer for the restoration of the nation.

1 Corinthians 1:3–9 — Paul thanks God for the grace and talent bestowed on the church at Corinth.

Mark 13:24–37 — Jesus warns his disciples to watch and wait, for the time of God's coming is at hand.

Theme(s) of lectionary texts: Be alert, and confident of God's grace.

CALL TO WORSHIP

Hear, O Shepherd of Israel,
  you who lead Joseph like a flock.
Restore us, O God of hosts;
  show us your light, and we shall be saved.
Let your hand be upon us, O Lord,
  and make us strong for your service.
Give us strength, that we may never turn from you;
  give us life, that we may call upon your name.

PRAYER OF CONFESSION

Almighty God,
in whom we live and move and have our being;
we are the clay, and you are the potter;
we are the work of your hand.
Yet we resist your purposes for us,
and have sought instead
to satisfy our own aims and desires.

Do not be exceedingly angry, O Lord,
and do not remember our iniquity forever.
We are your people; be merciful to us.
Come to us, revive us;
renew us, to your eternal honor and glory.

HYMN OF ASSURANCE

"Rejoice! Rejoice, Believers," *PH,* 15

SUGGESTED HYMNS

ENTRANCE/GATHERING HYMNS	HB	LBW	NCH	PH	RL	TFF	WOV
"All Hail to God's Anointed"	146	87	104	205	232	—	—
"Prepare the Way"	—	26	—	13	—	—	—
HYMNS RELATED TO SCRIPTURE							
O—"All My Hope on God Is Founded"	—	—	408	—	157	—	782
"Have Thine Own Way, Lord"	302	—	—	—	—	—	152
E—"Great Is Thy Faithfulness"	—	—	423	276	155	283	771
"Lord God of Hosts"	298	403	531	426	436	—	—
G—"Come, Thou Long-Expected Jesus"	151	30	122	1–2	183	—	—
"Wake, Awake, for Night Is Flying"	—	31	112	17	606	—	—
HYMNS OF THE TABLE							
"Jesus, Thou Joy of Loving Hearts"	215	356	329	510–11	273	—	—
SENDING FORTH							
"The Church's One Foundation"	437	369	386	442	394	—	—

First Sunday of Advent

Color: Blue/Purple

PSALM 80

METRICAL—
"O Hear Our Cry, O Lord" (SM with refrain), *PH*, 206
"O Shepherd Hear and Lead Thy Flock" (CMD), *PCW*, 94
RESPONSORIAL—
"Psalm 80," Hal Hopson, *Eighteen Psalms for the Church Year*, Hope
CHORAL—
"From Thy Throne, O Lord," Richard Proulx (SATB), GIA

ADDITIONAL SONGS

"Come Now, O Prince of Peace," Korean, various collections
"There Is a Longing," *Lift Up Your Hearts*, 141

CHORAL/VOCAL

"An Advent Carol," Jody Lindh (unison), Choristers Guild
"First Sunday in Advent B," Nancy Maeker (narrator/speech choir), Augsburg-Fortress
"Soon and Very Soon," Andraé Crouch/Jack Schrader (SATB), Hope
SOLO
"But Who May Abide," G. F. Handel (*Messiah*)
"Then Shall the Righteous Shine," Felix Mendelssohn (*Elijah*)
CHILDREN AND YOUTH
"O Come, O Come Emmanuel," Natalie Sleeth (unison/2-part), Choristers Guild
"Wake, Awake," John Horman (SAB), Hinshaw

ORGAN

"Jesus Comes with Clouds Descending" (HELMSLEY), Wilbur Held, *Four Advent Hymn Preludes, Set I*, MorningStar, 9
"Savior of the Nations, Come" (NUN KOMM, DER HEIDEN HEILAND)
J. S. Bach, *Leipzig Chorales* and *Orgelbuechlein*
Paul Manz, *Ten Chorale Improvisations*, MorningStar, 30
Charles W. Ore, *Eleven Compositions for Organ*, CPH, 17
"The Church's One Foundation" (AURELIA), Charles Callahan, *Six Meditations on English Hymn Tunes*, Organ Literature Foundation, 3

PIANO

"Let All Mortal Flesh Keep Silence," Angela Tipps, *Keys to the Kingdom*, vol. 4, Abingdon, 27
"Wake, Awake for Night Is Flying," Reginald Grieg, *Piano Preludes on Hymns and Chorales*, Hope, 20

HANDBELL

"Alleluia, He Comes to Us," Michael Keller (3 octaves), Agape
"Wake, Awake for Night Is Flying," Katherine Larson (3–5 octaves), Agape

STUDY CATECHISM

For today's questions and answers, see p. 214.

December 8, 2002

Isaiah 40:1–11	The Lord is coming to bring comfort to the people of God's choice.
Psalm 85:1–2, 8–13	God's blessing on the land of Israel.
2 Peter 3:8–15a	Wait with patience for the coming of God's new heaven and earth.
Mark 1:1–8	John the Baptist comes to announce the advent of Jesus Christ.

Theme(s) of lectionary texts: God's mercy and human preparation for Christ's coming.

CALL TO WORSHIP

You have been gracious to your land, O Lord;
  you have restored the good fortune of your people.
You have forgiven the sins of the people
  and have blotted out all their iniquities.
Mercy and truth have met together;
  righteousness and peace have embraced one
  another.
Truly, your salvation is very close to those who fear
  you,
  so that your glory may come to dwell in our
  land.

PRAYER OF CONFESSION

God of promise,
we come before you acknowledging that
we are not fully prepared for Christ's coming.
We have lived as though his coming is afar off,
spending ourselves to fulfill our own aims and
    desires,
rather than laying down our lives in love,
as he taught his disciples to do.

Forgive us for crowding Jesus out of our lives;
convict and empower us by your Spirit
to live according to his teaching and example,
so that we might be fully prepared for his coming.

HYMN OF ASSURANCE

"O Lord, How Shall I Greet You?" *PH,* 11

SUGGESTED HYMNS

ENTRANCE/GATHERING HYMNS	HB	LBW	NCH	PH	RL	TFF	WOV
"Hear the Good News of Salvation"	—	—	—	355	—	—	—
"Lift Up Your Heads, Ye Mighty Gates"	152	—	117	8	185	—	—
HYMNS RELATED TO SCRIPTURE							
O—"Comfort, Comfort You My People"	—	29	101	3	169	—	—
"Hallelujah, We Sing Your Praises"	—	—	—	—	—	158	722
E—"Love Divine, All Loves Excelling"	399	315	43	376	464	—	—
"The Lord Will Come and Not Be Slow"	230	318	—	—	165	—	—
G—"Blessed Be the God of Israel"	—	—	—	602	—	—	725
"On Jordan's Bank the Baptist's Cry"	—	36	—	10	187	—	—
HYMNS OF THE TABLE							
"Let All Mortal Flesh Keep Silence"	148	198	345	5	188	—	—
SENDING FORTH							
"Jesus Shall Reign"	496	530	300	423	233	—	—

Second Sunday of Advent

Color: Blue/Purple

PSALM 85

METRICAL—
"Lord, You Have Lavished on Your Land"
(8.8.8.8.8.8) *Psalter Hymnal*, 85
"The Lord Has Long with Favor Looked" (CMD)
PCW, 99
RESPONSORIAL—
Psalm 85, Hal Hopson, *Ten More Psalms*, Hope
CHORAL—
"A Psalm of Peace," Jane Marshall (SATB), Hinshaw
"Advent: Psalm 85," Dolores Hurby, *Season Psalms for Children* (unison), World Library

ADDITIONAL SONGS

"A Voice Cries Out," Michael Joncas, *Glory & Praise*, 294
"Canticle of the Turning," Irish Folk Song, *Worship & Praise*, 26
"Prepare Ye the Way," Tommy Walker, *Maranatha! Praise Band 7*, 13
"Wait for the Lord," *Taizé: Songs for Prayer*, 30

CHORAL/VOCAL

"Comfort, Comfort Ye My People," Claude Goudimel (SATB), GIA
"Every Valley," John Ness Beck (SATB), Beckenhorst
"Prepare the Royal Highway," W. A. Mozart/Hal Hopson (2–3, part mixed), Choristers Guild
"Prepare Ye the Way," Hart Morris (SATB/13 handbells), AGEHR
"The Glory of the Lord," Hal Hopson (unison/5 handbells), SMP
SOLOS
"All Earth Is Waiting," Alberto Taule (SSA), CPH
"Comfort Ye," G. F. Handel (*Messiah*)
"Every Valley," G. F. Handel (*Messiah*)

CHILDREN AND YOUTH

"Benedictus," Schubert/Lowe (unison/2-part), Choristers Guild
"Prepare the Way of the Lord," W. A. Mozart/Hal Hopson (2-part), Choristers Guild

ORGAN

"Comfort, Comfort You My People" (PSALM 42),
Egil Hovland, *Orgelkoraler, Set 5*, Norsk Musikverlag, 4
Paul Manz, *Ten Short Intonations on Well-Known Hymns*, Augsburg-Fortress, 3
"Prepare the Way, O Zion" (BEREDEN VAG FOR HERRAN)
Charles W. Ore, *Eleven Compositions for Organ, Set 5*, CPH, 8
Wilbur Held, *Four Advent Hymn Preludes, Set 1*, MorningStar, 3

PIANO

"Hail to the Lord's Anointed," Angela Tipps, *Keys of the Kingdom 5*, Abingdon, 2
"O Come, O Come Emmanuel," Angela Tipps, *Keys of the Kingdom 2*, Abingdon, 4

HANDBELL

"And the Glory of the Lord" (Messiah) Handel, arr. Kevin McChesney (3–5 octaves), Agape
"Comfort, Comfort Ye My People," Cynthia Dobrinski (3–5 octaves), Agape

STUDY CATECHISM

For today's questions and answers, see p. 214.

December 15, 2002

Isaiah 61:1–4, 8–11	Justice will be established with the coming of God's Anointed One.
Psalm 126 or	Those who sowed with tears now reap with songs of joy.
Luke 1:47–55	The Magnificat.
1 Thessalonians 5:16–24	Christians are to unite in prayer and joy, awaiting Christ's return.
John 1:6–8, 19–28	John the Baptist's witness to the person and work of Jesus Christ.

Theme(s) of lectionary texts: Testing, justice, and the Anointed One who comes to save.

CALL TO WORSHIP

When the Lord restored the fortunes of Zion,
   we were like those who dream.
Then was our mouth filled with laughter,
   and our tongues with shouts of joy.
Then it was said among the nations around us,
   "The Lord has done great things for them!"
The Lord has done great things for us,
   and we are glad indeed!

PRAYER OF CONFESSION

God of covenant,
we confess that our faith has been small.
We have doubted your promises,
and have denied your power
to free us from captivity,
and to establish us in security.
We have chosen instead
to trust in our own ways and strength.

By your tender mercy,
forgive our unbelief;
fill us with your Holy Spirit,
that we may fully trust and obey you.
Cast out our sin, and enter in;
be born in us today,
by our Lord and Savior, Jesus Christ.

HYMN OF ASSURANCE

"On Jordan's Bank the Baptist's Cry," *PH,* 10

SUGGESTED HYMNS

ENTRANCE/GATHERING HYMNS	HB	LBW	NCH	PH	RL	TFF	WOV
"Christ, Whose Glory Fills the Skies"	47	265	—	462–3	463	—	—
"When Morning Gilds the Skies"	41	545	86	487	365	—	—
HYMNS RELATED TO SCRIPTURE							
O—"Arise, Your Light Has Come"	—	—	164	411	418	—	652
"O Christ, the King Anointed"	—	—	—	—	—	294	—
E—"O Come, O Come Emmanuel"	147	34	116	9	184	—	—
"Rejoice, Ye Pure in Heart"	407	553	55	145/6	—	—	—
G—"Hark! A Thrilling Voice Is Sounding"	—	37	—	—	—	—	—
"Hark, the Herald Angels Sing"	163	60	144	31	196	—	—
"Word of God, Come Down to Earth"	—	—	—	—	—	—	716
HYMNS OF THE TABLE							
"Deck Yourself, My Soul, with Gladness"	—	224	—	506	536	—	—
SENDING FORTH							
"Rejoice, the Lord Is King"	140	171	303	15	596–97	—	—

Third Sunday of Advent

Color: Blue/Purple

PSALM 126

METRICAL—
"When God Arose to Bring Us Home" (CM), *Singing Psalms of Joy and Praise*, 66
RESPONSORIAL—
Psalm 126, *Psalter for Worship: Cycle B*, 8
CHORAL—
"Psalm 126," Roger Sherman (SAB), GIA
"They That Sow in Tears," Heinrich Schuetz (SSATB), G. Schirmer

LUKE 1:47–55

METRICAL—
"My Soul Proclaims Your Greatness" (CMD), *WOV*, 730
"Song of Mary" (CM), *PH*, 600
RESPONSORIAL—
"Magnificat," Alec Wyton, *Psalter (1993)*, 163
CHORAL—
"Magnificat and Nunc Dimittis," Ralph Vaughn Williams (SATB), G. Schirmer

ADDITIONAL SONGS

"Soon and Very Soon," Andraé Crouch, *Lift Up Your Hearts*, 142
"Magnificat," Anne Ward, *Glory & Praise*, 434
"My Soul Will Glorify the Lord," Maluku Folk Song, *World Praise*, 106
"Singing, We Gladly Worship," Guatemalan Folk Song, *Common Ground*, 114

CHORAL/VOCAL

"Arise, Shine, O Zion," Maurice Greene (SATB), Oxford
"How Shall We Know Him?" Gilbert Martin (SATB), Triune
"I Rejoice in the Lord," James Biery (SATB/string quartet), GIA
"O Day of Peace," K. Lee Scott (SAB), MorningStar

"The Eyes of All Wait Upon Me," Jean Berger (SATB), Augsburg-Fortress
"The Record of John" David Hurd (2-part, mixed), Chantry
SOLO
"Come with Me to Bethlehem," John Carter and Mary Kay Beall, *Come with a Singing Heart*, Hope
CHILDREN AND YOUTH
"With the Help of the Spirit of the Lord," Jayne Southwick Cool, Choristers Guild

ORGAN

"O Come, O Come Emmanuel" (VENI EMMANUEL)
Wilbur Held, *A Nativity Suite*, CPH, 2
Paul Sifler, *Four Nativity Tableau*, H. W. Gray, 1
"I'll Praise My Maker While I've Breath" (OLD 113TH)
Gerald Near, *Preludes on Four Hymn Tunes*, Augsburg-Fortress, 1
"Come, Thou Long-Expected Jesus" (HYFRYDOL)
Gerald Near, *Preludes on Four Hymn Tunes*, Augsburg-Fortress, 9
David A. Schack, *Nine Chorale Preludes*, CPH, 3
Ralph Vaughn Williams, *Three Preludes*, Stainer & Bell, 10

PIANO

"Hail to the Lord's Anointed" Angela Tipps, *Keys of the Kingdom 5*, Abingdon, 2
"Magnificat" Jackson Berkey, *Sacred Piano Devotions*, SDG Press

HANDBELL

"O Come, O Come Emmanuel" Alan Lohr (3–5 octaves), AGEHR
"Rejoice, Rejoice!" Cathy Mokeburst (2 octaves), Choirsters Guild

STUDY CATECHISM

For today's questions and answers, see p. 214.

December 22, 2002

2 Samuel 7:1–11, 16 — Nathan the prophet assures King David that his offspring will rule with the might and mercy of God.

Luke 1:47–55 or — The Magnificat.
Psalm 89:1–4, 19–26 — Singing the love of God.
Romans 16:25–27 — The revelation of God's gracious plan for salvation in Jesus Christ.
Luke 1:26–38 — The angel Gabriel tells Mary that she will bear God's child.

Theme(s) of lectionary texts: Annunciation of the coming birth. A child of royal lineage will bring joy to people of every class and race.

CALL TO WORSHIP

My heart magnified the Lord,
    and my soul is glad because of God my Savior.
For God has remembered me,
    and from now on, people will call me blessed.
God has brought down kings from their thrones
    but has lifted up the lowly and filled them with
        good things.
God has kept every promise made to our ancestors,
    and comes to our help when we are most in need.

PRAYER OF CONFESSION

God of glory and light,
you come to make your home among us,
yet we try to keep you at a distance,
in temples on the periphery of our lives.
You have drawn near to us,
but we have shrunk back from you.

In mercy, forgive our resistance to you.
By your Spirit, revive our love for you,
and put in us a new and willing spirit
that welcomes you and your purposes—
in us, among us, and through us;
for the sake of Emmanuel, God with us.

HYMN OF ASSURANCE

"Lift Up Your Heads, Ye Mighty Gates," *PH,* 8

SUGGESTED HYMNS

ENTRANCE/GATHERING HYMNS	HB	LBW	NCH	PH	RL	TFF	WOV
"O Come, O Come Emmanuel"	147	34	116	9	184	—	—
"People Look East"	—	—	—	12	—	—	626
HYMNS RELATED TO SCRIPTURE							
O—"Blessed Be the God of Israel"	—	—	—	601–2	—	—	725
"Hail to the Lord's Anointed"	146	87	104	205	232	—	—
E—"All Glory Be to God on High"	—	166	—	133	620	—	—
"Gentle Mary Laid Her Baby"	167	—	—	27	210	—	—
"For All the Faithful Women"	—	—	—	—	—	219	692
"Joy to the World"	161	60	144	31	196	—	—
HYMNS OF THE TABLE							
"O Word of God Incarnate"	251	231	315	327	387	—	—
SENDING FORTH							
"Lord, Dismiss Us with Your Blessing"	79	259	77	538	—	—	—

Fourth Sunday of Advent

Color: Blue/Purple

PSALM

Luke 1:47–55
  For Metrical and Responsorial versions, see December 15
CHORAL—
"Magnificat and Nunc Dimittis," Gerald Near (SATB/T), Aureole Editions
Psalm 89:1–4, 19–26
METRICAL—
"My Song Forever Shall Record" (8.8.8.8.8.8), *PH*, 209
Psalm 89b (CM), *PCW*, 104
RESPONSORIAL—
Psalm 89, Hal Hopson, *Psalter (1993)*, 81
CHORAL—
"I Will Forever Sing," Benedetto Marcello (SAB), Roger Dean
"I Will Sing of Thy Great Mercies," Felix Mendelssohn (*St. Paul*)

ADDITIONAL SONGS

"My Soul in Silence Waits," Marty Haugen, *Gather Comprehensive*, 328
"My Soul Proclaims," Bernadette Farrell, *Common Ground*, 15b

CHORAL/VOCAL

"A New Magnificat," Carolyn Jennings (SATB), Augsburg-Fortress
"Advent Processional," John Ferguson (SATB), Augsburg-Fortress
"Do Not Fear, Mary," Richard Weeks (SAB), Theodore Presser
"Festival Magnificat," Richard Proulx (SATB/brass), Selah
"Gabriel's Message," Gerald Near (SATB), MorningStar
"Magnificat," Robert Landes (SATB), MorningStar
"Mary Walks Amid the Thorns," David Cherwein (unison), Choristers Guild
"Mary's Song of Praise," Paul Bouman (unison or 2-part), *Six Anthems for the Church Year, Set 1*, CPH
"The Angel Gabriel," Alec Wyton (SATB/S), Roger Dean
SOLOS
"Behold, A Virgin," G. F. Handel (*The Messiah*)
"Who Would Send a Baby?" John Carter and Mary Beall, *Come with a Singing Heart*, Hope
CHILDREN AND YOUTH
"Love Enough to Give," John Horman (Unison/SATB), Choristers Guild
"Sing a Song of Praise," Alan Pote (unison/flute), Choristers Guild

ORGAN

"Come, Thou Long-Expected Jesus" (HYFRYDOL)
  David Cherwein, *Interpretations Based on Hymn Tunes, Book VII*, AMSI, 12
  William Held, *Those Wonderful Welsh, Set 1*, MorningStar, 12
"Hark! The Herald Angels Sing" (MENDELSSOHN)
  J. Wayne Kerr, *Three Carols for Epiphany*, CPH, 8

PIANO

"Lo, How a Rose E'er Blooming" John Carter, *Carols for Piano*, Hope, 6
"O Come, All Ye Faithful" Angela Tipps, *Keys of the Kingdom 2*, Abingdon, 7

HANDBELL

"Picardy" (Let All Mortal Flesh), Isabel McNeill Carley (2 octaves), Augsburg-Fortress
"Lo, How a Rose E'er Blooming," Douglas Warner (duet: 2 octaves/piano), Jeffers

STUDY CATECHISM

For today's questions and answers, see p. 214.

December 24, 2002

Isaiah 9:2–7	The day of justice is coming, overthrowing earthly oppression with the coming of God's child.
Psalm 96	The Lord will judge the world in righteousness and truth.
Titus 2:11–14	God's incarnation in Jesus Christ brings new life to believers.
Luke 2:1–14 (15–20)	The story of Christ's birth as told by Luke.

Theme(s) of lectionary texts: The nativity of Jesus.

CALL TO WORSHIP

Sing to the Lord a new song.
    Sing to the Lord, all the earth!
Sing to the Lord, and bless God's name,
    and proclaim salvation from day to day!
For the Lord is great, and greatly to be praised;
    it is God who made heaven and earth.
Worship the Lord in the beauty of holiness.
    Let the whole world tremble in awe!

PRAYER OF CONFESSION

God of grace and truth,
in Jesus Christ you came among us
as light shining in darkness.
We confess that we have not welcomed the light,
or trusted good news to be good.
We have closed our eyes to glory in our midst,
expecting little, and hoping for less.

Forgive our doubt, and renew our hope,
so that we may receive the fullness of your grace,
and live in the truth of Christ the Lord.

HYMN OF ASSURANCE

"O Little Town of Bethlehem," *PH, 43*

SUGGESTED HYMNS

ENTRANCE/GATHERING HYMNS	HB	LBW	NCH	PH	RL	TFF	WOV
"Come, Thou Long-Expected Jesus"	151	30	122	1–2	183	—	—
HYMNS RELATED TO SCRIPTURE							
O—"Isaiah the Prophet Has Written of Old"	—	—	108	337	—	—	—
"The Race That Long in Darkness Pined"	153	—	—	—	167	—	—
E—"All My Heart"	172	46	—	21	202	—	—
"From Heaven Above to Earth I Come"	—	51	130	54	207	—	—
G—"O Little Town of Bethlehem"	171	41	133	43–44	193	—	—
"'Twas in the Moon of Wintertime"	—	72	151	61	—	—	—
HYMNS OF THE TABLE							
"Jesus, Thou Joy of Loving Hearts"	215	—	—	510–11	273	—	—
SENDING FORTH							
"Silent Night, Holy Night"	154	65	134	60	216	—	—

Christmas Eve

Color: White/Gold

PSALM 96

METRICAL—
"O Sing New Songs unto the Lord," (7.6.7.6 D),
PCW, 111
RESPONSORIAL—
"Psalm 96," Hal Hopson, *Ten More Psalms*, Hope
CHORAL—
"O Sing Unto the Lord a New Song," Jan Bender
(SATB), CPH
"Psalm 96," John Bell (SATB/congregation), GIA
"Psalm 96," John Ogasapian (unison), Augsburg-
Fortress
"Sing to the Lord," Johann Hermann Schein (SAB),
Aureole

ADDITIONAL SONGS

"A Babe Was Born in Bethlehem," Ivor Golby, *World
Praise*, 1
"God's Love Made Visible," Dave and Iola Brubeck,
Lift Up Your Hearts, 140
"Hear the Angels," Robin Cain/Phil Kadidlo, *Worship
& Praise*, 57
"Iona Gloria," Traditional, *Common Ground*, 64
"Song of the Stable," David Haas, *Gather
Comprehensive*, 364

CHORAL/VOCAL

"Before the Marvel of This Night," Carl Schalk
(SATB), Augsburg-Fortress
"Hush, Do Not Wake the Infant King," Walter Ehret
(SATB), Theodore Presser
"Nativity Carol," John Rutter (SATB/strings), Oxford
"O Come, All Ye Faithful," Christopher Dedrick
(SATB/brass/congregation), Brookfield Press
"Unto Us a Child Is Born," Nancy Roberts
(SSAATTBB), Flammer

ORGAN

"O Come, All Ye Faithful" (ADESTE FIDELES), Bruce
Neswick, *Fantasia on Adeste Fideles*, Paraclete Press
"O Little Town of Bethlehem" (FOREST GREEN)
Emma Lou Diemer, *Ten Hymn Preludes for
Meditation and Praise*, Carl Fisher, 12
Richard Purvis, *Seven Chorale Preludes*, Carl Fisher
"Silent Night" (STILLE NACHT)
Samuel Barber, *Chorale Prelude*, G. Schirmer
Wilbur Held, *A Nativity Suite*, CPH, 4

VIOLIN AND ORGAN

"Triptych on FOREST GREEN," Kevin Hildebrand,
MorningStar

PIANO

"Joy to the World," Chuck Marohnic, *5 Carols for the
Piano*, MorningStar, 2
"Silent Night, Holy Night," Angela Tipps, *Keys of the
Kingdom*, vol. 2, Abingdon, 24
"The First Noel," John Carter, *Carols for Piano*,
Hope, 14

HANDBELL

"Christmas Joy Fanfare," Douglas Warner (2–3
octaves), Choristers Guild
"I Wonder as I Wander," Karen Buckwalter (3–5
octaves), Hal Leonard
"Silent Night," Cynthia Dobrinski (3–5 octaves),
Agape

December 25, 2002

Isaiah 52:7–10 | Even in a time of deep trouble, Isaiah reassures the nation that "Your God reigns!"

Psalm 98 | All the earth sings a new song to the Lord.

Hebrews 1:1–4 (5–12) | To make sure the message is clear, the Word has come to us in the person of God's own child.

John 1:1–14 | The prologue to John's Gospel: "In the beginning was the Word."

Theme(s) of lectionary texts: The Word became flesh and dwelt among us, full of grace and truth.

CALL TO WORSHIP

Shout with joy to the Lord, all you nations!
    Lift up your voice, rejoice, and sing!
Sing to the Lord with the harp;
    with the harp and the voice of song!
Let the sea make a noise, and all the creatures in it;
    and also the land, with its people and animals.
Let the rivers clap their hands in praise,
    and let the hills and mountains ring with joy!

PRAYER OF CONFESSION

God of light,
shine brightly in our world
through the glory of our Lord Jesus Christ.
Your grace is more abundant than our sinfulness
so that the light continues to shine
despite our world's love of darkness.
We have been too preoccupied in this season
to concentrate on giving you praise
for the birth of your Son.
We have refused his peace
and have failed to live in a spirit of goodwill.

Forgive our sin, doubt, and preoccupation,
and renew in us the spirit of wonder
so that we may hear with renewed attention
the great good news of the coming of our Savior,
Jesus Christ the Lord. Amen.

HYMN OF ASSURANCE

"In Bethlehem a Newborn Boy," *PH,* 35

SUGGESTED HYMNS

ENTRANCE/GATHERING HYMNS	HB	LBW	NCH	PH	RL	TFF	WOV
"O Come, All Ye Faithful"	170	45	135	41	195	—	
HYMNS RELATED TO SCRIPTURE							
O—"Joy to the World"	161	39	132	40	198	—	—
"O Sing to the Lord"	—	—	—	472	—	—	795
E—"In the Bleak Midwinter"	—	—	128	36	—	—	—
"O Splendor of God's Glory Bright"	46	271	87	474	76	—	—
G—"At the Name of Jesus"	143	179	—	148	336	—	—
"O Word of God Incarnate"	251	231	315	327	387	—	—
HYMNS OF THE TABLE							
"My Song Is Love Unknown"	—	—	222	76	284	—	661
SENDING FORTH							
"Go, Tell It on the Mountain"	—	70	154	29	224	52	—

Christmas Day

Color: White

PSALM 98

METRICAL—
"Psalm 98," Hal Hopson, *Eighteen Psalms for the Church Year*, Hope
RESPONSORIAL—
"Psalm 98," Hal Hopson, *Ten Psalms*, Hope
"Psalm 98," Presbyterian tone 3, *The Psalter* (1993), 94
CHORAL—
"Cantate Domino," David Hurd (SATB/congregation), Augsburg-Fortress
"New Songs of Celebration Render," Dale Gotenhuis (SATB/congregation/brass), Selah
"Psalm 98," Jane Marshall (unison), Choristers Guild

ADDITIONAL SONGS

"A Child Is Born for Us this Day," Weston Priory, *Glory & Praise*, 330
"God Sent His Son," Zimbabwe folk song, *World Praise*, 70
"He Came Down," Cameroonian folk song, *World Praise*, 56
"Sent by the Lord Am I," John Bell, arr., *Common Ground*, 105
"The Virgin Mary Had a Baby Boy," West Indies carol, *Gather Comprehensive*, 345

CHORAL/VOCAL

"And the Word Became Flesh," Paul Bouman (SATB), MorningStar
"Ding Dong Merrily on High," Michael Neaum (SSAA), Theodore Presser
"In the Beginning Was the Word," Paul Sjolund (SATB), Fred Bock
"The Word Was God," Rosephanye Powell (SSAATTBB), Gentry

ORGAN

"Go, Tell It on the Mountain"
    Wilbur Held, *Christmas Comes Again*, MorningStar, 13
    J. Wayne Kerr, *Three Carols for Epiphany*, CPH, 2
"O Come, All Ye Faithful" (ADESTE FIDELES)
    Bruce Neswick, *Fantasia on Adeste Fideles*, Paraclete Press
    Charles Ives, *Adeste Fideles* (published with *Variations on America*), Mercury
"Of the Father's Love Begotten" (DIVINUM MYSTERIUM), Wilbur Held, *Six Carol Settings*, CPH, 6

PIANO

"Of the Father's Love Begotten," Matthew Weston, *Hymns of the Holy Child*, MorningStar, 10
"Patapan," David L. Mennicke (SATB with flute/triangle/hand drum/tambourine/piano), MorningStar

HANDBELL

"Carol of the Bells," Charles Maggs, arr. (quartet, 3 octaves), Cantabile
"Christmas Trilogy," Karen Buckwalter (3–5 octaves), Flammer
"Ding Dong Merrily on High," Cynthia Dobrinski (3–5 octaves), Agape
"I Saw Three Ships," Barbara Kinyon (2 octaves), Agape
"In the Bleak Midwinter," Steven Kerin, *Christmas Trios* (trio), Jeffers
"West Indies Carol," Hart Morris (4 octaves/percussion), Ring Out!

December 29, 2002

Isaiah 61:10–62:3 — The prophet proclaims the restoration of Jerusalem.

Psalm 148 — The universal sovereignty of God the Creator.

Galatians 4:4–7 — The coming of God's child makes possible our adoption as children of God, sisters and brothers in Jesus Christ.

Luke 2:22–40 — The infant Jesus is dedicated at the Temple in Jerusalem.

Theme(s) of lectionary texts: Christ is both the Redeemer of Israel and a light to all nations.

CALL TO WORSHIP

Praise the Lord in the heavens;
    praise God with the hosts on high!
Praise the Lord, sun and moon;
    praise God, all you shining stars!
Praise the Lord from earth to sky,
    for God commanded, and all was created.
The name of the Lord alone is exalted,
    and God's splendor covers heaven and earth!

PRAYER OF CONFESSION

God of grace and truth,
in Jesus Christ you came among us
as light shining in darkness.
We confess that we have not welcomed the light,
or trusted good news to be good.
We have closed our eyes to glory in our midst,
expecting little, and hoping for less.

Forgive our doubt, and renew our hope,
so that we may receive the fullness of your grace,
and live in the truth of Christ the Lord.

HYMN OF ASSURANCE

"O Little Town of Bethlehem," *PH*, 43

SUGGESTED HYMNS

ENTRANCE/GATHERING HYMNS	HB	LBW	NCH	PH	RL	TFF	WOV
"Angels from the Realms of Glory"	168	50	126	22	229	—	—
"Good Christian Friends, Rejoice"	165	55	129	28	218	—	—
HYMNS RELATED TO SCRIPTURE							
O—"O Lord, How Shall I Meet You?"	—	23	—	11	368	—	—
"O That I Had a Thousand Voices"	—	—	—	475	—	—	—
E—"From Heaven Above"	—	51	130	54	207	—	—
"To God Be the Glory"	—	—	—	485	355	264	—
G—"Blessed Be the God of Israel"	—	—	—	601–602	—	—	725
"O Sing a Song of Bethlehem"	177	—	51	308	356	—	—
HYMNS OF THE TABLE							
"What Child Is This?"	159	40	148	53	217	—	—
SENDING FORTH							
"God Who Stretched the Spangled Heavens"	—	463	556	268	29	—	—

First Sunday after Christmas

Color: White

PSALM 148

METRICAL—
"Glory to God Above!" John Bell (SATB or unison), *Psalms of Patience, Protest and Praise,* GIA
"Praise God in the Highest Heaven" (8.7.8.7.8.7), *PCW,* 170
RESPONSORIAL—
"Psalm 148," Hal Hopson, *The Psalter* (1993), 155
"Psalm 148," *Psalter for Worship: Cycle B,* 14
CHORAL—
"O Praise the Lord of Heaven," William Billings (SATB), CPH
"Psalm 148," Gustav Holst (SATB, div.), *Two Psalms,* Galliard (Galaxy)

ADDITIONAL SONGS

"I've Waited Long," Scottish folk song, *Common Ground,* 55
"Nunc dimittis," *Taizé: Songs for Prayer,* 16
"We're Told He Was Born," Malawi folk tune, *World Praise,* 114

CHORAL/VOCAL

"Depart in Peace," John Rutter (SATB), Hinshaw
"In Peace and Joy I Now Depart," Deborah Govenor (SATB), Beckenhorst
"Nunc dimittis," Roger Sherman (two voices/handbells), GIA
"Nunc dimittis," Thomas Tallis (SSAA), Carl Fisher
"Song of Simeon," Jane Marshall (SATB), Augsburg-Fortress
"We Are His Children," Richard Wienhorst (2-part/handbells/brass), Mark Foster

ORGAN

"Prelude on KINGSFOLD (O Sing a Song of Bethlehem)," Robert Cundick and John Longhurst, *Twelve Hymns Settings from the Tabernacle,* Sonos Music Resources, 10
"Prelude on PICARDY (Let All Mortal Flesh Keep Silence)," Henry Coleman, *Twenty-four Interludes Based on Communion Hymn Tunes,* Oxford, 11

PIANO

"Deck Yourself, My Soul, with Gladness," Angela Tipps, *Keys of the Kingdom 4,* Abingdon, 20
"He Is Born!" John Carter, *Carols for Piano,* Hope, 10
"What Child Is This?" Chuck Marohnic, *Christmas Jazz: 5 Carols for the Piano,* MorningStar, 4
"What Child Is This?" Anglea Tipps, *Keys of the Kingdom,* vol. 2, Abingdon, 14

HANDBELL

"Bring a Torch," Christine Anderson (solo), Agape
"Bring a Torch," Douglas Wagner (3 octaves), Agape
"Of the Father's Love Begotten," Richard Gieseke (2 octaves), CPH
"What Child Is This?" Michael Helman (3–5 octaves), AGEHR

OTHER INSTRUMENTAL

"What Child Is This?" Dale Elmshaeuser (strings/woodwind quartet), Lorenz

STUDY CATECHISM

For today's questions and answers, see p. 215.

January 5, 2003

Jeremiah 3:7–14   Jeremiah implores the nation to turn from worship of false gods.

Psalm 147:12–20   The Lord's judgment and truth are revealed to those whom God chooses.

Ephesians 1:3–14   Believers share the depth of the riches and grace of God in Jesus Christ.

John 1:(1–9) 10–18   The coming of Jesus Christ into the world reveals the fullness of God's grace and truth.

Theme(s) of lectionary texts: Thanksgiving for our unity and calling in Christ.

CALL TO WORSHIP

God gives snow like wool and scatters hail like bread-crumbs;
then the Word of the Lord is sent forth and melts them away.
God strengthens the walls that keep you secure and blesses the children within your gates.
The Lord will establish peace on our borders, and God will feed us with the finest wheat.
God's command is sent out across the earth; and the Word of the Lord travels swiftly.

SUGGESTED HYMNS

ENTRANCE/GATHERING HYMNS	HB	LBW	NCH	PH	RL	TFF	WOV
"Blessed Jesus, at Your Word"	—	248	74	454	—	—	—
"Joyful, Joyful, We Adore Thee"	21	551	4	464	521	—	—
HYMNS RELATED TO SCRIPTURE							
O—"Be Thou My Vision"	303	—	451	339	67	—	776
"Guide My Feet"	—	—	497	354	—	153	—
"Spirit"	—	—	286	319	—	—	—
E—"All Glory Be to God on High"	—	166	—	133	620	—	—
"Amazing Grace"	275	448	547	280	456	—	—
"I Greet Thee Who My Sure Redeemer Art"	144	—	251	457	366	—	—
G—"Born in the Night, Mary's Child"	—	—	152	30	—	—	—
"Once in Royal David's City"	462	—	145	49	201	—	643
"We All Believe in One True God"	—	374	—	137	609	—	—
HYMNS OF THE TABLE							
"Jesus, Thou Joy of Loving Hearts"	215	—	—	510–11	273	—	—
"Lord, We Have Come at Your Own Invitation"	—	—	—	516	—	—	—
SENDING FORTH							
"Come, Thou Fount of Every Blessing"	379	499	459	356	—	—	—

Second Sunday after Christmas

Color: White

PRAYER OF CONFESSION

God of steadfast love,
we have forsaken you,
and find ourselves exiled—
far from the land of promise.
We yearn to return to your dwelling place,
to our true and abiding home.

Forgive our sins,
and remove all that separates us
from the place you have prepared for us.
We would be your holy people.
By your Spirit, cleanse us and renew us,
so that we may honor and serve you well,
for the sake of our Lord and Savior, Jesus Christ.

HYMN OF ASSURANCE

"Breathe on Me, Breath of God," *PH*, 316

PSALM 147

METRICAL—
"Now Praise the Lord" (CM), *PH*, 255
RESPONSORIAL—
"Praise the Lord, O Jerusalem," Malcolm Williamson
    (unison/congregation), Boosey & Hawkes
"Psalm 147," Hal Hopson, *The Psalter* (1993), 154
CHORAL—
"Sing to the Lord, Rejoice!" Georg Philipp Telemann
    (2-part mixed), Alfred

ADDITIONAL SONGS

"Mourning into Dancing," Tommy Walker, *Worship
    & Praise*, 99
"The King of Glory Comes," Israeli Traditional,
    Worship & Praise, 136
"The Lord Is Come," John Foley, *Glory & Praise*, 326
"To Christ the Seed," Sean O'Riada, *Common
    Ground*, 135

CHORAL/VOCAL

"Deep Within," David Haas (2-part mixed), GIA
"Messenger to Ephesus," Eugene Butler (SATB),
    Agape
"O Sing Unto the Lord," William Harris (SATB),
    Novello
"Sing Praises to Our God," Robert Powell (SA), CPH

ORGAN

"Prelude on ST. ANNE (Now Praise the Lord),"
    C. Hubert H. Parry, *Seven Chorale Preludes*,
    Novello
"Prelude on PUER NOBIS NASCITUR (O Splendor of
    God's Glory Bright)," Geoffrey Shaw, *Variations on
    an Old Carol Tune*, J. B. Cramer & Co.

PIANO

"Go, Tell It on the Mountain," John Carter, *Carols for
    Piano*, Hope, 4

HANDBELL

"An English Carol," Arnold Sherman (3–5 octaves),
    Agape
"Fount of Blessings," Christine Anderson (solo),
    Alfred
"Joy to the World," Debra Colkins, *Three Duets for
    Christmas* (duet, 3 octaves), National
"Joy to the World," Robert Ivey, *Ring Noel* (3 octaves
    to 3+ octaves), Flammer

STUDY CATECHISM

For today's questions and answers, see p. 215.

January 6, 2003

Isaiah 60:1–6   Even in the deepest gloom, God's light prevails.

Psalm 72:1–7, 10–14   The Son of David will reign in justice and righteousness.

Ephesians 3:1–12   In Jesus Christ, every nation is invited to know the living God of all.

Matthew 2:1–12   Three seekers of wisdom come from the East to do homage to Jesus in Bethlehem.

Theme(s) of lectionary texts: The manifestation of Christ's glory.

CALL TO WORSHIP

Give the king your justice, O God,
    and entrust righteousness to the Son of David.
All kings will one day bow before him,
    and nations will serve his purposes.
And he will redeem human lives from oppression,
    and violence will be banished from his sight.
May his name be established as long as the sun
    endures,
    and may all the nations come to call him
    blessed.

SUGGESTED HYMNS

ENTRANCE/GATHERING HYMNS	HB	LBW	NCH	PH	RL	TFF	WOV
"Arise, Your Light Is Come"	—	—	164	411	918	—	652
"O Morning Star, How Fair and Bright"	415	76	158	69	367	—	—
HYMNS RELATED TO SCRIPTURE							
O—"O Gladsome Light"	61	279	—	549	623	—	—
"O Light Whose Splendor Thrills"	—	—	—	550	—	—	—
"Shine, Jesus, Shine"	—	—	—	—	—	64	651
E—"Here I Am, Lord"	—	—	—	525	—	230	752
"I'm Gonna Live So God Can Use Me"	—	—	—	369	—	—	—
"When I Had Not Yet Learned of Jesus"	—	—	—	410	—	—	—
"Ye Servants of God, Your Master Proclaim"	27	252	305	477	598	—	—
G—"Bright and Glorious Is the Sky"	—	75	—	—	—	—	—
"Brightest and Best"	175	84	156–57	67	230	—	—
"Midnight Stars Make Bright the Sky"	—	—	—	65	—	—	—
"From a Distant Home (De Tierra Lejana)"	—	—	155	64	—	—	—
HYMN OF THE TABLE							
"Deck Yourself, My Soul, with Gladness"	—	—	—	506	536	—	—
SENDING FORTH							
"Go, Tell It on the Mountain"	—	70	154	29	124	52	—
"We Are Marching in the Light of God"	—	—	526	—	—	63	650

Epiphany

PRAYER OF CONFESSION

God of glory,
you sent Jesus among us as the light of the world,
to reveal your love for all people.
We confess that our sin and pride
hide the brightness of your light.
We turn away from the poor;
we ignore cries for justice;
we do not strive for peace.

In your mercy, cleanse us of our sin,
and baptize us once again with your Spirit,
that, forgiven and renewed,
we may show forth your glory
shining in the face of Jesus Christ.

HYMN OF ASSURANCE

"As with Gladness Men of Old," *PH,* 63

PSALM 72

METRICAL—
"Hail to the Lord's Anointed," *Psalter Hymnal,* 72
RESPONSORIAL—
"Psalm 72," Laurence Bevenot/John Schiavone,
   PH, 72
"Psalm 72," Peter Hallock, *The Psalter* (1993), 204
CHORAL—
"Hail to the Lord's Anointed," Roy Hopp (SATB/
   congregation/brass), Selah
"He Shall Come Down Like Rain," Robert Edward
   Smith (SSA), GIA

ADDITIONAL SONGS

"Lord Jesus, Your Light Shines," *Taizé: Songs for Prayer,* 15
"Star of the Morning," Un-yung La, *World Praise,* 53
"The Lord Is Come," John Foley, *Glory & Praise,* 326
"There Is a Redeemer," Keith Green, *Renew,* 232
"We Bow Down," Twila Paris, *Renew,* 38

CHORAL/VOCAL

"All Shall Come from East and West," Hal Hopson
   (SATB/5 handbells), Hope
"Arise, Shine!" Jane Marshall (SATB), CPP/Belwin
"Epiphany Alleluias," John Weaver (SATB), Boosey &
   Hawkes
"Visit of the Magi," David H. Williams (SATB/S),
   H. W. Gray
SOLO
"The People That Walked in Darkness," G. F. Handel
   (*Messiah*)
"Where Is the Child?" Craig Courtney, *Sacred Songs of
   John Ness Beck,* Beckenhorst, 39
CHILDREN AND YOUTH
"Set the Sun Dancing," Helen Kemp, Choristers
   Guild
"Shining Brightly, Christmas Star," Shute, Abingdon

ORGAN

"We Three Kings of Orient Are," Wilbur Held, *A
   Nativity Suite,* Concordia
"Prelude on WIE SCHOEN LEUCHTET (O Morning Star,
   How Fair and Bright)"
   Dietrich Buxtehude (various publishers)
   Dupre, *Seventy-nine Chorales,* H. W. Gray

PIANO

"The First Noel," John Carter, *Carols for Piano,* Hope,
   14
"We Three Kings," Angela Tipps, *Keys of the Kingdom,*
   vol. 2, Abingdon, 34

HANDBELL

"Beautiful Savior," James Klein (2 octaves), National
"Siyahumba (We Are Marching)," Robert Ward (4–6
   octaves), AGEHR
"We Three Kings," Cynthia Dobrinski (3–5 octaves),
   Agape

January 12, 2003

Genesis 1:1–5 — God creates all things, taming the primordial waters.

Psalm 29 — The sovereignty of the Lord whose voice resounds on land and sea.

Acts 19:1–7 — As Paul baptizes Ephesian converts with water, the fire of the Holy Spirit descends from heaven.

Mark 1:4–11 — John the Baptist prophesies the coming into the world of a baptism greater than that which he practices in the wilderness.

Theme(s) of lectionary texts: The covenantal waters of baptism.

CALL TO WORSHIP

Ascribe to the Lord the glory that is due God's name; worship the Lord in the beauty of holiness.

The voice of the Lord carries across the waters; the God of glory thunders upon the mighty oceans.

In the temple of the Lord, all are crying, "Glory!"

For the Lord sits enthroned above the flood and will give strength and peace to the people of God.

SUGGESTED HYMNS

ENTRANCE/GATHERING HYMNS	HB	LBW	NCH	PH	RL	TFF	WOV
"All Glory Be to God on High"	—	166	—	133	620	—	—
"Morning Has Broken"	464	—	—	469	—	—	—
HYMNS RELATED TO SCRIPTURE							
O—"I Sing the Mighty Power of God"	84	—	12	272	—	—	—
"Spirit"	—	—	286	319	—	—	684
"Thy Strong Word Did Cleave the Darkness"	—	233	—	—	386	—	—
A—"Come Holy Ghost, Our Souls Inspire"	237	472–73	268	125	385	—	—
"O Christ, the Great Foundation"	—	—	387	443	—	—	—
G—"O Love, How Deep, How Broad"	—	88	209	83	342–43	—	—
"When Jesus Came to Jordan"	—	—	—	72	—	—	647
HYMNS OF THE TABLE							
"Many and Great"	—	—	3	271	—	—	794
"O Spirit of the Living God"	242	388	263	—	378	—	—
SENDING FORTH							
"Love Divine, All Loves Excelling"	399	315	43	376	464	—	—
"Mothering God, You Gave Me Birth"	—	—	467	—	—	—	—

Baptism of Our Lord

Color: White

PRAYER OF CONFESSION

God who formed the heavens and earth,
And all that dwell in them—
we gratefully acknowledge that by your Word
you created us,
and that by your Spirit,
you continue to sustain us.
Yet we have lived as though we were our own,
and as though your world belonged to us.
We have failed to be good stewards of your creation,
and have conducted ourselves as though
we belonged to ourselves.

Forgive our resistance to your life-giving Spirit.
Fill our hearts with gratitude and humility.
Empower us to embrace and display
your holy claims on our lives,
to the honor of our Lord and Savior,
Jesus Christ, your Beloved Son.

HYMN OF ASSURANCE

"God, You Spin the Whirling Planets," *PH,* 285

PSALM 29

METRICAL—
"Psalm 29" (8.7.8.7 D), *PCW,* 40
"The God of Heaven Thunders" (irregular), *PH,* 180
RESPONSORIAL—
"Psalm 29," Hal Hopson, *The Psalter* (1993), 26
"The Lord Will Bless His People," Tom Booth,
Singing the Psalms: Book Four, 12
CHORAL—
"The Voice of the Lord," Heinrich Schuetz, Mercury

ADDITIONAL SONGS

"Come, Spirit, Come," Walt Harrah, *Lift Up Your
Hearts,* 151

"Song Over the Waters," Marty Haugen, *Worship &
Praise,* 127
"Spirit Song," John Wimber, *Renew,* 248
"The River Is Here," Andy Park, *Lift Up Your
Hearts,* 98

CHORAL/VOCAL

"Carol of the Baptism," George Brandon (SAB), CPH
"Come Down, O Love Divine," Daniel Gawthrop
(SATB), H. W. Gray
"The Creation," Willy Richter (SATB or TTBB),
Flammer

ORGAN

"Prelude on BUNESSEN (Morning Has Broken)," Dale
Wood, *Wood Works,* Sacred Music Press, 20
"Prelude on CAITHNESS (Christ, When for Us You
Were Baptized)," Healey Willan, *Thirty-six Short
Preludes and Postludes, 1,* C. F. Peters, 6

PIANO

"God That Madest Earth and Heaven," Daniel Kane,
More Selectable Delectables, 3
"I Sing the Mighty Power of God," Mark Sedio,
Dancing in the Light of God, 16
"This Is the Spirit's Entry Now," John Carter, *Hymns
for Piano,* Hope, 2

HANDBELL

"Breathe on Me, Breath of God," Douglas Warner,
Service Music for Bells (3 octaves), Beckenhorst
"Genesis," William Payne (3 octaves), Flammer
"Spirit Wind," John Bartsch (3–5 octaves), Fred Bock

STUDY CATECHISM

For today's questions and answers, see pp. 215–16.

January 19, 2003

1 Samuel 3:1–10 (11–20) As a child, Samuel hears God's voice in the night.
Psalm 139:1–6, 13–18 God has knowledge of our innermost thoughts.
1 Corinthians 6:12–20 Paul responds to reports of sexual impurity in the church at Corinth.
John 1:43–51 Jesus calls disciples to become his followers.
Theme(s) of lectionary texts: Vocation and discipleship.

CALL TO WORSHIP

Lord, you have searched me, and you know me;
    you know my sitting down and my rising up.
You discern my thoughts from afar,
    and you are acquainted with all my ways.
There is not a word that comes to my lips
    but that you, O Lord, know it altogether.
Knowledge like yours is too wonderful to me,
    and so I give you thanks and praise.

PRAYER OF CONFESSION

Lord and Shepherd of us all,
you have called us to serve you cheerfully,
and to follow you faithfully.
But we have turned a deaf ear to your call;
we have been so occupied with our own concerns
that we have not stopped to listen for you.

Forgive us for insisting upon our own way,
when you have called us to a better way.
By your Spirit, give us the minds and hearts of true
    disciples.
Be glorified in our glad obedience to your call,
as we walk in free submission to your will,
according to the pattern of our Lord, Jesus Christ.

HYMN OF ASSURANCE

"O Thou, My Soul, Return in Peace," *PH,* 228

SUGGESTED HYMNS

ENTRANCE/GATHERING HYMNS	HB	LBW	NCH	PH	RL	TFF	WOV
"Be Thou My Vision"	303	—	451	339	67	—	—
"Come Thou Fount of Every Blessing"	379	499	459	356	449	—	—
HYMNS RELATED TO SCRIPTURE							
O—"Here I Am, Lord"	—	—	—	525	—	230	752
"Lord, Speak to Me That I May Speak"	298	403	531	426	436	—	—
E—"Hear the Good News of Salvation"	—	—	—	355	—	—	—
"Make Me a Captive, Lord"	308	—	—	378	442	—	—
G—"I Sing a Song of the Saints of God"	—	—	295	364	401	—	—
"Jesus Calls Us"	269	494	171	—	258	—	—
HYMNS OF THE TABLE							
"Lord, You Have Come to the Lakeshore"	—	—	173	377	—	154	784
"Seek Ye First"	—	—	—	333	—	149	783
SENDING FORTH							
"Blessed Assurance, Jesus Is Mine"	139	—	473	341	453	118	699
"O Jesus, I Have Promised"	307	503	493	388–89	471	—	—

Second Sunday in Ordinary Time

Color: Green

PSALM 139

METRICAL—
"Lord, You Have Searched My Life and Know"
    (8.8.8.8.8.8), *Psalter Hymnal*, 139
"Psalm 139" (8.7.8.7. D), *PCW*, 160
REPONSORIAL—
"Lord, You Have Searched Me," David Hurd
    (SATB/congregation), GIA
"Psalm 139," Hal Hopson, *The Psalter* (1993), 143
CHORAL—
"Lord, Thou Hast Searched Me," Alice Parker (unison), Hinshaw
"Lord, Thou Hast Searched Me," David Friedell
    (SATB), H. W. Gray

ADDITIONAL SONGS

"Grace Greater than Our Sin," Julia Johnston/Daniel
    Towner, *Lift Up Your Hearts*, 76
"Lay It All Down," Brian March, *Lift Up Your
    Hearts*, 92
"Lord, Be Glorified," Bob Kilpatrick, *Renew*, 172
"The Summons," John Bell, *Worship & Praise*, 137

CHORAL/VOCAL

"He Comes to Us," Jane Marshall (SATB), Carl Fisher
"Here I Am, Lord," John Ness Beck and Craig
    Courtney (SATB), Beckenhorst
"How Clear Is Our Vocation," Russell Schultz-
    Widmer (SATB), Augsburg-Fortress
"Samuel Lay Down," Max Exner (unison/triangle),
    Augsburg-Fortress

ORGAN

"Be Thou My Vision" (SLANE)
    Paul Schwartz, *Reflections on an Irish Hymn Tune*,
    H. W. Gray
    Hal Hopson, *Five Preludes on Familiar Hymns*,
    Flammer, 12
"Come, Holy Ghost" (VENI CREATOR SPIRITUS)
    Wilbur Held, *Hymn Preludes for the Pentecost
    Season*, CPH, 3
    Maurice Durufle, *Prelude, Adagio, et Choral Varie
    sur Veni Creator*, Durand

PIANO

"Be Thou My Vision," Angela Tipps, *Keys of the
    Kingdom*, vol. 1, Abingdon, 26
"Here I Am, Lord," John Carter, *Today's Hymns and
    Songs*, Hope, 5

HANDBELL

"He Leadeth Me," Cynthia Dobrinski (3–5 octaves),
    Agape
"Prelude on NETTLETON," Robert Scheiblhofer
    (4 octaves), Hinshaw

STUDY CATECHISM

For today's questions and answers, see p. 216.

January 26, 2003

Jonah 3:1–5, 10 — After his resistance, Jonah gives into God's calling and goes to deliver his prophecy *that* in Nineveh.

Psalm 62:5–12 — The believer waits in silence for the knowledge of God's presence.

1 Corinthians 7:29–31 — Paul reminds the Corinthians that this world will ultimately pass away.

Mark 1:14–20 — Jesus calls Simon, Andrew, James, and John to be disciples.

Theme(s) of lectionary texts: Dependence on the Lord God. Repentance.

CALL TO WORSHIP

M: God alone is our rock and our salvation,
    our stronghold in whom we dwell secure.
In God alone is our safety and our honor;
    God is our strong defense and our refuge.
P: May we Put your trust in God always,
    and pour out your hearts before God in prayer.
Power belongs to the Lord alone,
    and steadfast love is God's promise to us.

PRAYER OF CONFESSION

Most holy Lord, ~~our Judge and Advocate,~~ *we confess*
we ~~have cared~~ *care* more for our own pleasure and power
than for your peace and justice.
~~We deserve your judgment,~~
~~yet we call upon you for mercy.~~

Awaken us to our need for repentance, *and*
convict us by your Holy Spirit
of those words, thoughts, and actions
which have separated us from you. *and from one another.*
Remember your steadfast love,
and forgive us for the sake of your Son,
Jesus Christ, our Savior and Redeemer. *Amen*

HYMN OF ASSURANCE

"O My Soul, Bless Your Redeemer," *PH*, 223

SUGGESTED HYMNS

ENTRANCE/GATHERING HYMNS	HB	LBW	NCH	PH	RL	TFF	WOV
"Come, Ye Thankful People, Come"	525	407	422	551	18	—	—
HYMNS RELATED TO SCRIPTURE							
O—"As Morning Dawns"	—	—	—	161	—	—	—
"Comfort, Comfort You My People"	—	29	161	3	169	—	—
E—"God of Grace and God of Glory"	358	415	436	420	416	—	—
"It's Me, O Lord (Standin' in the Need)"	—	—	519	—	—	240	—
G—"Take My Life, and Let It Be Consecrated"	310	406	448	391	475	—	—
"They Cast Their Nets in Galilee"	421	449	—	—	—	—	—
HYMN OF THE TABLE							
"Rock of Ages"	271	327	596	—	447	—	—
SENDING FORTH							
"Lord, You Give the Great Commission"	—	—	—	429	—	—	756
"O Jesus, I Have Promised"	307	503	493	388–89	471	—	—

Third Sunday in Ordinary Time

Color: Green

PSALM 62

METRICAL—
"On God Alone I Wait Silently," John Bell (SATB or unison), *Psalms of Patience, Protest and Praise*, GIA
"Psalm 62" (LM), *PCW*, 75
RESPONSORIAL—
"Psalm 62:5–12," Robert Bastastini, *The Psalter* (1993), 52
CHORAL—
"For God Alone My Soul in Silence Waits," Frank Boles (SATB), Paraclete
"Leave It All Quietly to God," Jean Berger (SATB), Fred Bock

ADDITIONAL SONGS

"From the Sun's Rising," Graham Kendrick, *Lift Up Your Hearts*, 25
"Jesus, We Are Here," Patrick Matsikenyiri, *Lift Up Your Hearts*, 9
"Jonah's Song," Vicki Williams, *Renew*, 125
"The God Who Sings," Douglas Galbraith, *Common Ground*, 123

CHORAL/VOCAL

"Jonah," Dale Wood (SATB), Carl Fisher
"O for a Closer Walk with God," Anthony Baldwin (SATB), Oxford
"The Kingdom of God," Austin Lovelace (SATB), Hope
SOLO
"I Am Free," Chris Christiansen, *Hosanna! Songbook 4*, 299
CHILDREN AND YOUTH
"God Is Like a Rock," Natalie Sleeth, Choristers Guild

ORGAN

"God of Grace and God of Glory" (CWM RHONNDA), Paul Manz, *Ten Chorale Improvisations, Set 5*, MorningStar
"Take Up Your Cross, the Savior Said" (BOURBON), Gilbert Martin, *Early American Folk Hymns for Organ*, Lorenz, 28

PIANO

"He Leadeth Me," Angela Tipps, *Keys of the Kingdom*, vol. 3, Abingdon, 26
"Lord of the Dance," John Carter, *Folk Hymns for the Piano*, Hope, 8

HANDBELL

"God of Grace and God of Glory" (CWM RHONNDA) Anna Laura Page (3–5 octaves), AGEHR
Albert Zabel, *Seventeen Handbell Processionals* (3 octaves), Agape

STUDY CATECHISM

For today's questions and answers, see p. 216.

February 2, 2003

Deuteronomy 18:15–20	Considering his own death, Moses assures the people that God will raise up another prophet.
Psalm 111	A psalm contemplating the grandeur of all God's works.
1 Corinthians 8:1–13	Paul explains that the liberty of Christians must be tempered by the love they learned in Jesus.
Mark 1:21–28	Jesus demonstrates his divine authority through the sign of healing.

Theme(s) of lectionary texts: God's authority and love as the basis for community.

CALL TO WORSHIP

Let us give thanks to the Lord with willing hearts,
offering praise in the midst of the congregation.
Great are God's works;
the ways of the Lord are studied by all who
delight in them.
The deeds of the Lord are full of majesty and splendor;
God performs acts of justice and mercy across the
whole earth.
The fear of the Lord is the beginning of wisdom;
thanks and praise endure among God's people for-
ever!

PRAYER OF CONFESSION

Gracious God,
You have given us a sure Word—
sealed by your Spirit in the free gift of your Son.
In him you have set us free from bondage,
bound up and healed our wounds,
and led us into paths of peace.
But still we listen to other voices,
as though your word were just one among others.

In mercy, forgive us, O Lord.
Enable us by your Spirit,
to demonstrate our gratitude for all your blessings,
by following Jesus with undivided hearts,
and by bearing his liberating good news
wherever there is brokenness and bondage,
to the glory of your holy name.

HYMN OF ASSURANCE

"Jesus, Lover of My Soul," *PH, 303*

SUGGESTED HYMNS

	HB	LBW	NCH	PH	RL	TFF	WOV
ENTRANCE/GATHERING HYMNS							
"The God of Abraham Praise"	89	544	24	488	595	—	—
HYMNS RELATED TO SCRIPTURE							
O—"Draw Us in the Spirit's Tether"	—	—	337	504	—	—	703
E—"O Master, Let Me Walk with Thee"	304	492	503	357	428	—	—
G—"Christ Whose Glory Fills the Skies"	47	265	—	462–63	463	—	—
HYMN OF THE TABLE							
"There Is a Balm in Gilead"	—	—	553	394	465	—	737
SENDING FORTH							
"Blest Be the Tie That Binds"	473	370	393	438	407–08	—	—

Fourth Sunday in Ordinary Time

Color: Green

PSALM 111

METRICAL—
"Psalm 111," Heinrich Schuetz, *Eight Psalms*,
    Augsburg-Fortress
RESPONSORIAL—
"Psalm 111," Hal Hopson, *The Psalter* (1993), 111
CHORAL—
"I Will Give Thanks," Ronald A. Nelson (SATB),
    Augsburg-Fortress
"My Heart Is Full Today," Richard Proulx (SS),
    Augsburg-Fortress
"Praise Ye the Lord," Peter Prelleur (SAB/solo),
    Broude

ADDITIONAL SONGS

"Awesome God," Rich Mullins, *Renew*, 245
"I Sing Praises," Terry MacAlmon, *Lift Up Your
    Hearts*, 35
"Majesty," Jack Hayford, *Renew*, 63

CHORAL/VOCAL

"All You Works of the Lord," Kenneth Jennings
    (SATB), Augsburg-Fortress
"Draw Us in the Spirit's Tether," Harold Friedell
    (SATB), H. W. Gray
"I Am the Bread of Life," Suzanne Toolan (SATB),
    GIA
"There Is a Balm in Gilead," William Dawson
    (SATB/S), Tuskegee Institute
CHILDREN AND YOUTH
"Tell All the World," John Horman, Choristers Guild

ORGAN

"Prelude on DARWELL'S 148th (Rejoice, the Lord Is
    King)," Percy Whitlock, *Six Hymn Preludes*,
    Oxford, 1
"All Creatures of Our God and King" (LASST UNS
    ERFREUEN)
    Wilbur Held, *Hymn Preludes for the Autumn
    Festivals*, CPH, 6
    Charles W. Ore, *Eleven Compositions for Organ*,
    CPH, 26

PIANO

"All Creatures of Our God and King," Fred Bock,
    Bock's Best 4, Fred Bock Music, 80

HANDBELL

"All Creatures of Our God and King," Cynthia
    Dobrinski (3–5 octaves), Agape
"Majesty," Jack Schrader (3–5 octaves), Agape
"There Is a Balm in Gilead," Jeffery Honore (3–5
    octaves), CPH

STUDY CATECHISM

For today's questions and answers, see pp. 216–17.

February 9, 2003

Isaiah 40:21–31 — All things come from the Creator alone, including the community of God's people.

Psalm 147:1–11, 20c — A psalm of thanksgiving to God for restoration and plenty.

1 Corinthians 9:16–23 — The greatest treasure is God's calling to proclaim good news.

Mark 1:29–39 — Jesus heals Peter's mother-in-law.

Theme(s) of lectionary texts: Proclamation of the good news of God.

CALL TO WORSHIP

How good it is to sing praises to our God;
  how pleasant it is to honor the Lord with praise!
The Lord rebuilds the fallen city,
  and gathers the victims and exiles into homes.
The Lord heals the brokenhearted
  and binds up the wounds of the injured.
Great is our God, and mighty in power;
  God's wisdom is beyond our understanding.
    Alleluia!

PRAYER OF CONFESSION

Faithful Shepherd:
In seasons of struggle and distress,
we forget your steadfast love;
we complain that you have not met our needs,
and we question your care for us.
We rush to other saviors,
rather than waiting patiently for your salvation.

In your tender mercy,
forgive us for charging you with neglect—
as though we could not trust your promises
of goodness, mercy, and justice
to all who trust in you.
Help us by your Spirit
to hold fast to the sure hope
that every promise you make is reliable,
confirmed forever by the redeeming love
of our Savior and Lord, Jesus Christ.

HYMN OF ASSURANCE

"Now Thank We All Our God," *PH,* 555

SUGGESTED HYMNS

ENTRANCE/GATHERING HYMNS	HB	LBW	NCH	PH	RL	TFF	WOV
"Praise to the Lord, the Almighty"	—	543	22	482	145	—	—
"Sing Praise to God"	15	542	6	483	146	—	—
HYMNS RELATED TO SCRIPTURE							
O—"Give to the Winds Thy Fears"	364	—	404	286	149	—	—
"Immortal, Invisible, God Only Wise"	85	526	1	263	7	—	—
E—"I Love to Tell the Story"	383	390	522	—	—	—	—
"Lift High the Cross"	—	377	198	371	415	—	—
G—"O Christ the Healer"	—	360	175	380	—	—	—
"What a Friend We Have in Jesus"	385	439	506	403	507	—	—
HYMN OF THE TABLE							
"Precious Lord"	—	—	472	404	—	193	—
SENDING FORTH							
"Lord, Dismiss Us with Thy Blessing"	79	259	77	538	—	—	—

Fifth Sunday in Ordinary Time

Color: Green

PSALM 147

METRICAL—
"Hallelujah! How Good It Is" (CM) *A New Metrical Psalter*, 231
"Psalm 147a" (10.10.10.4) *PCW*, 168
RESPONSORIAL—
"Psalm 147," C. Kelly and S. Weber, *The Psalter* (1993), 153
CHORAL—
"Praise Ye the Lord," Johann Geisler (SSAB or SATB), Boosey & Hawkes
"Sing Praises to Our God," Robert J. Powell (SS), CPH

ADDITIONAL SONGS

"Beauty for Brokenness," Graham Kendrick, *Worship & Praise*, 17
"On Eagles' Wings," Michael Joncas, *Lift Up Your Hearts*, 87
"Sing Out, Earth and Skies," Marty Haugen, *Worship & Praise*, 126

CHORAL/VOCAL

"Hast Thou Not Known?" David Hugh Jones (SATB), Carl Fisher
"Have You Not Known?" Randall Thompson, *Peaceable Kingdom* (SATB), ECS
"They That Wait Upon the Lord," Jean Berger (SATB), Augsburg-Fortress
"They That Wait Upon the Lord," Gerald Near (SATB), Aureole
CHILDREN AND YOUTH
"Have You Not Known?" John Horman, Choristers Guild

ORGAN

"If Thou But Trust in God to Guide Thee (WER NUR DEN LIEBEN GOTT)"
  J. S. Bach, Schuebler Chorales (various editions) and Orgelbuechlein (various editions)
  Jan Bender, *Kleine Choralvorspiele, 1*, Baerenreiter, 51
  Helmut Walcha, *Chorale Preludes, 1*, Peters, 44
"Praise to the Lord, the Almighty (LOBE DEN HERREN)," Emma Lou Diemer, *Ten Hymn Preludes for Meditation and Praise*, Carl Fisher, 2

PIANO

"Lift High the Cross," Fred Bock, *Bock's Best, 4*, Fred Bock Music
"To God Be the Glory," John Carter, *Hymns for Piano*, Hope, 10

HANDBELL

"Lift High the Cross," Cynthia Dobrinski (3–5 octaves), Agape
"Praise to the Lord, the Almighty," Kevin McChesney (2–3 octaves), Agape
"Wondrous Love," Jeffery Honore (3–4 octaves), Augsburg-Fortress

STUDY CATECHISM

For today's questions and answers, see p. 217.

February 16, 2003

2 Kings 4:1–14 — Naaman, a Syrian general, comes to Elisha in hope of being cured of his skin disease.

Psalm 30 — Thanksgiving to God for healing and renewal.

1 Corinthians 9:24–27 — Paul discusses the self-discipline necessary in living the Christian life.

Mark 1:40–45 — Jesus becomes known throughout the region as he undertakes his ministry.

Theme(s) of lectionary texts: Disciplines of service.

CALL TO WORSHIP

We will exalt you, O Lord,
 for you have lifted us up in time of need.
**O Lord our God, when we cry out to you,
 you restore the very things we lack.**
The Lord turns our mourning into dancing;
 God bids us replace our sackcloth with joy.
**Therefore our hearts sing to God;
 O Lord, may we give you thanks forever!**

PRAYER OF CONFESSION

Gracious Redeemer:
Your touch has healed our wounds,
your peace has quieted our strife,
and your grace has cleansed our hearts.
Yet our hope in you has faltered.
We have turned away from you,
and have sought out other healers,
and heeded other voices.

In your mercy, forgive us for forsaking you,
whom alone to know is life eternal.
By your Spirit, quicken our faith,
and renew us in steadfast hope,
that we look to you with confident reliance,
and listen to you with certain assurance
that your Word, made incarnate in our Lord Jesus,
is never empty or powerless.

HYMN OF ASSURANCE

"O Savior, in This Quiet Place," *PH*, 390

SUGGESTED HYMNS

	HB	LBW	NCH	PH	RL	TFF	WOV
ENTRANCE/GATHERING HYMNS							
"Awake, My Soul"	346	269	491	474	174	—	—
"Praise, My Soul, the King of Heaven"	31	549	—	478–79	144	—	—
HYMNS RELATED TO SCRIPTURE							
O—"If Thou but Trust in God to Guide Thee"	344	453	410	282	151	—	—
"Whate'er My God Ordains Is Right"	266	446	—	—	153	—	—
E—"Christ of the Upward Way"	295	—	—	344	—	—	—
"Fight the Good Fight"	359	461	—	307	—	—	—
G—"Creating God, Your Fingers Trace"	—	—	462	134	—	—	—
"Immortal Love, Forever Full"	229	—	166	—	254	—	—
HYMN OF THE TABLE							
"Just As I Am"	272	296	207	370	467	—	—
SENDING FORTH							
"My Hope Is Built on Nothing Less"	368	293	404	379	459	—	—

Sixth Sunday in Ordinary Time

Color: Green

PSALM

METRICAL—
"Psalm 30," Heinrich Schuetz, *Eight Psalms*,
    Augsburg-Fortress
"Psalm 30" (8.7.8.7 D), *PCW*, 41
RESPONSORIAL—
"Psalm 30," Peter Merrick/Ralph Vaughan Williams,
    The Book of Psalms
CHORAL—
"I Will Exalt You, O Lord," Raymond Chenault
    (2-part mixed) GIA
"Thou Hast Turned My Laments into Dancing,"
    Daniel Pinkham (SATB), C. F. Peters

ADDITIONAL SONGS

"God Has Smiled on Me," Isaiah Jones Jr., *Lift Up
    Your Hearts*, 69
"God Is So Good," unknown author, *Lift Up Your
    Hearts*, 24
"How Can I Keep from Singing?" Robert Lowry, *Lift
    Up Your Hearts*, 34

CHORAL/VOCAL

"Awake Our Souls," George Brandon (2-part mixed),
    CPH
"Springs in the Desert," Arthur Jennings (SATB/T),
    H. W. Gray
CHILDREN AND YOUTH
"Now Is the Time for Singing," John Horman,
    Choristers Guild
"Then Will I Jehovah Praise," G. F. Handel/R. Powell,
    Choristers Guild

ORGAN

"Chorale Prelude on ST. BRIDE (Give to the Winds
    Thy Fears)"
    Alec Rowley, *Chorale Preludes Based on Famous
    Hymn Tunes*, C. F. Peters, 17
    Healey Willan, *Thirty-six Short Preludes and
    Postludes 3*, C. F. Peters, 22

PIANO

"Just As I Am," Fred Bock, *Bock's Best 4*, Fred Bock
    Music, 66

HANDBELL

"Immortal, Invisible," Barbara Kinyon (3 octaves),
    Choristers Guild
"Praise, My Soul, the King of Heaven," Cynthia
    Dobrinski (3–5 octaves), Agape

STUDY CATECHISM

For today's questions and answers, see p. 217.

February 23, 2003

Isaiah 43:18–25   The people of God are warned not to neglect the worship of God.

Psalm 41   God's care for the poor and for all who reach out to the needy.

2 Corinthians 1:18–22   Jesus is the Word of God, and that Word is "Yes!"

Mark 2:1–12   Friends of a crippled man bring him to Jesus for healing of body and spirit.

Theme(s) of lectionary texts: Gifts of God are intended for the people of God.

CALL TO WORSHIP

Happy are those who remember the poor and the needy, for the Lord will deliver them in time of trouble.
The Lord preserves their lives and protects them, so that one day they may prosper in the land.
The Lord sustains them on their sickbed and ministers to them in their illness.
The Lord is merciful and will raise up those who fall; blessed be the Lord our God forever! Amen.

SUGGESTED HYMNS

	HB	LBW	NCH	PH	RL	TFF	WOV
ENTRANCE/GATHERING HYMNS							
"I Come with Joy"	—	—	349	507	534	—	—
"O for a Thousand Tongues to Sing"	141	559	42	466	362	—	—
HYMNS RELATED TO SCRIPTURE							
O—"Camina Pueblo de Dios (Walk On, People of God)"	—	—	614	296	—	—	—
"Lift Every Voice and Sing"	—	562	593	563	—	—	—
"When God Delivered Israel"	—	—	—	237	133	—	—
E—"Amen, Amen"	—	—	161	299	—	—	—
"My Song Forever Shall Record"	516	—	—	209	113	—	—
G—"O Christ the Healer"	—	360	175	380	—	—	—
"Pass Me Not, O Gentle Savior"	—	—	551	—	—	150	—
"Thine Arm, O Lord, in Days of Old"	179	431	—	—	—	—	—
HYMNS OF THE TABLE							
"Every Time I Feel the Spirit"	—	—	282	315	—	241	—
"O Morning Star"	—	76	—	69	367	—	—
SENDING FORTH							
"Canto de Esperanza (Song of Hope)"	—	—	—	432	—	—	—
"How Firm a Foundation"	369	507	407	361	172	—	—
"Savior, Like a Shepherd Lead Us"	380	481	252	387	—	254	—

Seventh Sunday in Ordinary Time

Color: Green

PRAYER OF CONFESSION

Renewer of life:
You call us to embrace the new, but we prefer the old.
You call us to beware resting at "ease in Zion,"
but we clutch closely the coziness of familiar places.
You invite us to join you as you do new things;
we'd prefer to keep a safe distance from the upheaval
    of it all.
You seek to renew us in your image;
we do all we can to cling to our old ways of life.
We confess that we oppose your work in us;
we resist being conformed to your will.

Loving God, have mercy on us.
Forgive us for clutching tightly
when you would have us let go.
Stir us by your Spirit,
who makes all things new,
for the sake of your Son,
our Savior and Lord, Jesus Christ.

HYMN OF ASSURANCE

"Breathe on Me, Breath of God," *PH*, 316

PSALM

METRICAL—
"How Blest Are They" (CMD), *Psalter Hymnal*, 41
"Psalm 41" (LM), *PCW*, 53
RESPONSORIAL—
"Psalm 41," *A Hymn Tune Psalter, Book 1*, 23
CHORAL—
"Blessed Is He That Considereth," Michael Wise
    (SATB), *New Church Anthem Book*, Oxford

ADDITIONAL SONGS

"Love Is a Circle," Peggy Brown, *Lift Up Your Hearts*,
    94
"One More Step," Sydney Carter, *Common Ground*,
    100
"Say Yes," Graham Kendrick, *Hosanna! Songbook 6*,
    524

CHORAL/VOCAL

"Blessed Is He," Marjorie Harper (SATB or SSA),
    Mercury
"No Need," Michael Ward (unison/trumpet), Word
"O for a Thousand Tongues," John Ness Beck
    (SATB/S/B), Fred Bock Music

ORGAN

"Chorale Prelude on NUN DANKET ALL' UND BRINGET
    EHR (Spirit Divine, Attend Our Prayers," Helmut
    Walcha, *Choralvorspiele, 3*, C. F. Peters, 39
"Processional on 'Lift High the Cross' (CRUCIFER),"
    Donald Bussarow, CPH

PIANO

"Lift High the Cross," Fred Bock, *Bock's Best, 4*, Fred
    Bock Music, 88

HANDBELL

"Savior, Like a Shepherd Lead Us," Linda McKechnie
    (3 octaves), Agape

STUDY CATECHISM

For today's questions and answers, see pp. 217–18.

March 2, 2003

2 Kings 2:1–12   Elijah the prophet is taken to heaven in a fiery chariot, and his mantle passes to Elisha.

Psalm 50:1–6   The people of God's covenant give testimony to the Creator's glory.

2 Corinthians 4:3–6   Paul tells the Christians of Corinth that they themselves serve as the most convincing letter of reference attesting his zeal for the gospel.

Mark 9:2–9   Mark's account of the transfiguration of the Lord Jesus Christ.

Theme(s) of lectionary texts: Glory, tinged with intimations of suffering to come.

CALL TO WORSHIP

The Lord shines forth in glory.
>Our Lord, the God of all, has spoken.

God will come and not keep silent;
>**the heavens reveal the glory of the Lord.**

God calls heaven and earth to bear witness,
>to testify that the covenant has been sealed.

Let the heavens declare God's justice,
>**and let the people give honor to the Lord.**

PRAYER OF CONFESSION

Exalted Savior,
we have set our affections on the things of this
>world,
when you challenge us to set our hearts on things
>above.
We pray for your kingdom to come,
yet we turn away from your light
when it reveals how we have stumbled
in our chosen darkness.

Forgive us for the many ways
we deny your rightful rule.
Teach us to fear you well,
and lead us in your paths of righteousness.
We lay our lives before you in repentance,
that you may work your holy purposes in us,
for your honor and glory.

HYMN OF ASSURANCE

"Lord, Enthroned in Heavenly Splendor," *PH,* 154

SUGGESTED HYMNS

ENTRANCE/GATHERING HYMNS	HB	LBW	NCH	PH	RL	TFF	WOV
"All Hail the Power of Jesus' Name"	132	328–29	304	142–43	593–94	—	—
HYMNS RELATED TO SCRIPTURE							
O—"Hail to the Lord's Anointed"	146	87	104	205	232	—	—
"Swing Low, Sweet Chariot"	—	—	—	—	—	171	—
E—"Blessed Jesus, at Your Word"	—	—	74	454	530	—	—
"O Splendor of God's Glory Bright"	46	271	87	474	76	—	—
G—"Christ Whose Glory Fills the Skies"	—	265	—	462	463	—	—
"Jesus on the Mountain Peak"	—	—	—	74	257	—	653
HYMN OF THE TABLE							
"I Heard the Voice of Jesus Say"	280	497	489	—	—	62	—
SENDING FORTH							
"Come Down, O Love Divine"	—	508	289	313	444	—	—
"Shine, Jesus, Shine"	—	—	—	—	—	64	651

Transfiguration of the Lord

Color: White or gold

PSALM 50

METRICAL—
"Psalm 50" (CMD), *PCW*, 63
"The Mighty God and Sovereign Lord" (8.8.8.8.8.8),
  Psalter Hymnal, 50
RESPONSORIAL—
"Psalm 50," Peter Hallock, *The Psalter (1993)*, 45
CHORAL—
"The Lord Has Spoken," F. J. Haydn (SAB), CPH
"The Mighty God," Benedetto Marcello (SAB), CPH

ADDITIONAL SONGS

"Come to the Mountain," Kathy Donlan Tunseth,
  Worship & Praise, 29
"He Is Exalted," Twila Paris, *Lift Up Your Hearts*, 33
  "Shine, Jesus, Shine," Graham Kendrick, *Lift Up
Your Hearts*, 50
"'Tis Good to Be Here," *Gather Comprehensive*, 778
"Transfiguration," Carey Landry, *Glory & Praise*, 443

CHORAL/VOCAL

"God of the Prophets," Emse Engle (SATB),
  Augsburg-Fortress
"Prayer for Transfiguration Day," John Weaver
  (SATB), Hope
"The Transfiguration of the Lord," Nancy Maeker
  (unison/Orff), Augsburg-Fortress
"This Is My Son, My Beloved," Kathy Powell (SATB),
  GIA
"Transfiguration," Allan Hovhanes (SATB/T), C. F.
  Peters
"Transfiguration," Alec Wyton (SATB), Flammer
"We Shall Be Changed," Michael Ward (SATB), Word

ORGAN

"I Greet Thee, Who My Sure Redeemer Art"
  (TOULON), Wilbur Held, *Three Pieces for Organ*,
  Augsburg-Fortress, 13
"Lord of Light, Your Name Outshining" (ABBOTS
  LEIGH)
  Austin C. Lovelace, *Abbot's Leigh*, Hope
  Robert J. Powell, *Three New Hymn Settings for
  Organ*, Hope, 2

PIANO

"Swing Low, Sweet Chariot," John Carter, *Spirituals
  for Piano*, Hope, 5

HANDBELL

"How Firm a Foundation," Tammy Waldrop (3–4
  octaves), Red River Music
"The God of Heaven," Hal Hopson, *Creative Use of
  Handbells in Worship*, Hope, 96

STUDY CATECHISM

For today's questions and answers, see p. 218.

March 5, 2003

Joel 2:1–2, 12–17 or Isaiah 58:1–12 — The prophet warns of the coming Day of the Lord. Isaiah calls on the people to be just: that is the fasting that God desires from them.

Psalm 51:1–17 — A psalm of repentance and confession of sin.

2 Corinthians 5:20b–6:10 — God was in Christ, inaugurating a ministry of reconciliation.

Matthew 6:1–6, 16–21 — Jesus teaches that personal piety must be paired with humility. The reward for faithfulness does not come from the culture, but treasures are stored in heaven.

Theme(s) of lectionary texts: Fasting and repentance as essential in giving one's life to God.

CALL TO WORSHIP

My tongue will sing your righteousness,
   O God of my salvation.
Open my lips, O Lord,
   and my mouth shall proclaim your praise.
If you desired it, I would offer a sacrifice,
   but you take no delight in burnt offerings.
The sacrifice of God is a troubled spirit;
   a sorrowful and contrite heart O God you will
      not despise.

SUGGESTED HYMNS

ENTRANCE/GATHERING HYMNS	HB	LBW	NCH	PH	RL	TFF	WOV
"Forty Days and Forty Nights"	—	—	205	77	—	—	—
"Sweet Hour of Prayer"	398	—	505	—	—	242	—
HYMNS RELATED TO SCRIPTURE							
O—"Come, Let Us to the Lord Our God"	125	—	—	—	37	—	—
"Out of the Depths I Cry to You"	—	295	483	240	134	—	—
"There's a Wideness in God's Mercy"	110	290	23	298	349	—	—
E—"Dust and Ashes Touch Our Face"	—	—	186	—	—	—	—
G—"I Want Jesus to Walk with Me"	—	—	490	363	—	—	606
"There Is a Place of Quiet Rest"	318	—	—	527	—	—	—
"Time Is Filled with Swift Transition"	—	—	—	—	—	231	—
HYMNS OF THE TABLE							
"Just As I Am"	472	296	207	370	467–68	—	—
"Lord, Who Throughout These Forty Days"	181	99	211	81	—	—	—
"Our Father, We Have Wandered"	—	—	—	—	—	—	733
"What Can Wash My Sins Away?"	—	—	—	—	—	69	—
SENDING FORTH							
"Love Divine, All Loves Excelling"	399	315	43	376	464	—	—

Ash Wednesday

Color: Purple

PRAYER OF CONFESSION

Exalted Savior,
we have set our affections on the things of this
    world,
when you challenge us to set our hearts on things
    above.
We pray for your kingdom to come,
yet we turn away from your light
when it reveals how we have stumbled
in our chosen darkness.

Forgive us for the many ways
we deny your rightful rule.
Teach us to fear you well,
and lead us in your paths of righteousness.
We lay our lives before you in repentance,
that you may work your holy purposes in us,
for your honor and glory.

HYMN OF ASSURANCE

"Lord, Enthroned in Heavenly Splendor," *PH*, 154

PSALM 51

METRICAL—
"Have Mercy on Us, Living Lord" (CM), *PH*, 195
"Psalm 51" (CM), *PCW*, 64
RESPONSORIAL—
"Psalm 51," David Clarke Isele, *PH*, 196
"Psalm 51," *Hymn Tune Psalter, 2*, 88
CHORAL—
"Have Mercy On Me, O God," Peter Pindar Stearns
    (SATB), Paraclete Press
"Create in Me a Clean Heart, O God," Carl Mueller
    (SATB), G. Schirmer
"Create in Me a Clean Heart, O God," John V.
    Mochnik (SATB), Augsburg-Fortress
"Create in Me, O God," Johannes Brahms (SATBB),
    G. Schirmer

ADDITIONAL SONGS

"Change My Heart, O God," E. Espinosa, *Lift Up
    Your Hearts*, 61
"Create in Me a Clean Heart," *Renew*, 181–82
"Healing Grace," G. Sadler and M. Chisum, *Lift Up
    Your Hearts*, 68

CHORAL/VOCAL

"Blow the Trumpet in Zion," Frances Jackson (SATB),
    Oxford
"Out of the Depths," Carl Schalk (SAB), MorningStar
"Thy Holy Wings," Daniel Kallman (unison), Mark
    Foster
"Treasures in Heaven," Joseph Clokey (SATB),
    Summy Birchard
"True Fasting," George Brandon (2-part), Abingdon

ORGAN

"Prelude to ST. FLAVIAN (Lord, Who Throughout
    These Forty Days)," C. Peeters, *Hymn Preludes for
    the Liturgical Year, 24*, C. F. Peters, 19

PIANO

"Out of the Depths I Cry to You," Richard Gerig,
    Piano Preludes on Hymns and Chorales, Hope, 18

HANDBELL

"O for a Thousand Tongues to Sing," John
    Yarrington, *Ten Hymntune Intradas* (various), Art
    Masters

March 9, 2003

Genesis 9:8–17	God gives the rainbow sign to seal the covenant with Noah and his family.
Psalm 25:1–10	A prayer for wisdom, understanding, and guidance in God's ways.
1 Peter 3:18–21	Peter explains baptism in terms of Noah's flood and the ark.
Mark 1:9–15	The baptism of Jesus.

Theme(s) of lectionary texts: The baptism, followed by forty days of temptation in the wilderness.

CALL TO WORSHIP

To you, O Lord, I lift up my soul;
  my God, I put my trust in you.
Let none who trust in you be put to shame;
  let the evil be disappointed in all their schemes.
Show me your ways, O Lord,
  and teach me to follow in your paths.
You guide the humble in doing right, O God,
  and all your ways are love and faithfulness.

PRAYER OF CONFESSION

Covenant-making God,
as heirs of your covenant,
which was sealed for us in baptism,
we have been promised your grace and forgiveness,
and been called to live as your holy people.
But we have taken your promises for granted,
neglecting the way of life to which you have called us.

Melt us, mold us, and saturate us anew
with your Holy Spirit into which we were baptized.
Empower us to embrace the way of the cross,
that we may be faithful to our calling,
as disciples of our Savior and Lord, Jesus Christ.

HYMN OF ASSURANCE

"Spirit of the Living God," *PH,* 322

SUGGESTED HYMNS

ENTRANCE/GATHERING HYMNS	HB	LBW	NCH	PH	RL	TFF	WOV
"Come, Thou Almighty King"	244	522	275	139	618	—	—
"Lord, Who Throughout These Forty Days"	181	99	211	81	—	—	—
"The Glory of These Forty Days"	—	—	—	87	242	—	657
HYMNS RELATED TO SCRIPTURE							
O—"Heaven and Earth and Sea and Air"	6	—	566	—	—	—	—
"Thank You, God, for Water, Soil, and Air"	—	—	559	266	22	—	—
E—"Baptized into Your Name Most Holy"	—	—	324	—	529	—	—
"Dearest Jesus, We Are Here"	—	248	74	493	530	—	—
G—"Forty Days and Forty Nights"	—	—	205	77	—	—	—
"O Love, How Deep"	—	88	209	83	342–44	—	—
HYMN OF THE TABLE							
"Ah, Holy Jesus"	191	123	218	93	285	—	—
SENDING FORTH							
"God of the Sparrow, God of the Whale"	—	—	32	272	—	—	—

First Sunday in Lent

Color: Purple

PSALM 25

METRICAL—

"Lord, to You My Soul Is Lifted" (8.7.8.7.7.8.7.8), *PH*, 78

"Psalm 25" (CM), *PCW*, 36

RESPONSORIAL—

"Psalm 25," Presbyterian tone 8, *The Psalter* (1993), 23

"Psalm 25," Hal Hopson, *Twenty-five Psalms for the Church Year*, 6

CHORAL—

"Call to Remembrance," Richard Farrant (TTBB), G. Schirmer

"Show Me Thy Ways," Walter Pelz (SATB), Augsburg-Fortress

ADDITIONAL SONGS

"Out in the Wilderness," Jay Beech, *Worship & Praise*, 115

"The Steadfast Love of the Lord," Edith McNeill, *Renew*, 23

"What Shall We Pray?" John Bell, *Common Ground*, 141

CHORAL/VOCAL

"O Love That Wilt Not Let Me Go," Robert Wetzler (SATB/T), Selah

"The Baptism of Christ," Peter Hallock (SATB/Solo), GIA

"To Thee, O Lord," Sergei Rachmaninov (SATB/S), Oxford

"Unto Thee, O Lord," Virgil Ford (SATB), G. Schirmer

ORGAN

"Chorale Prelude on ERHALT UNS HERR (The Glory of These Forty Days)," J. Pachelbel, *The Church Organist's Golden Treasury, 1*, Oliver Ditson, 151

"Prelude on ST. FLAVIAN (Lord, Who Throughout These Forty Days)," C. S. Lang, *Twenty Hymn-Tune Preludes, 1*, Oxford, 14

PIANO

"Come, Thou Almighty King," Reginald Gerig, *Piano Preludes on Hymns and Chorales*, Hope, 8

"O Love, How Deep," Angela Tipps, *Keys of the Kingdom*, vol. 5, Abingdon, 32

HANDBELL

"Nearer to the Cross," Sharon Elery Rogers (2–3 octaves), MorningStar

STUDY CATECHISM

For today's questions and answers, see p. 218.

March 16, 2003

Genesis 17:1–7, 15–16   God establishes a covenant with Abraham.

Psalm 22:23–31   A proclamation of the sovereignty of God.

Romans 4:13–25   Paul's teaching that God's covenant was established because of Abraham's faith, not because of good works on his part.

Mark 8:31–38   Jesus prophesies his suffering and death, calling his disciples to follow him.

Theme(s) of lectionary texts: The covenant with Abraham. Jesus as Suffering Servant.

CALL TO WORSHIP

Praise the Lord, you who worship the Lord;
     stand in awe of God, and give glory to the Lord.
For the Lord does not despise the poor and needy,
     but when they cry out, God answers them.
The hungry shall eat and be satisfied,
     and those who love the Lord shall offer praise.
All the ends of the earth shall worship God,
     for the Lord rules over every nation.

SUGGESTED HYMNS

ENTRANCE/GATHERING HYMNS	HB	LBW	NCH	PH	RL	TFF	WOV
"O Wondrous Sight, O Vision Fair"	182	80	184	75	256	—	—
"The God of Abraham Praise"	89	544	24	488	595	—	—
HYMNS RELATED TO SCRIPTURE							
O—"Deep in the Shadows of the Past"	—	—	320	330	—	—	—
"God of Our Life"	108	—	366	275	58–59	—	—
E—"Christ of All My Hopes the Ground"	314	—	—	—	455	—	—
"New Songs of Celebration Render"	—	—	—	218	119	—	—
"O God, Our Faithful God"	—	504	—	277	69	—	—
"O Praise the Gracious Power"	—	—	54	471	—	—	—
G—"All to Jesus I Surrender"	—	—	—	—	—	235	—
"Lord Christ, When First You Came to Earth"	—	421	—	7	608	—	—
"Take Up Thy Cross"	293	398	204	393	268	—	—
HYMNS OF THE TABLE							
"Beneath the Cross of Jesus"	190	107	190	92	310–11	—	—
"Jesus Walked This Lonesome Valley"	—	—	—	80	—	—	—
"Must Jesus Bear the Cross Alone?"	290	—	—	—	—	237	—
"We Have Come at Christ's Own Bidding"	—	—	182	—	—	—	—
SENDING FORTH							
"Lead On, O King Eternal"	332	495	573	447–48	423	—	—
"The Church of Christ in Every Age"	—	443	306	421	—	—	—

Second Sunday in Lent

Color: Purple

PRAYER OF CONFESSION

God of compassion,
look upon us in mercy,
for we have not walked in the way of Jesus, your Son.
We have not laid down our lives for the Gospel,
but have sought to advance and defend ourselves.
Our faith in you has wavered;
we have trusted more
in our own strength and understanding.

In loving kindness, forgive us.
Strengthen our faith by your Spirit,
that we would be courageous enough
to embrace the way of the cross.
Enable us to trust that this way of life,
proclaimed and lived by Jesus,
displays your glory most faithfully
and profits us best
both now, and in ages to come.

HYMN OF ASSURANCE

"Christ Is Made the Sure Foundation," *PH*, 416–7

PSALM 22

METRICAL—
"Psalm 22b" (CMD), *PCW*, 33
RESPONSORIAL—
"Psalm 22:23–31," Presbyterian tone 3, *The Psalter* (1993), 17
CHORAL—
"When We Are Tempted to Deny Your Son," Sally Ann Morris (SATB), GIA

ADDITIONAL SONGS

"In the Bulb There Is a Flower," Natalie Sleeth, *Lift Up Your Hearts*, 88

"How Long, O Lord," Christopher Norton, *Renew*, 68
"My Tribute," Andraé Crouch, *Renew*, 68
"Take Up Your Cross," Kinley Lange, *Lift Up Your Hearts*, 117

CHORAL/VOCAL

"Faith," Terry Kirkland (unison), Abingdon
"Follow Me," Alex Hegenbart (SATB), Brodt
"O Lord, Increase My Faith," Orlando Gibbons (SATB), H. W. Gray

ORGAN

"My Faith Looks Up to Thee" (OLIVET), Hal Hopson, *Praise to the Lord*, Sacred Music Press, 6
"Prelude on ROCKINGHAM (When I Survey the Wondrous Cross)," C. S. Lang, *Twenty Hymn-Tune Preludes*, Oxford, 13

PIANO

"Be Thou My Vision," Matthew Weston, *Visions, Set 1*, MorningStar
"Beneath the Cross of Jesus," Angela Tipps, *Keys of the Kingdom*, vol. 5, Abingdon, 22

HANDBELL

"Beneath the Cross of Jesus," Christine Anderson (solo), Agape
"Lenten Meditation," Paul McKleen (2–3 octaves), CPH

STUDY CATECHISM

For today's questions and answers, see pp. 218–19.

March 23, 2003

Exodus 20:1–7 — The Ten Commandments.

Psalm 19 — Throughout the whole creation, God sets the standard for order, truth, and righteousness.

1 Corinthians 1:18–25 — The cross of Jesus Christ is the power and wisdom of God.

John 2:13–22 — Jesus drives the moneychangers from the Temple in Jerusalem.

Theme(s) of lectionary texts: The standards of God, contrasted with worldly, cultural values.

CALL TO WORSHIP

The heavens declare the glory of God;
    the sky above is testimony to the Creator.
One day tells earth's story to another,
    and one night imparts knowledge to the next.
God has set a pavilion for the sun,
    and nothing is hidden from its brilliant light.
Let the words of our mouths, and the meditations
    of our hearts,
be acceptable in your sight, O Lord, our strength
    and Redeemer.

SUGGESTED HYMNS

ENTRANCE/GATHERING HYMNS	HB	LBW	NCH	PH	RL	TFF	WOV
"In the Cross of Christ I Glory"	195	104	193	84	297–98	—	—
"Rejoice, Ye Pure in Heart"	407	553	55	145–46	—	—	—
HYMNS RELATED TO SCRIPTURE							
O—"God Marked a Line and Told the Sea"	—	—	568	283	—	—	—
"How I Love Thy Law, O Lord"	253	—	—	—	—	—	—
E—"Jesus, Keep Me Near the Cross"	376	—	197	—	—	73	—
"Nature with Open Volume Stands"	—	119	—	—	294–95	—	—
G—"Draw Nigh to Thy Jerusalem"	—	—	—	—	269	—	—
"With Joy I Heard My Friends Exclaim"	—	—	—	235	132	—	—
HYMNS OF THE TABLE							
"Beneath the Cross of Jesus"	190	107	190	92	310–11	—	—
"O God of Earth and Altar"	511	428	582	291	—	—	—
"On a Hill Far Away"	—	—	195	—	—	77	—
"When I Survey the Wondrous Cross"	198	482	224	100–101	292–93	—	—
SENDING FORTH							
"All My Hope Is Firmly Grounded"	—	—	408	—	156–57	—	782
"God of Grace and God of Glory"	358	415	436	420	416	—	—

Third Sunday in Lent

Color: Purple

PRAYER OF CONFESSION

God of mighty deliverance,
we gratefully embrace the redemption
you have offered us through Jesus our Savior,
who was lifted high on the cross for our sake.
Yet we have dishonored his sacrifice for us;
we have not followed his example of loving service,
and have spurned his call to honor your life-giving
   law.

In mercy, forgive us for rejecting his way of life.
Quicken us by your Spirit to take up our cross,
that we may walk purposefully and joyously
in the ways of life and peace you have set before us,
loving you with all our heart and strength,
and our neighbors as ourselves.

HYMN OF ASSURANCE

"Beneath the Cross of Jesus," *PH*, 92

PSALM 19

METRICAL—
"God's Law Is Perfect and Gives Life" (CMD), *PH*,
   167
"The Heavens Above Declare God's Praise" (CM),
   PH, 166
RESPONSORIAL—
"Psalm 19," Hal Hopson, *Eighteen Psalms for the
   Church Year*, 3
CHORAL—
"A Psalm of Praise," Judy Hunnicutt (unison),
   Choristers Guild
"Most Perfect Is the Law of God," *HB*, 257

ADDITIONAL SONGS

"At the Foot of the Cross," Derek Bond, *Worship &
   Praise*, 11

"Lord of All," Danny Daniels, *Lift Up Your Hearts*, 42
"Refiner's Fire," Brian Doerksen, *Lift Up Your Hearts*,
   66
"Tree of Life," Marty Haugen, *Common Ground*, 136

CHORAL/VOCAL

"Ah, Holy Jesus," John Ferguson (SATB), Augsburg-
   Fortress
"Jesus and the Traders," Zoltan Kodaly (SATB),
   Boosey & Hawkes
"The Foolishness Carol," Austin Lovelace (SATB),
   Somerset
"The Holy Ten Commandments," F. J. Haydn (3-part
   canon), Mercury

ORGAN

"Prelude on DUNDEE (The Lord Moves in Mysterious
   Ways)," G. Young, *Fourteen Pieces for Organ*,
   Sacred Music Press, 11
"Prelude on SLANE (Be Thou My Vision)," Dale
   Wood, *Wood Works*, Sacred Music Press, 17

PIANO

"Beneath the Cross of Jesus," Angela Tipps, *Keys of the
   Kingdom*, 5, 22
"In the Cross of Christ I Glory," Angela Tipps, *Keys of
   the Kingdom*, 5, 26

HANDBELL

"When I Survey the Wondrous Cross," Hal Hopson
   (2 octaves), Lorenz
"When I Survey the Wondrous Cross," Kevin
   McChesney (quartet), Cantabile

STUDY CATECHISM

For today's questions and answers, see p. 219.

March 30, 2003

Numbers 21:4–9 — Moses is told to display the image of a serpent on a tree, thus ending a plague of fiery serpents threatening the people as they wandered in the wilderness.

Psalm 107:1–3, 17–22 — Thanksgiving to God for salvation from tribulations.

Ephesians 2:1–10 — It is through God's grace alone that we receive salvation.

John 3:14–21 — God loved the world so much that Jesus came to be lifted up on the cross, like the serpent in the wilderness, so that those who believe in him may be saved.

Theme(s) of lectionary texts: The love of God and the salvation offered in Christ.

CALL TO WORSHIP

Give thanks to the Lord, for God is good.
　　God's mercy endures forever.
Let the redeemed of the Lord proclaim
　　that it is God who saves us from the hand of the foe.
In our troubles, we cry to the Lord
　　who saves us from every distress.
Let us give thanks for the mercy of God,
　　and for all the wonders of the Lord.

SUGGESTED HYMNS

ENTRANCE/GATHERING HYMNS	HB	LBW	NCH	PH	RL	TFF	WOV
"Guide Me, O Thou Great Jehovah"	339	343	18–19	281	—	—	—
"Lord God, Your Love Has Called Us Here"	—	—	—	353	503	—	—
HYMNS RELATED TO SCRIPTURE							
O—"As Moses Raised the Serpent Up"	—	—	605	—	—	—	—
"If Thou But Trust in God to Guide Thee"	344	453	410	282	151	—	—
E—"Rock of Ages, Cleft for Me"	271	327	596	—	447	—	—
"Savior, Like a Shepherd Lead Us"	380	481	252	387	—	254	—
"To God Be the Glory"	—	—	—	485	—	264	—
"We Walk by Faith and Not by Sight"	—	—	—	399	—	—	675
G—"God Loved the World"	—	292	208	—	—	—	—
"Of the Father's Love Begotten"	7	42	118	309	190	—	—
HYMNS OF THE TABLE							
"I Greet Thee, Who My Sure Redeemer Art"	144	—	251	457	366	—	—
"My Song Is Love Unknown"	—	94	222	76	284	—	—
SENDING FORTH							
"Amazing Grace"	275	488	547–48	280	456	—	—
"There's a Wideness in God's Mercy"	110	290	23	298	349	—	—

Fourth Sunday in Lent

Color: Purple

PRAYER OF CONFESSION

God of holy majesty,
we lift our hearts and eyes to you,
acknowledging that we have disobeyed your holy
    law;
we have been sorely wounded by our sin,
and call upon you to bind us up.

Have mercy upon us in our distress;
heal us, restore us, shine your light into our darkness.
Be glorified in us and through us;
that with gladness of heart we may testify
of your merciful kindness and steadfast love to us.
Help us by your Spirit to bear witness
to your healing grace and restoring mercy,
wherever we find brokenness and ruin;
through Jesus Christ, our saving Lord.

HYMN OF ASSURANCE

"My Song Is Love Unknown," *PH,* 76

PSALM 107

METRICAL—
"Psalm 107" (11.11.11.11), *PCW,* 124
RESPONSORIAL—
"Psalm 107," *Psalter for Worship—Cycle B,* 33
CHORAL—
"Be Joyful in the Lord," F. Couperin, K. Jewel, arr.
    (2-part), Concordia
"O Give Thanks Unto the Lord," Jean Berger (SATB,
    div.), Augsburg-Fortress

ADDITIONAL SONGS

"Come and Fill," Taizé community, *Lift Up Your
    Hearts,* 4
"He Is Lord," unknown author, *Lift Up Your Hearts,*
    150

"Love Is a Circle," Peggy Brown, *Lift Up Your Hearts,*
    94

CHORAL/VOCAL

"As Moses Lifted Up," Ralph Johnson (unison/flute),
    Choristers Guild
"As Moses Lifted Up the Serpent," Edward C.
    Bairstow (SATB), Banks
"God So Loved the World," John Stainer (SATB),
    various editions
"We Are God's Work of Art," Marty Haugen (SATB),
    GIA

ORGAN

"Prelude on O QUANTA QUALIA (Blessing and Honor),"
    R. Hillert, *Concordia Hymn Prelude Series,* 35,
    Concordia
"Prelude on ST. MAGNUS (The Head That Once Was
    Crowned with Thorns)," Healey Willan, *Thirty-six
    Short Preludes and Postludes,* C. F. Peters

PIANO

"As Moses Raised the Serpent Up," John Carter,
    Today's Hymns and Songs for Piano, 9
"Variations on Salvation Unto Us," Curt Oliver,
    MorningStar

HANDBELL

"Amazing Grace," Charles Maggs (3–4 octaves),
    Genesis Press
"Jesus, Lover of My Soul," Christine Anderson (solo),
    Agape

STUDY CATECHISM

For today's questions and answers, see p. 219.

April 6, 2003

Jeremiah 31:31–34 — The prophet proclaims the establishment of a new covenant.

Psalm 51:1–7 or Psalm 119:9 — A psalm of penitence. Commitment to study of Holy Scripture.

Hebrews 5:5–10 — God has appointed Jesus Christ to be our great high priest.

John 12:20–33 — As he draws near Jerusalem, Jesus prophesies his death and rising.

Theme(s) of lectionary texts: The new covenant between God and the people of God.

CALL TO WORSHIP

Blessed are you, O Lord:
   Instruct us in your Word.
**With our lips we will recite
   the teachings of the Scripture.**
We will meditate on your commandments
   and pay attention to what you ask of us.
**For our delight is in your Word;
   let you teaching never be far from our thoughts.**

PRAYER OF CONFESSION

Have mercy on us, O God,
according to your unfailing love;
according to your great compassion blot out our
   transgressions.
Wash away all our iniquity and cleanse us from sin.
Create in us a pure heart, O God,
and renew a steadfast spirit within us.
Do not cast us from your presence
or take your Holy Spirit from us.
Restore to us the joy of your salvation
and grant a willing spirit to sustain us.

HYMN OF ASSURANCE

"God of Compassion, in Mercy Befriend Us," *PH*, 261

SUGGESTED HYMNS

ENTRANCE/GATHERING HYMNS	HB	LBW	NCH	PH	RL	TFF	WOV
"The Church's One Foundation"	437	369	386	442	394	—	—
HYMNS RELATED TO SCRIPTURE							
O—"Camina, Pueblo de Dios (Walk On, People of God)"	—	—	614	296	—	—	—
"God of Compassion, in Mercy Befriend Us"	122	—	—	261	39	—	—
E—"At the Name of Jesus"	143	179	—	148	336	—	—
"When Jesus Came from Jordan"	—	—	—	72	—	—	647
G—"Now the Green Blade Rises"	—	148	238	—	—	—	—
The Word of God Is Source and Seed"	—	—	—	—	—	—	658
HYMN OF THE TABLE							
"Here I Am, Lord"	—	—	—	525	—	230	752
SENDING FORTH							
"Jesus Shall Reign Where'er the Sun"	496	530	300	423	233	—	—

Fifth Sunday in Lent

Color: Purple

PSALM 51

Psalm 51:1–7
METRICAL—
"Have Mercy on Us, Living Lord" (CM) *PH*, 195
RESPONSORIAL—
"Psalm 51," Hal Hopson, *Ten Psalms*, Hope
CHORAL—
"Miserere," Gregorio Allegri (SSATB), Novello
"Wash Me Thoroughly from My Wickedness," G. F. Handel (SA or TB), Hinshaw

PSALM 119

Psalm 119:9–16
METRICAL—
"Psalm 119a" (CM), *PCW*, 136
RESPONSORIAL—
"How Shall a Young Man Cleanse His Way?" Peter R. Hallock, *The Ionian Psalter: Fifteen Psalms for the Seasons of the Church Year*, 4
CHORAL—
"Blest Are the Uncorrupt in Heart," *PH*, 233

ADDITIONAL SONGS

"Glorify Your Name," Donna Adkins, *Renew*, 37
"O Lord, Hear My Prayer," Taizé community, *Lift Up Your Hearts*, 111
"Thy Word," Amy Grant and Michael Smith, *Lift Up Your Hearts*, 85

CHORAL/VOCAL

"A Great Harvest," Alexander Peloquin (SATB), GIA
"The New Covenant," David Stanley York (SATB/T), Presser
"This Is the Covenant," Jean Berger (SATB), Augsburg-Fortress

ORGAN

"Prelude on ST. CHRISTOPHER (Beneath the Cross of Jesus)," Robert Elmore, *Three Miniatures for Organ*, Flammer, 2
"Prelude on ST. MAGNUS (The Head That Once Was Crowned with Thorns)," Alec Rowley, *Chorale Preludes Based on Famous Hymn Tunes, 2*, Edwin Ashdown, 8

PIANO

"Here I Am, Lord," John Carter, *Today's Hymns and Songs for Piano*, Hope, 5
"Lift High the Cross," Fred Bock, *Bock's Best, 4*, Fred Bock Music, 88

HANDBELL

"O the Deep, Deep Love of Jesus," Christine Anderson (solo), Agape
"Reflections on AURELIA" (The Church's One Foundation), Donald Allured (4 octaves), Hinshaw

STUDY CATECHISM

For today's questions and answers, see pp. 219–20.

April 13, 2003

LITURGY OF THE PALMS

| Mark 11:1–11 or John 12:12–16 | Jesus enters Jerusalem on Palm Sunday. |
| Psalm 118:1–2, 19–29 | A psalm of ascent for keeping festival in Jerusalem. |

LITURGY OF THE PASSION

Isaiah 50:4–9a	A song of the Servant of the Lord who give his life for the nation.
Psalm 31:9–16	A psalm expressing trust in the Lord.
Philippians 2:5–11	An early Christian hymn extolling the life and sacrifice of Jesus.
Mark 14:1–15:47 or Mark 15:1–39, (40–47)	The Last Supper, followed by the passion of our Lord Jesus Christ, according to Mark's Gospel. The trial, suffering, and death of Jesus, according to Mark.

Theme(s) of lectionary texts: The final week of the life of Jesus, from the triumphal entry into Jerusalem to his death on the cross.

CALL TO WORSHIP

O Lord, open to us the gates of righteousness
   so that we may enter them, and give you praise.
We will give thanks to you, for you hear our prayer, and you have become our salvation.
Blessed is the One who comes in the Lord's name.
   We bless your name from the sanctuary!
Hosanna in the highest!
   Blessed is the One who comes in the name of the Lord.

SUGGESTED HYMNS

ENTRANCE/GATHERING HYMNS	HB	LBW	NCH	PH	RL	TFF	WOV
"Hosanna, Loud Hosanna"	185	—	213	89	282	—	—
"Rejoice, the Lord Is King"	140	171	303	155	596–97	—	—
HYMNS RELATED TO SCRIPTURE							
O—"He Never Said a Mumblin' Word"	—	—	—	95	—	80	—
"O God, Our Faithful God"	—	504	—	277	69	—	—
E—"All Hail to God's Anointed"	146	87	104	205	232	—	—
"At the Name of Jesus"	143	179	—	148	336	—	—
G—"Ah, Holy Jesus"	191	123	218	93	285	—	—
"Sing, My Tongue, the Glorious Battle"	—	118	222	—	289–90	—	—
HYMN OF THE TABLE							
"O Sacred Head, Now Wounded"	194	116–17	226	98	300	—	—
SENDING FORTH							
"When I Survey the Wondrous Cross"	198	482	224	100–101	292–93	79	—

Palm/Passion Sunday

Color: Red

PRAYER OF CONFESSION

Merciful God,
as we enter this Holy Week,
solemnly gathering at your house of prayer,
we turn our hearts toward Jerusalem,
to the peace demonstrated for us and offered to us
in the words and deeds, in the suffering and death,
of Jesus, your anointed One.

Forgive our stubborn resistance to his work and
    witness;
impel us by your Spirit to follow in his way,
until we enter with him into the city not made by
    human hands,
the new Jerusalem, eternal in the heavens,
where we shall ever live to your praise and glory.

HYMN OF ASSURANCE

"Ah, Holy Jesus," *PH*, 93

PSALM 118

Psalm 118:1–2, 19–29
METRICAL—
"This Is the Day the Lord Hath Made," (CM) *PH*, 230
RESPONSORIAL—
"Psalm 118," Hal Hopson, *Eighteen Psalms for the
    Church Year*, 19
CHORAL—
"Let Us Rejoice and Sing," Larry E. Schultz (unison/
    2-part), Choristers Guild
"Open to Me the Gates of Righteousness," K. Lee
    Scott (SATB), CPH

PSALM 31

METRICAL—
"In You, Lord, I Have Put My Trust," *PH*, 183
RESPONSORIAL—
"Psalm 31," Hal Hopson, *The Psalter (1993)*, 28

CHORAL—
"In Thee, O Lord, Do I Put My Trust," Jan Bender
    (unison), Augsburg-Fortress
"In Thee, O Lord, Have I Trusted," G. F. Handel
    (SAB), Presser

ADDITIONAL SONGS

"Hosanna," Carl Tuttle, *Lift Up Your Hearts*, 145
"Lift Up Your Heads," Mimi Farra, arr., *Cry Hosanna*,
    123
"Meekness and Majesty," Graham Kendrick, *Common
    Ground*, 86

CHORAL/VOCAL

"A Palm Sunday Anthem," Eugene Hancock
    (SATB/youth), H. W. Gray
"Behold the Savior of Mankind," S. Drummond Wolf
    (SATB), Concordia
"Welcome the Glorious King," Jean Berger (SATB),
    Augsburg-Fortress

ORGAN

"All Glory, Laud, and Honor (VALET WILL ICH DIR
    GEBEN)," J. S. Bach, various editions, including
    versions in hymnals
"Prelude on THE KING'S MAJESTY (Ride On, Ride On
    in Majesty)," Leo Sowerby, H. W. Gray

PIANO

"All Glory, Laud, and Honor," Angela Tipps, *Keys of
    the Kingdom*, vol. 5, Abingdon, 38
"Sing, My Tongue," Angela Tipps, *Keys of the
    Kingdom*, vol. 4, Abingdon, 27

HANDBELL

"Hosanna, Loud Hosanna," Barbara Kinyon (2–3
    octaves), Agape

STUDY CATECHISM

For today's questions and answers, see p. 220.

April 17, 2003

Exodus 12:1–4 (5–10) 11–14	Moses tells the story of the first Passover.
Psalm 116:1–2, 12–19	A festival psalm for the festival of Passover in Jerusalem.
1 Corinthians 11:23–26	Paul hands on the tradition he received concerning the Last Supper.
John 13:1–17, 31b–35	At table with the disciples, Jesus washes their feet.

Theme(s) of lectionary texts: Celebration of the Passover and the Lord's Supper.

CALL TO WORSHIP

How shall we repay you, Lord,
    for all your goodness to us?
**We will lift up the cup of salvation
    and call upon the name of the Lord.**
We are your servants, Lord,
    help us to celebrate this sacrifice of thanksgiving.
**Help us to fulfill all you intend for us
    as members of the community of God.**

PRAYER OF CONFESSION

Eternal God,
whose covenant with us is never broken,
we confess that we fail to fulfill your will.
Though you have bound yourself to us,
we will not bind ourselves to you.
In Jesus Christ you serve us freely,
but we refuse your love
and withhold ourselves from others.
We do not love you fully
or love one another as you command.

In your mercy, forgive and cleanse us.
Lead us once again to your table
and unite us to Christ,
who is the bread of life
and the vine from which we grow in grace.

HYMN OF ASSURANCE

"An Upper Room Did Our Lord Prepare," *PH*, 94

SUGGESTED HYMNS

	HB	LBW	NCH	PH	RL	TFF	WOV
ENTRANCE/GATHERING HYMNS							
"An Upper Room Did Our Lord Prepare"	—	—	346	586	568	—	—
HYMNS RELATED TO SCRIPTURE							
O—"Behold the Lamb of God"	—	—	—	—	291	—	—
"O Lamb of God, Most Holy"	585	111	—	82	—	—	—
E—"Truth Whom We Adore"	—	—	339	—	—	—	—
"When Twilight Comes"	—	—	—	—	—	—	663
G—"A New Commandment"	—	—	—	—	—	—	664
"Jesu, Jesu, Fill Us with Your Love"	—	—	498	367	—	83	765
HYMNS OF THE TABLE							
"Bread of the World"	445	—	346	502	551	—	—
"It Happened on That Fateful Night"	—	127	—	—	283	—	—
"The Blood That Jesus Shed for Me"	—	—	—	—	—	210	—
SENDING FORTH							
"Go to Dark Gethsemane"	193	109	219	97	—	—	—

Maundy Thursday

Color: Red

PSALM 116

METRICAL—
"O Thou, My Soul" (CM), *PH*, 228
RESPONSORIAL—
"Psalm 116," Samuel Weber, *The Psalter* (1993), 116
CHORAL—
"Our Blessed Cup," Bob Moore (SATB), GIA
"What Shall I Render to My God," Austin Lovelace
   (SATB), Canyon Press

ADDITIONAL SONGS

"Come to the Table," Martin Nystrom, *Worship &
   Praise*, 32
"Here Is Bread," Graham Kendrick, *Worship & Praise*,
   58
"Jesus Took a Towel," Chrysogonus Waddell, *Lift Up
   Your Hearts*, 146
"One Bread, One Body," John Foley, *Lift Up Your
   Hearts*, 130
"Remember Me," Traditional, *Lift Up Your Hearts*,
   112
"Sent by the Lord Am I," John Bell, *Common Ground*,
   105

CHORAL/VOCAL

"I Give You a New Commandment," John Shepherd
   (ATBB or TTBB), RSCM
"In Remembrance," Austin Lovelace (SATB),
   Augsburg-Fortress
"Take, Eat," Kenneth Lowenberg (unison or 2-part),
   Selah
"This Do in Remembrance of Me," Austin Lovelace
   (SATB), Hope

ORGAN

"Chorale Prelude on RENDEZ A DIEU (Bread of the
   World)," Helmut Walcha, *Choralvorspiele*, 3, C. F.
   Peters, 36
"Prelude on MARYTON (O Master, Let Me Walk with
   Thee)," Flor Peeters, *Hymn Preludes for the
   Liturgical Year*, 17, C. F. Peters, 22

PIANO

"Be Known to Us in Breaking Bread," Fred Bock,
   Bock's Best, 4, Fred Bock Music, 63
"Bread of the World," Angela Tipps, *Keys of the
   Kingdom*, vol. 4, Abingdon, 7
"Jesu, Jesu, Fill Us with Your Love," Mark Sedio,
   Dancing in the Light of God, Augsburg-Fortress, 10
"One Bread, One Body," John Carter, *You Satisfy the
   Hungry Heart*, Hope, 15

HANDBELL

"Ave Verum Corpus," W. A. Mozart/Arnold Sherman
   (3–4 octaves), Agape
"Requiem," William Payne (4–5 octaves), AGEHR

April 18, 2003

Isaiah 52:13–53:12 — A song of the Suffering Servant of the Lord.

Psalm 22 — A cry of desolation, followed by the promise of help.

Hebrews 10:16–25 or Hebrews 4:14–16; 5:7–9 — Jesus our great high priest gives us confidence in the day of trial. Jesus, who was fully human, knows what it is to suffer as we do.

John 18:1–19:42 — The passion and death of Jesus, according to John's Gospel.

Theme(s) of lectionary texts: Jesus' suffering and death for our sake.

CALL TO WORSHIP

My God, my God, why have you forsaken me?
　Why are you so far from helping me?
O God, we cry in the daytime, but hear no answer;
we lie awake at night, and find no rest.
Yet our ancestors cried out, and you delivered them;
　they trusted you, and they were not put to shame.
Be not far from me, Lord God, for trouble is near,
and there is no one else who can truly help.

SUGGESTED HYMNS

ENTRANCE/GATHERING HYMNS	HB	LBW	NCH	PH	RL	TFF	WOV
"O Love, How Deep, How Broad, How High"	—	88	209	83	342–43	—	—
"When I Survey the Wondrous Cross"	198	482	224	100–101	292–93	79	—
HYMNS RELATED TO SCRIPTURE							
O—"Deep Were His Wounds, and Red"	—	100	—	103	—	—	—
"He Never Said a Mumblin' Word"	—	—	—	95	—	80	—
E—"Ah, Holy Jesus"	191	123	218	93	285	—	—
"O Sacred Head, Now Wounded"	194	116–17	226	98	300	—	—
G—"Alas, and Did My Savior Bleed?"	199	98	200	78	—	—	-
"Calvary"	—	—	—	96	—	85	—
"Throned Upon the Awful Tree"	197	—	—	99	—	—	—
"Were You There?"	201	92	229	102	—	81	—
SENDING FORTH							
"In the Cross of Christ I Glory"	195	104	193–94	84	297–98	—	—
"My Song Is Love Unknown"	—	94	222	76	284	—	661

Good Friday

Black, or stripped of color

PRAYER OF CONFESSION

Triune God,
revealed to us in the perfect love of Christ:
Because of the world's sin,
your eternal Word became flesh
and dwelt among us,
and showed us your love,
and died the death of a criminal
nailed to a cross.
It was for our sin that Jesus died,
and he is our only hope.

Convince and convict us of our sinfulness, O God,
that we may appreciate what you have done for us.
By the power of your Holy Spirit,
reform and renew our hearts,
that we may truly be grateful for Christ's sacrifice
and for the promise of eternal life he brought to
    your children.
We pray in his name. Amen.

HYMN OF ASSURANCE

"What a Friend We Have in Jesus," *PH,* 403

PSALM 22

METRICAL—
"Lord, Why Have You Forsaken Me?" (LM), *PH,* 168
RESPONSORIAL—
"Psalm 22," *Psalter for Worship—Cycle B,* 38
CHORAL—
"My God, My God, Why Hast Thou Forsaken Me?"
    Gerald Near (SATB), H. W. Gray
"My God, My God, Why Hast Thou Forsaken Me?"
    Maurice Greene (SSATB), Broude Bros.

ADDITIONAL SONGS

"Behold the Wood," Dan Schutte, *Lord Be Glorified,*
32

"Come and See," Graham Kendrick, *Lift Up Your
    Hearts,* 147
"There Is a Redeemer," Keith Green, *Renew,* 232

CHORAL/VOCAL

"Good Friday," Bernard Naylor (SSATB), Novello
"He Was Despised," G. F. Handel (*Messiah*), various
    editions
"Seeing That We Have a Great High Priest," Robert
    Powell (SAB), Abingdon
"Surely He Hath Borne Our Griefs," G. F. Handel
    (*Messiah*), various editions
"'Tis Finished," Robert Shaw/Alice Parker (SA(T)B),
    Lawson Gould

ORGAN

"Were You There?" (with flute), Paul Nicholson,
    Augsburg-Fortress
"Prelude on RATHBUN" (In the Cross of Christ I
    Glory), Seth Bingham, *Twelve Hymn Preludes,*
    Grey-Belwin

PIANO

"Alas, and Did My Savior Bleed?" Angela Tipps, *Keys
    of the Kingdom,* vol. 5, Abingdon, 20
"O Sacred Head, Now Wounded" Fred Bock, *Bock's
    Best, 4,* Fred Bock Music, 86

HANDBELL

"He Never Said a Mumblin' Word," Arnold Sherman
    (3–5 octaves), Agape
"Were You There?" Kevin McChesney (quartet),
    Cantabile
"When I Survey the Wondrous Cross," Hal Hopson
    (2 octaves), Lorenz

April 20, 2003

Acts 10:34–43   At the home of Cornelius, Peter recounts how his own life and the life of the world have been transformed by the power of the risen Christ.

Psalm 118:1–2, 14–24   Good news of salvation.

1 Corinthians 15:1–11   Witnesses to the resurrection of Jesus Christ.

John 20:1–18   Christ's followers discover the empty tomb, and Mary Magdalene meets Christ in the garden.

Theme(s) of lectionary texts: Jesus Christ is risen from the grave, giving hope to all who believe.

CALL TO WORSHIP

The Lord is my strength and my song
    and has become my salvation.
I shall not die, but I shall live
    and declare the goodness of the Lord!
I will give thanks to the Lord, for God has answered me
    and assured me of the good news of salvation.
The same stone the builders rejected
    has become the chief cornerstone.
This is the Lord's doing;
    it is marvelous in our eyes.
The Lord has acted on this day:
    we will rejoice, and be glad in it!

PRAYER OF CONFESSION

God of Life,
You reveal yourself to us
in ways and in places where we least expect to find
    you.
Amidst the decay of death and the paralysis of fear,
we discover your bold and living presence among us,
and begin to see just how good
the story of our salvation really is.
Yet we turn away from you,
refusing to acknowledge your gracious presence
    among us.
We prefer clinging to our fears
to embracing your hope;
forgive us for turning away from you.

Captivate us with the Good News
of your sure salvation,
through Jesus Christ, our Risen Lord.
Cause our hearts to burn within us
as we walk with him,
that we may declare with assurance
and live in confidence
that all is well, and all shall be well.

HYMN OF ASSURANCE

"God of Our Life," *PH,* 275

SUGGESTED HYMNS

ENTRANCE/GATHERING HYMNS	HB	LBW	NCH	PH	RL	TFF	WOV
"Jesus Christ Is Risen Today"	204	151	240	123	312	—	—
HYMNS RELATED TO SCRIPTURE							
A—"We Know That Christ Is Raised"	—	189	—	495	528	—	—
E—"Christ Is Risen, Shout Hosanna"	—	—	—	104	—	—	672
G—"The Day of Resurrection"	208	141	245	118	317	—	—
HYMN OF THE TABLE							
"Christ Jesus Lay in Death's Strong Bonds"	—	134	—	110	342	—	—
SENDING FORTH							
"Thine Is the Glory"	209	145	—	122	327	—	—

Easter Day: Resurrection of the Lord

Color: White

PSALM 118

METRICAL—
"This Is the Day the Lord Has Made," *PH*, 230
RESPONSORIAL—
"Psalm 118," *The Psalter* (1993), 120 (Jacques Berthier)
CHORAL—
"Easter Antiphon," Robert J. Powell (2-part), Augsburg (A)
"Easter Alleluia" (Psalm 118 and Gospel Acclamation), Rory Cooney, arr. (unison choir/congregation, organ, optional flute, bass, or strings), GIA G-5019 (A/SC)

ADDITIONAL SONGS

"Christ the Lord Is Risen," Ghanaian folk song, Tom Colvin and Kevin R. Hackett, arr., *The Faith We Sing*, 2115
"He Is Lord," *LUYH*, 150
"This Is the Day," *LUYH*, 15

CHORAL/VOCAL

"Christ Is Living"/"Christo Vive," Robert Buckley Farlee (SATB, organ, percussion, guitar, and optional congregation), Augsburg 11-11021
"Christ the Lord Is Risen Again," John Rutter (SATB), Oxford E124 (M)
"Earth, Earth Away," Sally Ann Morris (SATB/congregation/organ/trumpet) GIA G-4394 (SC)
"Easter: Rise, Heart, Thy Lord Is Risen," Ralph Vaughn Williams. *Five Mystical Songs* 1 (SATB/baritone solo/piano or organ), ESC Publishing (C)
"Resurrection Dance," Russel Schulz-Widmar (SAB/Handbells), GIA (SC)
"Ye Choirs of New Jerusalem," C. V. Stanford (SATB/organ), GIA G-4188 (C)

ORGAN

"Christ Lag in Todesbanden," G. P. Telemann. *Seasonal Choral Preludes for Manuals Only,* Oxford, 6
"Erscheinen ist der Herrliche Tag," J. G. Walther. *Seasonal Choral Preludes for Manuals Only,* Oxford, 2

PIANO

"Christ the Lord Is Risen Today," Charles Webb, arr., *Keys of the Kingdom: Easter, Ascension, Pentecost,* Abingdon, 6
"The Risen Lord," Eugene Butler, *Journeys to Easter,* Lorenz, 29
"Thine Be the Glory," Wallace Hornibrook, arr., *Keys of the Kingdom: Easter, Ascension, Pentecost,* Abingdon, 2

HANDBELL

"An Easter Festival," Sharon Elery Rogers (2–3 octaves), Lorenz
"The Church's One Foundation," Jane McFadden (3–5 octaves), AGEHR

THE EASTER SEASON: VISUAL ARTS, DRAMA, DANCE

Use visual arts and drama to make the worship space noticeably different from the time of Lent. Banners and printed explanations in the bulletin can heighten the joy and majesty of this season of the church year. Visual motifs are an excellent way to engage children.
GATHERING—
Festive music plays as the congregation enters the sanctuary: trumpets and other brass instruments. Flowers and banners may be brought forward as part of an entrance processional.
DRAMA—
Eyewitness accounts of the experiences of Mary and Peter, based on the Scriptures.

STUDY CATECHISM

For today's questions and answers, see pp. 220–21.

April 20, 2003

Isaiah 25:6–9	The Lord spreads a feast for the people of God.
Psalm 114	A song of exodus and liberation.
1 Corinthians 5:6b–8	The sacrifice of the Lamb of God.
Luke 24:13–49	The road to Emmaus, and Christ is made known to disciples in the breaking of bread.

Theme(s) of lectionary texts: The joyous feast of the people of God.

CALL TO WORSHIP

When Israel came out of Egypt,
the house of Israel delivered from a people of a foreign tongue,
Judah become God's sanctuary,
and Israel became God' dominion.
The sea beheld this sight, and fled;
the Jordan River turned and flowed back.
The mountains skipped like rams,
and the hills like young sheep.
Tremble, O earth, at the presence of the Lord,
at the presence of the God of liberation.
For the Lord turned hard rock to water,
and flint became a flowing stream.
Praise the Lord!

SUGGESTED HYMNS

ENTRANCE/GATHERING HYMNS	HB	LBW	NCH	PH	RL	TFF	WOV
"Alleluia, Alleluia, Give Thanks"	—	—	—	106	—	—	671
"Because You Live, O Christ"	—	—	231	105	—	—	—
HYMNS RELATED TO SCRIPTURE							
O—"Come, Ye Faithful, Raise the Strain"	205	132	230	114–15	315–16	—	—
"The Strife Is O'er"	203	135	242	119	319	—	—
E—"Celebrate with Joy and Singing"	—	—	—	107	—	—	—
"Christ Is Risen, Shout Hosanna"	—	—	—	104	—	—	672
G—"Alleluia! Jesus Is Risen"	—	—	—	—	—	91	674
"Amidst Us Our Beloved Stands"	—	—	—	—	543	—	—
"O Word of God Incarnate"	251	231	315	327	387	—	—
HYMNS OF THE TABLE							
"Be Known to Us in Breaking Bread"	446	—	342	504	—	—	—
"Come, Risen Lord"	—	209	—	503	550	—	—
SENDING FORTH							
"Lift High the Cross"	—	377	198	371	415	—	—

Easter Evening

Color: White

PRAYER OF CONFESSION

God of Life,
You reveal yourself to us
in ways and in places where we least expect to find
    you.
Amidst the decay of death and the paralysis of fear,
we discover your bold and living presence among us,
and begin to see just how good
the story of our salvation really is.
Yet we turn away from you,
refusing to acknowledge your gracious presence
    among us.
We prefer clinging to our fears
to embracing your hope;
forgive us for turning away from you.
Empower us by your Spirit
to embrace your word of Life
in a world still ruled by death.
Captivate us with the Good News
of your sure salvation,
through Jesus Christ, our Risen Lord.
Cause our hearts to burn within us
as we walk with him,
that we may declare with assurance
and live in confidence
that all is well, and all shall be well.

HYMN OF ASSURANCE

"God of Our Life," *PH,* 275

PSALM 114

METRICAL—
"When Israel Came, and Judah's House," *A New Metrical Psalter,* 183
"When Israel Fled from Egypt Land," *The Psalter Hymnal,* 114

RESPONSORIAL—
"Psalm 114," Helen L. Wright, *The Psalter* (1993), 114
CHORAL/VOCAL—
"Psalm 114," Zoltan Kodaly (SATB, organ), Boosey & Hawkes 5328
"When Israel Came out of Egypt," S. S. Wesley (SATB/SATB, organ ad lib.), Novello, 786

ADDITIONAL SONGS

"Laphalala Igazi (Christ Is Risen)," David Dargie, South Africa, *Halle, Halle,* 31
"We Are Marching," South African traditional, *Common Ground,* 139

CHORAL/VOCAL

"Stay with Us," Walter Pelz (SATB, flute), Concordia (M)
"The Way to Emmaus," Jaromir Weinberger, solo cantata for soprano and piano (14 minutes, challenging), Belwin
"Verse/Easter Evening," Walter Pelz (SATB, organ), Augsburg (A)

ORGAN

Toccata on "O FILII ET FILIAE," Lynnwood Farnham, Theodore Press Co. 113-25819

PIANO

"Breathe on Me, Breath of God," Angela Tipps, *Keys of the Kingdom,* vol. 6, Abingdon, 37

HANDBELL

"Christ the Lord Is Risen Today," Barbara Kinyon (2 octaves), Agape
"Fantasy on an Easter Hymn," Charles Maggs (quartet), Cantabile

April 27, 2003

Acts 4:32–35 — Mutual support within the earliest church.
Psalm 133 — The unity of believers.
1 John 1:1–2:2 — The coming of the Word of God, bringing us into light.
John 20:19–31 — Doubting Thomas and the blessedness of faith.

Theme(s) of lectionary texts: Communion (koinonia) among believers in response to the revelation of Christ as Lord and Savior.

Jesus breathes the Holy Spirit upon the disciples; empowerment, new creation, springtime.

CALL TO WORSHIP

How good and pleasant it is
    when the community dwells together as one.
It is like the sensation of fine oil,
    the oil of anointing, running down the head.
The oil of anointing ran down the beard of Aaron
    and perfumed the collar of his robe.
Unity is like the dew on Mount Hermon,
    falling softly upon the hills of Zion.
For there the Lord has ordained the blessing:
    Peace forevermore! Amen.

PRAYER OF CONFESSION

God of love and light,
you have called us to live by your light,
in unity of heart and mission;
yet we have continued in ways of darkness.
We hide from you and from one another,
rather than joining hands, hearts, and resources
to live and work for your peace and justice.
Though called and chosen to live in confident hope
that Christ's resurrection assures us of abundant life,
we anxiously strive instead to preserve and increase
our personal well-being and profit.

Forgive us for denying the light of Easter's hope,
and empower us by your Holy Spirit to walk in the
    light,
freely laying down our lives for Christ's sake,
even as he did for us.

HYMN OF ASSURANCE

"Good Christians All, Rejoice and Sing!" *PH,* 111

SUGGESTED HYMNS

ENTRANCE/GATHERING HYMNS	HB	LBW	NCH	PH	RL	TFF	WOV
"Here, O Lord, Your Servants Gather"	—	—	72	465	—	—	—
HYMNS RELATED TO SCRIPTURE							
A—"As Those of Old Their Firstfruits Brought"	—	—	—	414	—	—	—
E—"Eternal Light, Shine in My Heart"	—	—	—	340	—	—	—
"I Want to Walk as a Child of the Light"	—	—	—	—	—	—	649
G—"O Sons and Daughters, Let Us Sing"	206	139	244	116–17	—	—	—
"We Walk by Faith and Not by Sight"	—	—	—	399	—	—	675
HYMNS OF THE TABLE							
"Draw Us in the Spirit's Tether"	—	—	337	504	—	—	703
"You Satisfy the Hungry Heart"	—	—	—	521	—	—	711
SENDING FORTH							
"O Splendor of God's Glory Bright"	46	271	87	474	76	—	—

Second Sunday of Easter

Color: White and gold

PSALM 133

METRICAL—
"Behold the Goodness of the Lord," *PH,* 241
RESPONSORIAL—
"Psalm 133," Hal Hopson, *The Psalter* (1993), 137
CHORAL/VOCAL—
Psalm 133, "Ecce quam bonan," Richard Proulx
    (SATB/organ/optional strings), Hope, FPC, 136
    (M)
"Together in Unity" (unison choir/congregation/
    organ), Malcolm Williamson, Boosey & Hawkes,
    W-003

ADDITIONAL SONGS

"Our God Reigns," Lenny Smith, S. A. Beddia, arr.,
    LUYH, 84

CHORAL/VOCAL

"Easter Carol," Richard Proulx (unison/2-part, organ,
    flute) GIA G-4465 (A)
"I Believe, This Is Jesus," Lawrence Bennett, ed.
    (SATB/solo), *West Wind Songbook,* Flammer GA-
    5041, 9 (A)(SC)
"I Know That My Redeemer Liveth," G. F. Handel,
    Messiah (various editions)
"O Sons and Daughters," Alice Parker and Robert
    Shaw, arr. (SATB), G. Schirmer, The Shaw-Parker
    Easter Carol Collection HL50481433, 12 (A) (SC)
"These Things Did Thomas Count as Real," Carol
    Doran/Thomas Troeger (unison/keyboard), *New
    Hymns for the Lectionary to Glorify the Maker's
    Name,* Oxford, 33 (A) (SC)
"The Whole Bright World Rejoices Now," Carl Schalk
    (unison), Choristers Guild CGA-560 (A) (SC)
"We Walk by Faith," Michael Helman (SATB, piano,
    optional flute and handbells), Augsburg/Gladsong
    11-11114 (M)

ORGAN

"Christ Lag in Todesbanden," G. P. Telemann in
    Seasonal Choral Preludes for Manuals Only, S. H.
    Trevor, ed., 6

PIANO

"The Risen Lord," Eugene Butler, *Journey to Easter,* 29

HANDBELL

"This Joyful Day," Douglas Wagner (3–5 octaves),
    Agape

THE EASTER SEASON: VISUAL ARTS, DRAMA, DANCE

COLOR—
To the traditional colors of white and gold, a touch of
    red might be added on this day to symbolize the
    breath of the Spirit.
DRAMA—
A conversation between Thomas and Jesus.

STUDY CATECHISM

For today's questions and answers, see p. 221.

May 4, 2003

Acts 3:12–19 — Peter urges the people to repent.

Psalm 4 — God hears our prayers and redeems us.

1 John 3:1–7 — Transformation through the power of love.

Luke 24:36b–48 — The risen Lord appears again to the disciples.

Theme(s) of lectionary texts: The process of personal change as believers come to reflect more clearly the image of Christ.

CALL TO WORSHIP

Answer me when I call on you, O God,
    for you are the defender of my cause.
Have mercy on me and hear my prayer,
    for you have the power to set me free.
The Lord does wonders for the faithful;
    when I cry out, the Lord hears me.
Many are saying,
    "Oh, that we might see better times!"
Put your trust in the Lord,
    pray that the light of God's face will shine on us.
For the Lord puts gladness in my heart;
    in God alone may I dwell in safety.

SUGGESTED HYMNS

ENTRANCE/GATHERING HYMNS	HB	LBW	NCH	PH	RL	TFF	WOV
"Blessed Jesus, at Your Word"	—	—	—	454	530	—	—
"That Easter Day with Joy Was Bright"	—	154	—	121	313	—	—
HYMNS RELATED TO SCRIPTURE							
A—"Have Mercy on Us, Living Lord"	—	—	—	195	—	—	—
"Were You There?"	201	92	229	102	—	81	—
E—"Children of the Heavenly Father"	—	474	—	—	585	—	—
"Lord, Speak to Me"	298	403	531	426	436	—	—
"What Wondrous Love Is This?"	—	385	223	85	—	—	—
G—"I Greet Thee, Who My Sure Redeemer Art"	144	—	251	457	366	—	—
HYMNS OF THE TABLE							
"Come, Let Us Eat"	—	214	—	—	—	119	—
"Here, O My Lord, We See You"	442	211	336	520	549	—	—
"O Lord, We Praise You"	—	215	—	—	—	—	—
SENDING FORTH							
"To God Be the Glory"	—	—	—	485	355	264	—

Third Sunday of Easter

Color: White and gold

PRAYER OF CONFESSION

Everlasting Father,
by your Spirit you raised your holy child Jesus from
  the dead,
and by that same Spirit you raise us up with him,
calling and adopting us as your own.
Like a mother who never ceases caring for her children,
you continue to comfort, shelter, and nurture us.
Yet we live as though your sustaining provision and
  protection
were neither trustworthy nor sufficient.

Forgive us for denying and disowning you
as our Source and Sustainer.
Renew us in faith, hope, and love;
that we may proclaim
with joyous words and integrity of life
the good news of your sure salvation,
through Jesus, our Risen Lord.

HYMN OF ASSURANCE

"Great Is Thy Faithfulness," *PH*, 276

PSALM 4

METRICAL—
"O God, Defender of My Cause," *A New Metrical
  Psalter*, 42
RESPONSORIAL—
"Psalm 4," Helen Wright, *PH*, 160, and *The Psalter*
  (1993), 3
CHORAL/VOCAL—
"Lead Me, Lord," S. S. Wesley (SATB), E. C.
  Schirmer (A)

ADDITIONAL SONGS

"Refiner's Fire," Brian Doerksen, *LUYH*, 66

CHORAL/VOCAL

"In All These You Welcomed Me," William Bradley
  Roberts (unison/organ/optional oboe or C instru-
  ment), Augsburg 111–10661 (A) (SC)
"Love Is Come Again," Alice Parker and Robert Shaw,
  arr. (SATB), The Shaw Parker Carol Collection, G.
  Schirmer (A)
"See What Love," Felix Mendelssohn (SATB/organ),
  Augsburg 11–1281 (M)

ORGAN

"All Menschen muessen Sterben," J. Pachelbel,
  Seasonal Chorale Preludes, 8

PIANO

"What Wondrous Love Is This," John Leavitt, arr.,
  How Sweet the Sound, 44
"Wondrous Love," Eugene Peterson, *Journey to Easter*, 7

HANDBELL

"Children of the Heavenly Father," Douglas Wagner
  (3 octaves), Agape

THE EASTER SEASON: DRAMA

The third appearance of Jesus, once again eating with
the disciples. An atmosphere of peace, forgiveness,
trust.

STUDY CATECHISM

For today's questions and answers, see pp. 221–22.

May 11, 2003

Acts 4:5–12   Peter and John are put on trial for their proclamation.

Psalm 23   The psalm of the good shepherd.

1 John 3:18–24   The commandment to love one another.

John 10:11–18   Jesus tells his followers, "I am the good shepherd."

Theme(s) of lectionary texts: The shepherd of Israel, and the duty to love and care for one another.

CALL TO WORSHIP

The Lord is my shepherd,
    I shall want for nothing.
You, O Lord, make me lie down in green pastures
    and lead me beside still waters.
You revive my soul
    and guide me in the pathways that are right.
Though I walk in death's presence, I will not fear,
    for you are with me always.
You spread a feast for me; you anoint my head;
    my cup overflows with goodness.
Your goodness and mercy will follow me forever,
    and I will dwell secure in your house. Amen.

PRAYER OF CONFESSION

Faithful Shepherd,
you lead us and guide us in the way we should go.
You have set before us the way of life,
having borne upon yourself our sin and death,
so that we might live forever.
Yet we have wandered from your fold
and strayed from your path;
we have chosen to stumble in darkness,
rather than walking in your light.

By your merciful Spirit,
draw us back unto yourself,
and set our feet on your sure path,
that step by step, and day by day,
we may truly glorify your holy name.

HYMN OF RESPONSE

"Savior, Like a Shepherd Lead Us," *PH,* 387

SUGGESTED HYMNS

ENTRANCE/GATHERING HYMNS	HB	LBW	NCH	PH	RL	TFF	WOV
"O Day of Radiant Gladness"	—	—	66	470	—	—	—
"Praise the Lord, Rise Up Rejoicing"	—	196	—	—	—	—	—
HYMNS RELATED TO SCRIPTURE							
A—"At the Name of Jesus"	143	179	—	148	—	—	—
"Christ Is Made the Sure Foundation"	433	367	400	416–17	392	—	
E—"My Song Is Love Unknown"	—	94	222	76	284	—	661
"When a Poor One"/"Cuando Un Pobre"	—	—	—	407	—	—	—
G—"Savior, Like a Shepherd Lead Us"	380	481	252	387	—	254	—
"The King of Love My Shepherd Is"	106	456	248	171	266–67	—	—
HYMNS OF THE TABLE							
"Lord, I Want to Be a Christian"	317	—	454	372	—	234	—
SENDING FORTH							
"Jesu, Jesu, Fill Us with Your Love"	—	—	498	367	—	83	765

Fourth Sunday of Easter

Color: White and gold

PSALM 23

METRICAL—
"The King of Love My Shepherd Is," *PH,* 171
"The Lord's My Shepherd," *PH,* 174
"The Lord's My Shepherd, I'll Not Want," *PH,* 170
RESPONSORIAL—
"Christ Jesus, Lord and Savior"/"O Christe, Domine Jesu" (SATB ostinato/cantor), *Songs and Prayers from Taizé,* GIA, 32
"My Shepherd Is the Lord" *PH,* 173
Psalm 23, *The Psalter (1993),* 18–20
Psalm 23, *Psalms Together,* Choristers Guild
"The Lord Is My Shepherd," *The Ionian Psalter,* 12
CHORAL/VOCAL—
Psalm 23, Heinz Werner Zimmerman (SATB/organ/string bass), Augsburg 11-0638 (C)
Psalm 23, "The Lord Is My Shepherd," David Hurd (SAATTB with option of congregation), Augsburg 11–10172 (M)
"The Lord Is My Shepherd," Old Round, C. Wetzel, arr. (unison), *Cry Hosanna,* 114
"The Lord Is My Shepherd," John Rutter (SATB/oboe/organ), Oxford 94.216 (M)
"The Lord Is My Shepherd," Thomas Matthews (SATB/organ), Fitzsimmons F2137 (M)

ADDITIONAL SONGS

"Gentle Shepherd, Come and Lead Us," Gloria and William Gaither, *LUYH,* 102

CHORAL/VOCAL

"A Single Unmatched Stone," Carol Doran (unison/keyboard), *New Hymns for the Lectionary,* 49 (A) (SC)
"Do You Know Your Shepherd's Voice?" Suzanne Lord (unison/2-part/piano), Choristers Guild CGA673 (A)
"I Am the Good Shepherd," Thomas Matthews (2-part/keyboard), Mercury MC460-3 (A)
"Savior, Like a Shepherd Lead Us," William Bradley Roberts (unison/optional flute or C instrument/organ), Augsburg 11-2558 (A) (SC)

ORGAN

"Suite of Easter Hymns," Emma L. Diemer, Sacred Music Press

PIANO

"Brother James' Air," Dale Wood, *Wood Works,* 4
"My Shepherd Will Supply My Need," Dale Wood, *Wood Works,* 18

HANDBELL

"Savior, Like a Shepherd Lead Us," Linda McKechnie (3 octaves), Agape

VISUAL ARTS, DRAMA, DANCE

Visual motifs: Shepherd, sheep, rod, staff; cornerstone

STUDY CATECHISM

For today's questions and answers, see p. 222.

May 18, 2003

Acts 8:26–40   Philip baptizes an official of the Ethiopian court.
Psalm 22:25–31   The saving deeds of God.
1 John 4:7–21   God is love.
John 15:1–8   The true vine and the branches.

Theme(s) of lectionary texts: Giving glory to God in response to the many gracious gifts we have received.

CALL TO WORSHIP

I will praise the Lord in the midst of the assembly;
    I will worship with all those who gather in God's name.
The poor shall eat and be satisfied,
    and those who seek the Lord shall give praise.
All the ends of the earth shall worship the Lord,
    and all the families of nations shall bow down to God.
For sovereignty belongs to God alone;
    it is the Lord who rules over the nations.
My descendants shall serve the Lord;
    they shall be known as God's forever.
They shall make known to a people yet unborn
    the saving deeds that God has done. Amen.

PRAYER OF CONFESSION

God of our Life,
you have called us to bear witness
to the cross and resurrection of Jesus,
in whose love we have found abundant life.
We confess that we keep this good news to ourselves;
Neither our words nor our actions
have faithfully proclaimed his saving goodness.
We have failed to show and tell
the love by which we so richly live.

Forgive us for denying the divine love and power
in which we live, move, and have our being.
Quicken us by your Holy Spirit,
in all that we say and do,
to bear faithful witness
to the love, mercy, and justice
of our Lord and Savior, Jesus Christ.

HYMN OF ASSURANCE

"When We Are Living," *PH,* 400

SUGGESTED HYMNS

ENTRANCE/GATHERING HYMNS	HB	LBW	NCH	PH	RL	TFF	WOV
"Celebrate with Joy and Singing"	—	—	—	107	—	—	—
"Great God, Your Love Has Called Us Here"	—	—	—	353	—	—	666
HYMNS RELATED TO SCRIPTURE							
A—"Deep in the Shadows of the Past"	—	—	320	330	—	—	—
"We Know That Christ Is Raised"	—	189	—	495	—	—	—
E—"How Like a Gentle Spirit"	—	—	443	—	—	—	—
"Jesus, Thy Boundless Love to Me"	404	336	—	369	—	—	—
"Stand Up and Bless the Lord"	—	—	—	491	499	—	—
G—"God, Bless Your Church with Strength"	—	—	—	418	—	—	—
"How Firm a Foundation"	369	507	407	361	172	—	—
HYMNS OF THE TABLE							
"Bread of Heaven, On Thee We Feed"	—	—	—	501	—	—	—
"You Satisfy the Hungry Heart"	—	—	—	521	—	—	711
SENDING FORTH							
"Lord, Dismiss Us with Thy Blessing"	79	259	77	538	—	—	—

Fifth Sunday of Easter

Color: White and gold

PSALM 22

METRICAL—
"All Hail to God's Anointed" (Psalm 72), *PH*, 205
"My God! O My God!" *Psalter Hymnal*, 22 (stanzas 8–10)
RESPONSORIAL—
"Psalm 22," A New Zealand Prayer Book, *The Psalter* (1993), 17

ADDITIONAL SONGS

"In the Presence of Your People" (Psalm 22:3, 22), Brent Chambers, *LUYH*, 37

CHORAL/VOCAL

"Beloved, Let Us Love One Another," Jean Langlais (unison or solo voice/organ), *Three Short Anthems*, Hinshaw HMC-423 (M)
"Love One Another," John Bell (SAB), GIA G-5158 (A) (SC)
"O Blessed Spring," Robert Bucklee Farlee (SATB/ organ/oboe/optional congregation), Augsburg 11-10544 (A)
"The Branch That Bends," Carol Doran/Thomas Troeger (unison/organ), Oxford in *New Hymns for the Lectionary*, 41
"We Have Met Christ Raised and Living," Sally Ann Morris/Thomas H. Troege (unison or SATB), GIA, in *Giving Thanks in Song and Prayer*, 18

ORGAN

"Ubi Caritas," Charles Callahan, *Music for Manuals: Chant-Based Hymns*, 3

PIANO

"My Jesus I Love Thee," Angela Tipps, *Keys of the Kingdom*, vol. 1, Abingdon, 18

HANDBELL

"Come Thou Fount of Every Blessing," Dan Miller (quartet), Hinshaw

VISUAL ARTS, DRAMA, DANCE

DRAMA—
The conversation between Philip and the Ethiopian official.
VISUAL MOTIFS—
Vine and vineyard, pruned branches, fruit. Baptismal water.

STUDY CATECHISM

For today's questions and answers, see p. 223.

May 25, 2003

Acts 10:44–48 — The Holy Spirit is poured out on the Gentiles.

Psalm 98 — A song of praise to the Lord of all creation.

1 John 5:1–6 — The unity of the children of God.

John 15:9–17 — Jesus gives his followers a new commandment.

Theme(s) of lectionary texts: The universal love and providence of God.

CALL TO WORSHIP

Sing to the Lord a new song,
> for the Lord has done marvelous things.

The right hand of the Lord
> **has secured victory for God's people.**

Shout with joy to the Lord, all you lands!
> Lift up your voice, rejoice, and sing!

Sing to the Lord with a harp,
> **with trumpets and the voice of song!**

Let the sea make a noise, the rivers clap their hands,
> and let the hills ring out with joy before the Lord.

For the Lord alone is judge of all the world,
> **and God shall treat all people with equity.**
> **Amen.**

SUGGESTED HYMNS

ENTRANCE/GATHERING HYMNS	HB	LBW	NCH	PH	RL	TFF	WOV
"Blessed Jesus, at Your Word"	—	—	—	454	530	—	—
"Here, O Lord, Your Servants Gather"	—	—	72	465	—	—	—
"Love Divine, All Loves Excelling"	399	315	43	376	464	—	—
HYMNS RELATED TO SCRIPTURE							
A—"Baptized in Water"	—	—	—	492	—	—	693
"Like the Murmur of a Dove's Song"	—	—	270	314	—	—	685
"Spirit of the Living God"	—	—	283	322	—	101	—
"There's a Sweet, Sweet Spirit"	—	—	293	398	—	102	—
E—"Blessed Assurance, Jesus Is Mine"	—	—	—	341	—	118	699
"Take Me to the Water"	—	—	322	—	—	117	
G—"Give to Me, Lord, a Thankful Heart"	—	—	—	351	462	—	—
"Help Us Accept Each Other"	—	—	388	358	—	—	—
HYMNS OF THE TABLE							
"I Come with Joy to Meet My Lord"	—	—	349	507	534	—	—
"Lord, We Have Come at Your Own Invitation"	—	—	—	516	—	—	—
SENDING FORTH							
"In Christ There Is No East or West"	479	359	394–95	439–40	410	214	—

Sixth Sunday of Easter

Color: White and gold

PRAYER OF CONFESSION

Tender Savior,
we receive with gratitude your love,
which you demonstrated by
laying down your life for us.
You have chosen us as your own,
and called us to love one another as you have loved us.
But we fall far short of your life-giving command;
we cling in fear to the little we have,
rather than laying it down so that your riches of love
may fill us and flow through us.

Pour out your Spirit on us anew,
that we may know and proclaim
the depth, the breadth, the height, and the length
of your love that passes all measure.
Cause us to abide in that love so fully
that it will overflow among us,
and through us to the world around us;
that we would be faithful children of our heavenly
    Father,
who loves us with everlasting love.

HYMN OF ASSURANCE

"Hear the Good News of Salvation," *PH,* 355

PSALM 98

METRICAL—
"Cantad al Senor"/"O Sing to the Lord," *PH,* 472
"New Songs of Celebration Render," *PH,* 218
"Sing to the Lord a New Song," *The Faith We Sing,*
    Abigingdon 2045
"To God Compose a Song of Joy," *PH,* 219
RESPONSORIAL—
"All the Ends of the Earth," David Haas (2–3 part
    choir/congregation), GIA, in *Celebration Series*
    G-2703 (A)
Psalm 98, *The Psalter* (1993), 94 or 95

CHORAL/VOCAL—
"Clap Your Hands and Sing!" Allen Pote (SATB/key-
    board/optional flute), Hinshaw HMC-920 (M)
"O Sing to the Lord," Jane Marshall (unison),
    Choristers Guild CGA-427
Psalm 98, Noel Piercy (cantor/congregation and/or
    unison choir/handbells), AGEHR AGC 008

ADDITIONAL SONGS

"Sing Unto the Lord," Tom Fettke, arr., *LUYH,* 53

CHORAL/VOCAL

"I Give You a New Commandment," Peter Aston (2-part
    or unison/SA or all voices), GIA G-4331 (A) (SC)
"If Ye Love Me," Philip Wilby (SSATB/organ), Banks
    Museum/Hal Leonard ECS 191 (A) (SC)

ORGAN

"Lord Jesus, Think on Me," Allan Mahnke,
    Concordia, in *The (Really) Little Organ Book*

PIANO

"Every Time I Feel the Spirit," John Carter, Hope, in
    Spirituals for Piano

HANDBELL

"Love Divine, All Loves Excelling," Hal Hopson
    (2 octaves), Agape

EASTER SEASON: VISUAL MOTIFS

Water
Fruit
Banner: "Love One Another"

STUDY CATECHISM

For today's questions and answers, see p. 223.

Thursday, May 29, 2003

Acts 1:1–11 — With the apostles as witnesses, Jesus ascends into the clouds.

Psalm 47 — God is Lord over all the rulers of the earth.

Ephesians 1:15–23 — The Holy Spirit gives believers wisdom to perceive that Christ is Lord over earthly powers.

Luke 24:44–53 — The account of the ascension of Jesus from the Gospel according to Luke.

Theme(s) of lectionary texts: The ascension of Jesus to sit at the right hand of God.

CALL TO WORSHIP

The Lord is king over all the earth:
> shout to God with a cry of joy!

God has gone up with a shout,
> **the Lord arose with the sound of trumpets.**

Sing praise to God, sing praises;
> for God is Lord over all the earth.

God reigns over the nations,
> **God sits on heaven's exalted throne.**

The nobility of the earth will gather
> together with the children of Abraham,

for the rulers of the earth belong to God;
> **God alone is to be worshiped! Amen.**

PRAYER OF CONFESSION

Almighty God,
who raised Jesus from the dead into eternal glory,
we come before you as those who share in his hope
> **of glory—**

not on account of our own righteousness,
but through his obedience and sacrifice for us.
We have been raised to newness of life with him,
yet we continue to live as though death were the
> **final word.**

Confident that his intercession on our behalf
already rises before your holy throne,
we come before you freely confessing our sins,
trusting fully in your merciful forgiveness.
Strengthen us to live in a way that demonstrates
his abiding presence among us,
and the hope of glory within us,
through the power of your Holy Spirit.

HYMN OF ASSURANCE

"Alleluia! Sing to Jesus!" *PH,* 144

SUGGESTED HYMNS

ENTRANCE/GATHERING HYMNS	HB	LBW	NCH	PH	RL	TFF	WOV
"Come, Christians, Join to Sing"	131	—	—	150	357	—	—
"When Morning Gilds the Skies"	41	545–56	86	487	365	—	—
HYMNS RELATED TO SCRIPTURE							
A—"A Hymn of Glory Let Us Sing"	—	—	259	141	332	—	—
E—"He Is King of Kings"	—	—	—	153	—	—	—
G—"Crown Him with Many Crowns"	213	170	301	151	600	—	—
HYMN OF THE TABLE							
"Christ Jesus Lay in Death's Strong Bands"	—	134	—	110	324	—	—
SENDING FORTH							
"Lift High the Cross"	—	377	198	371	415	—	—

Ascension of the Lord

Color: White or gold

PSALM 47

METRICAL—
"Peoples, Clap Your Hands," *PH*, 194
RESPONSORIAL—
"Psalm 47," Hal Hopson, *The Psalter* (1993), 42
CHORAL/VOCAL—
"A Carol for Ascension," Lloyd Pfautsch (SATB), Augsburg 11-2496
"O Clap Your Hands," Harald Rohlig (SATB), Augsburg 11-0607
"Psalm for Ascension," Valerie Stegink Sterk (concertato for congregation, SATB, children's choir organ, tambourine), CRC Publications 24-1047 (A)

ADDITIONAL SONGS

"He Is Exalted," Twila Paris, *LUYH* 33
"Majesty," Jack W. Hayford, Eugene Thomas, arr., *LUYH* 46
"The Savior Leaves," John Bell (unison/organ), GIA G-3647, *Enemy of Apathy*, 103

CHORAL/VOCAL

"Alleluia! Sing to Jesus," Hal Hopson (unison), Augsburg (A) (SC)
"A Carol for Ascension," Lloyd Pfautsch (SATB), Augsburg 11-2496 (M)
"Come Away to the Skies," Alice Parker (SATB), Lawson-Gould 51334 (A)
"God Is Gone Up," Gerald Finzi (SATB/organ), Boosey & Hawkes CCs39 (C)
"Shout to God," Joseph M. Martin (SATB, accomp., optional brass and percussion), Flammer A6927

ORGAN

"Prelude on DIADEMATA (Crown Him with Many Crowns)," Wilbur Held, Concordia, in *Hymn Preludes for the Pentecost Season*

PIANO

"All Hail the Power of Jesus' Name," Charles Webb, *Keys of the Kingdom*, 25
"Beautiful Savior," Dale Wood, *Wood Works*, 30
"To God Be the Glory," Fred Bock, Fred Bock's Music in *Bock's Best*, vol. 4

HANDBELL

"Hail the Day That Sees Him Rise," Hal Hopson (2 octaves), Lorenz

EASTER SEASON: VISUAL MOTIFS AND DRAMA

DRAMA—
The disciples tell the story of the Ascension.
VISUAL EFFECTS—
Spotlights and textile drapery drawing the eyes to upper portions of worship space.

June 1, 2003

Acts 1:15–17, 21–26	The selection of a twelfth apostle.
Psalm 1	The righteous person is like a tree planted by the water.
1 John 5:9–13	The gift of eternal life is found in Christ.
John 17:6–19	Jesus prays for God to protect and consecrate those who have come to faith in him, and those who will come to believe through their words.

Theme(s) of lectionary texts: God's election, blessing, and protection of the righteous.

CALL TO WORSHIP

Happy are those who walk not in the counsel of the
    wicked,
      nor sit in the seats of scoffers.
**The delight of the righteous
    is in the law of the Lord our God.**
On the law of God, and all its teachings,
    they meditate by day and night.
**They are like trees planted by streams of water,
    bearing fruit in due season, with leaves that do
      not wither.**

PRAYER OF CONFESSION

Source of all wisdom—
You have called us to honor your word,
and showered us with blessing
when we have followed your counsel.
You have sent your Spirit to purify us deep within,
so that we may follow your way single-heartedly,
even when other voices and inner desires
call us away from you.
Yet we have disregarded your precepts,
and grieved your sanctifying Spirit.

In mercy, forgive us for resisting you.
By your boundless love,
draw us near to yourself,
that with joy and gratitude
we may honor you faithfully
in all that we do and say,
bearing abundant fruit of beauty and wholeness,
the inheritance of those who live by your holy wisdom,
through your Wisdom made flesh, Jesus our Lord.

HYMN OF ASSURANCE

"God of Compassion, in Mercy Befriend Us," *PH,*
    261

SUGGESTED HYMNS

ENTRANCE/GATHERING HYMNS	HB	LBW	NCH	PH	RL	TFF	WOV
"Celebrate with Joy and Singing"	—	—	—	107	—	—	—
"O Splendor of God's Glory Bright"	46	271	87	474	76	—	—
HYMNS RELATED TO SCRIPTURE							
A—"Christ Is Made the Sure Foundation"	433	367	400	416–17	392	—	—
E—"Alleluia, Alleluia, Give Thanks"	—	—	—	106	—	—	671
"I Greet Thee Who My Sure Redeemer Art"	144	—	251	457	366	—	—
G—"Help Us Accept Each Other"	—	—	388	358	—	—	—
"We All Are One In Mission"	—	—	—	435	—	—	755
HYMN OF THE TABLE							
"Draw Us in the Spirit's Tether"	—	—	337	504	—	—	703
SENDING FORTH							
"O Christ, the Great Foundation"	—	—	387	443	—	—	—

Seventh Sunday of Easter

Color: White and gold

PSALM 1

METRICAL—
"Happy Are They Who Walk," *RL*, 82
"How Blest Are They," *RL*, 81
"The One Is Blest," *PH*, 158
RESPONSORIAL—
"Happy Are Those Whose Delight," Peter R. Hallock, *The Ionian Psalter*
"Psalm 1 (1–4, 6)," Hal Hopson, *The Psalter* (1993), 1
CHORAL/VOCAL—
"Happy the Man Who Fears the Lord," Richard Proulx (SA, instr.), Augsburg 11-0312

ADDITIONAL SONGS

"Make Us One," Carol Cymbala. *The Faith We Sing*, 2224 (John 17)
"No One Will Ever Be the Same," Iona Community, *LUYH*, 137
"One Bread, One Body," John Foley (Unison/keyboard), *LUYH*, 130
"We Are One in Christ Jesus"/"Somos Uno en Christo" (SATB), *The Faith We Sing*, 2229

CHORAL/VOCAL

"Divided Our Pathways," Christopher Coelho, Erik Routley, arr. (unison/cantor/organ), Hope, in *Ecumenical Praise*, 59 (A) (SC)
"The Chosen Twelve, Now Lacking One," Christopher Tye and Carl Schalk, ed. (SATB), *Easter Motet Series B*, Augsburg 11-5750
"You Walk Along Our Shoreline," Sally Ann Morris/Sylvia Dunstan (unison/organ), GIA G-4930, *Giving Thanks in Song and Prayer*, 50 (A) (SC)

ORGAN

"Sing Praise to God Who Reigns Above," Charles W. Ore, Concordia, in *Eleven Compositions for Organ, Set 2*, 18

PIANO

"Jesus Shall Reign," Anne Krentz, *Keys of the Kingdom*, 22

HANDBELL

"Rise, Shine, You People!" Janet Linker (3–5 octaves), Augsburg-Fortress

VISUAL ARTS, DRAMA, DANCE

VISUAL MOTIFS—
Easter banners; springtime images.
DRAMA—
Jesus prays for his followers.

STUDY CATECHISM

For today's questions and answers, see p. 223.

June 8, 2003

Acts 2:1–21 or Ezekiel 37:1–14 — The events of Pentecost in Jerusalem. The valley of dry bones.

Psalm 104:24–34, 35b — God's Spirit is sent forth, renewing the earth.

Romans 8:22–27 — The Spirit prays in our prayers.

John 15:26–27; 16:4b–15 — Jesus promises to send the church an Advocate.

Theme(s) of lectionary texts: The coming of the Holy Spirit on the day of Pentecost.

CALL TO WORSHIP

Many are your works, O Lord,
  and you have made them all in wisdom.
The earth is full of God's creatures,
  as is the width and depth of the sea.
The ships move on it, and Leviathan swims beneath,
  for in goodness God has created it.
All creatures look to you, O Lord,
  for you give them their food in due season.
When you hide your face, they are terrified;
  when you take their breath, they turn to dust.
You send forth your Spirit, and they are created;
  and so you renew the face of the earth.

PRAYER OF CONFESSION

God of Pentecost:
As you have done in every age and place
you pour out your Spirit today upon your people,
loosening our tongues to declare your praise,
binding our hearts together in community,
and joining our hands in mission.
Yet we resist the work of your Spirit among us.
We'd rather die under our own control,
than live in the power of your Spirit.
Our lives deny the good news of your love,
and our life together betrays the unity of the Spirit.

Have mercy on us, O God.
Breathe new life into us,
and fill us with the fire of your love,
that we may proclaim with passion your glory
revealed to us in the face of Jesus Christ.

HYMN OF ASSURANCE

"On Pentecost They Gathered," *PH*, 128

SUGGESTED HYMNS

ENTRANCE/GATHERING HYMNS	HB	LBW	NCH	PH	RL	TFF	WOV
"Like the Murmur of the Dove's Song"	—	—	270	314	—	—	685
HYMNS RELATED TO SCRIPTURE							
A—"Breathe on Me, Breath of God"	235	488	292	316	—	—	—
"My Lord, What a Morning"	—	—	—	449	—	40	627
E—"Come, Holy Spirit, Heavenly Dove"	239	—	281	126	—	—	—
"Spirit"	—	—	286	319	—	—	684
"Spirit of God, Descend Upon My Heart"	236	486	290	326	445	—	—
G—"Come Down, O Lord Divine"	—	508	289	313	444	—	—
HYMN OF THE TABLE							
"Come Holy Spirit, Our Souls Inspire"	237	172–73	268	125	385	—	—
SENDING FORTH							
"Come, O Spirit"	—	—	—	127	—	—	—

Day of Pentecost

Color: Red (possibly with gold)

PSALM 104

METRICAL—
"Bless the Lord, My Soul and Being," *PH*, 224
RESPONSORIAL—
"Lord, Send Out Your Spirit," Robert Edward Smith, Cantor Congregation Series, GIA G-2122
"Psalm 104 (1–9)," *The Psalter* (1993), 104
CHORAL/VOCAL—
"Come, Holy Spirit, Blow Across the Waters," May Schwartz (SATB/congregation/optional brass quintet), Augsburg 11-10920 (A)

ADDITIONAL SONGS

"Come, Holy Spirit," the Iona Community, *LUYH*, 133
"Come, Spirit, Come," Walter Harrah, *LUYH*, 151
"Dance with the Spirit," Jim Strathdee, *LUYH*, 135
"God the Spirit Comes to Stay," John Bell, the Iona Community, GIA G-3647, *Enemy of Apathy*, 103
"Wa wa wa Emimimo," Samuel Solanke, *Halle, Halle*, 32

CHORAL/VOCAL

"And the Best Is Love," Richard Proulx (unison), Augsburg 11-1639
"Canticle for Pentecost," Erik Routley (SATB/cantor), *Two for Pentecost*, Hinshaw HMC-267 (A)
"Come Down, O Love Divine," David Ashley White (SATB/trumpet/organ/optional congregation), Selah 405-619 (A)
"Creator Spirit, Heavenly Dove," Robert J. Powell (SATB/handbells/organ), Paraclete Press PPM08607 (A)
"Pentecost Fire," Jayne Southwick Cool (unison), Choristers Guild CGA-502 (A)
"Sweet Delight, Most Lovely, Shining," Sally Ann Morris (SATB/organ), Pilgrim Press NCA06 (M)
"We Do Not Know How to Pray," Erik Routley (unison/cantor, organ), in *Ecumenical Praise*, Hope 110

"When the Counselor Comes," Jan Bender (SA/2 equal voices), Concordia 98-2055 (M)

ORGAN

"Komm, heiliger Geist, Herre Gott," J. Pachelbel, *Seasonal Chorale Preludes*, 9

PIANO

"Breathe on Me, Breath of God," John Innes, *Keys of the Kingdom*, 37
"I'm Goin' a Sing When the Spirit Says Sing," Charles Webb, *Keys of the Kingdom*, 44

HANDBELL

"Spirit in the Wind," Lee Afdahl (3 or 5 octaves), AGEHR

VISUAL ARTS, DRAMA, DANCE

In advance, invite the congregation to wear red on this Sunday. Provide simple, flame-shaped pins for those who forget to wear red.
GATHERING—
At this, the end of the Easter cycle, people may gather outside the church and process into the sanctuary by way of the baptismal font.
VISUAL MOTIFS—
Descending dove, tongues of flame, symbols of the church at its mission.
DRAMA—
Acts 2:1–21. Sounds of wind; illusion of fire—colorful streamers and pinwheels, for example. Use several languages in worship, if possible. Involve the children!

STUDY CATECHISM

For today's questions and answers, see p. 224.

June 15, 2003

Isaiah 6:1–8   The angels join in choruses of "Holy! Holy! Holy!" as Isaiah is called to be a prophet.

Psalm 29   Praise to the majesty of God's name.

Romans 8:12–17   The Spirit given by Christ enables us to cry, "Abba! Father!"

John 3:1–17   God's great love makes it possible for believers to be born anew in Christ by water and the Spirit.

Theme(s) of lectionary texts: The doctrine of the Tri-une God: three in one, and one in three.

CALL TO WORSHIP

Declare the majesty of God;
    declare the Lord's glory and power!
**Declare the glory that is due God's name,
    and worship the Lord in the beauty of holiness!**
The voice of the Lord sounds upon the waters;
    the God of glory thunders.
**The voice of the Lord shatters limbs of trees
    and fells the cedars of Lebanon.**
The voice of the Lord makes the oak trees writhe
    and strips the forest bare.
**In the temple of the Lord, all cry, "Glory!"
    For the Lord shall give us the blessing of peace.**

SUGGESTED HYMNS

ENTRANCE/GATHERING HYMNS	HB	LBW	NCH	PH	RL	TFF	WOV
"Come, Great God of All the Ages"	—	—	—	132	—	—	—
"Holy, Holy, Holy"	11	165	277	138	611	—	—
"O Day of Radiant Gladness"	—	—	66	470	—	—	—
HYMNS RELATED TO SCRIPTURE							
O—"Ye Watchers and Ye Holy Ones"	34	175	—	451	—	—	—
E—"Creating God, Your Fingers Trace"	—	—	462	134	—	—	757
"Every Time I Feel the Spirit"	—	—	282	315	—	241	—
"O God the Creator"	—	—	291	273	—	—	—
"The Lone, Wild Bird"	—	—	—	320	—	—	—
G—"Lift High the Cross"	—	377	198	371	415	—	—
HYMNS OF THE TABLE							
"God Is One, Unique and Holy"	—	—	—	135	—	—	—
"Holy, Holy"	—	—	—	140	—	289	—
SENDING FORTH							
"Holy God, We Praise Your Name"	—	535	276	460	619	—	—
"Stand Up and Bless the Lord"	—	—	—	491	499	—	—

Trinity Sunday

Color: White or gold

PRAYER OF CONFESSION

Eternal and Almighty God,
As we enter your holy presence,
we acknowledge that
    our lips are unclean,
    our hands are unclean,
    our hearts are unclean.
Our sins are too dark for us to face,
and too heavy for us to bear.
(pause for silent reflection)

In your tender compassion, show us mercy.
Purify us with the coals from your altar.
Fill our mouths with your word,
    our hands with your work,
    our hearts with your love,
according to your perfect will.

Sanctify us by your grace,
that we may be holy, even as you are holy:
eternally One God, with all power and majesty,
Father, Son, and Holy Spirit. Amen.

HYMN OF ASSURANCE

"Holy, Holy, Holy! Lord God Almighty!" *PH,* 138

PSALM 29

METRICAL—
"Ascribe to God, You Gods." *A New Metrical Psalter,*
  66
"The God of Glory Thunders," *PH,* 180
RESPONSORIAL—
"Psalm 29," Hal Hopson, *The Psalter* (1993), 26
CHORAL/VOCAL—
"Festal Anthem," Robert Leaf (SATB/trumpet),
  Augsburg (M)
"Psalm 29," James Marshal (unison), *Psalms Together
II,* Choristers Guild

ADDITIONAL SONGS

"Father, I Adore You," *The Faith We Sing,* 2038
"Holy, Holy," *The Faith We Sing,* 2039

CHORAL/VOCAL

"For God So Loved the World," Hugo Distler
  (SATB), Concordia 98-2239 (M)
"Holy, Holy, Holy Lord," Franz Schubert (SATB),
  various editions
"O God, O Lord of Heaven and Earth," Jan Bender
  (SATB/organ), Augsburg 11-10481

ORGAN

"Kyrie, Gott Vater in Ewigkeit," J. S. Bach, *Seasonal
  Chorale Preludes,* 16
"Vater Unser in Himmelreich," G. P. Telemann,
  Seasonal Chorale Preludes, 12

PIANO

"Ye Watchers and Ye Holy Ones," John Carter, in
  Carols for Piano, Hope, 7
"You Satisfy the Hungry Heart," Daniel Kane, in
  More Selectable Delectables, Augsburg-Fortress, 6

HANDBELL

"Festive Fanfare," Arnold Sherman (2–3 octaves), Agape

RECALLING THE TRINITARIAN NATURE OF GOD

Symbols of the three in one: equilateral triangle, inter-
twined circles, shamrock.
Use the Nicene Creed in worship on Trinity Sunday.

STUDY CATECHISM

For today's questions and answers, see p. 224.

June 22, 2003

1 Samuel 17:(1a, 4–11, 19–23) 32–49 or
1 Samuel 17:57–18:5, 10–16

David and Goliath.
The friendship of David and Jonathan, Saul's son.

Psalm 9:9–20 or Psalm 133

God is our refuge in time of trouble.
The blessings of unity.

2 Corinthians 6:1–13

Today is the day of salvation.

Mark 4:35–41

Jesus stills the storm at sea.

Theme(s) of lectionary texts: Even during the worst troubles and challenges, God is our refuge.

CALL TO WORSHIP

The Lord is a refuge for the oppressed,
    a haven in time of trouble.
**Those who know your name, O God,
    put their trust in you.**
Have pity on us, O Lord,
    for you alone have power to lift us from the gate of
    death.
**Sing praise to the Lord who is our help;
    proclaim to all peoples the great things God has
    done!**

PRAYER OF CONFESSION

Lord of hosts—
We confess that we are weak,
unable on our own to defeat the enemies of our souls.
We give in to our fears, and live in their darkness,
rather than living by faith in your promises of mercy
    and justice.

Even as you delivered your people of old from their
    enemies
by the hand of David, your anointed servant,
so deliver us also from all evil through the Son of
    David,
your anointed one and our Sovereign, Jesus of
    Nazareth.
By the same Spirit that strengthened them
both to believe and to act according to your promises,
strengthen us also to serve you faithfully,
that we may be victorious over all the forces of darkness
within us and around us,
to the praise of your glory and grace.

SUGGESTED HYMNS

ENTRANCE/GATHERING HYMNS	HB	LBW	NCH	PH	RL	TFF	WOV
"Lift Every Voice and Sing"	—	562	593	563	—	296	—
"O Day of God, Draw Nigh"	—	—	611	452	178	—	—
HYMNS RELATED TO SCRIPTURE							
O–"Gracious Spirit, Holy Ghost"	—	—	61	318	—	—	—
"Why Are Nations Raging?"	—	—	—	159	—	—	—
E–"God Moves in a Mysterious Way"	112	483	412	270	36	—	—
"How Can I Keep from Singing"	—	—	476	—	—	—	781
"It Is Well with My Soul"	—	346	438	—	—	194	—
G–"Jesus, Savior, Pilot Me"	336	334	441	—	—	—	—
"Lonely the Boat"	—	—	—	373	—	—	—
HYMNS OF THE TABLE							
"O Jesus, I Have Promised"	307	503	493	388–89	47	—	—
SENDING FORTH							
"Jesus, Lover of My Soul"	216	—	546	303	—	—	—

Twelfth Sunday in Ordinary Time

Color: Green

HYMN OF ASSURANCE

"My Faith Looks Up to Thee," *PH,* 383

PSALM 9

METRICAL—
"Wholehearted Thanksgiving to You I Will Bring,"
The Psalter Hymnal, 9
RESPONSORIAL—
"Psalm 9 (9–20)," Hal Hopson, *The Psalter* (1993), 6
CHORAL/VOCAL—
"They That Know Thy Name," Robert J. Powell
(SATB), Schmitt Hall McCreary (M)
(*For settings of Psalm 133, see lectionary aids for April
27, 2003.*)

ADDITIONAL SONGS

"Our God Is Mighty," Jim Gill, *LUYH,* 83

CHORAL/VOCAL

"A Rose Touched by the Sun's Warm Rays," Jean
Berger (SATB), Augsburg 11-953
"The Sails Were Spilling Wind," Carol
Doran/Thomas Troeger (unison/keyboard), *New
Hymns for the Lectionary,* 64
"When Peace Like a River," Philip Bliss, Dale
Grotenhuis, arr. (SATB/organ), Curtis Music Press
C8507 (A)

ORGAN

"Herre, wie Du Willst, so schick's mit Mir," F. W.
Marpurg, *Seasonal Chorale Preludes,* 23

PIANO

"It Is Well with My Soul," Angela Tipps, *Keys of the
Kingdom,* vol. 1, Abingdon, 30

HANDBELL

"The River," Ann Laura Page (3–5 octaves),
Augsburg-Fortress

STUDY CATECHISM

For today's questions and answers, see pp. 224–25.

June 29, 2003

2 Samuel 1:1, 17–27 — David mourns at the deaths of Saul and Jonathan.

Psalm 130 or Lamentations 3:23–33 — A psalm of lament and confession of sin. Grief lasts for a season.

2 Corinthians 8:7–15 — In response to Christ's great gift to us, Paul exhorts Christians to give generously to the poor.

Mark 5:21–43 — A young woman is restored to life, and a Gentile woman is healed.

Theme(s) of lectionary texts: The continuing struggle between the forces of death and the reality of restoration to life through Jesus Christ.

CALL TO WORSHIP

Out of the depths we cry to you, O Lord;
   Lord, hear our voice.
**If you kept account of all our sin,
   O Lord, who could stand?**
But there is forgiveness with you;
   therefore, you shall be feared and worshiped.
**I will wait for you, O Lord;
   my soul waits, for in your word is hope.**
Wait for the Lord, O people of God,
   for with the Lord there is mercy.
**The Lord is our salvation,
   for God has power to redeem us from our sin.**

SUGGESTED HYMNS

ENTRANCE/GATHERING HYMNS	HB	LBW	NCH	PH	RL	TFF	WOV
"Our God, Our Help"	111	320	25	210	1	—	—
"Praise, My Soul, the King of Heaven"	31	549	—	478–79	144	—	—
HYMNS RELATED TO SCRIPTURE							
O—"Abide with Me"	64	272	99	543	440	—	—
"Give Thanks for Life"	—	—	297	528	—	—	—
E–"As a Chalice Cast of Gold"	—	—	—	336	—	—	—
"Lord, I Want to Be a Christian"	317	—	454	372	—	234	—
G—"Draw Us in the Spirit's Tether"	—	—	337	504	—	—	703
"Many and Great, O God"	—	—	3	271	—	—	794
"Where Cross the Crowded Ways of Life"	507	429	543	408	482	—	—
HYMNS OF THE TABLE							
"If You But Trust in God to Guide You"	344	453	410	282	151	—	—
"Take My Life"	310	406	448	391	475	—	—
SENDING FORTH							
"I'm Gonna Live So God Can Use Me"	—	—	—	369	—	—	—
"On, My Children, with My Blessing"	—	—	—	—	—	—	721
"What Wondrous Love Is This"	—	385	223	85	—	—	—

Thirteenth Sunday in Ordinary Time

Color: Green

PRAYER OF CONFESSION

Compassionate Judge,
we thank you for graciousness to us,
dealing with us not according to our sin,
but according to your boundless mercy.
If you, Lord, should keep account of sin,
who could stand?
But with you is forgiveness.
Yet we deny the mercy by which we live:
We are slow to forgive,
yet quick to rise up in judgment.

Forgive our indifference and ingratitude
in face of your forbearance with us;
enable us by your Spirit to love one another as we
ought,
trusting each other to your generous mercy,
even as we cling to that mercy for our own hope,
through Jesus Christ, our Lord.

HYMN OF ASSURANCE

"There's a Wideness in God's Mercy," *PH,* 298

PSALM 130

METRICAL—
"Out of the Depths," *PH,* 240
"Psalm 130," *Psalms of Patience, Protest, and Praise,*
  GIA
RESPONSORIAL—
"Psalm 130," Peter Hallock, *Ionian Psalter,* PS-801
CHORAL/VOCAL—
"Out of the Depths," G. F. Handel (2-part mixed),
  Flammer

ADDITIONAL SONGS

"Come, My Way, My Truth, My Life," Ralph Vaughn
  Williams, *Common Ground,* 24
"Soon and Very Soon," Andraé Crouch, *LUYH,* 142

CHORAL/VOCAL

"The Scantest Touch of Grace Can Heal," Carol
  Doran/Thomas Troeger, *New Hymns for the*
  Lectionary, Oxford (M)
"When David Mourned," Thomas Tomkins (SSATB),
  C. F. Peters 6069 (C)

ORGAN

"If Thou but Trust in God to Guide Thee," George
  Boehm, in *The Church Organist's Golden Treasury,*
  vol. 3, Oliver Ditson Co.

PIANO

"I Come with Joy to Meet My Lord," John Carter, in
  You Satisfy the Hungry Heart, Hope, 18

HANDBELL

"Great Is Thy Faithfulness," Cynthia Dobrinski (3–5
  octaves), Agape

STUDY CATECHISM

For today's questions and answers, see p. 225.

July 6, 2003

2 Samuel 5:1–5, 9–10	The tribes of Israel hail David as their king.
Psalm 48	The Lord is a sure bulwark and defense.
2 Corinthians 12:2–10	Paul teaches, "When I am weak, then I am strong."
Mark 6:1–13	Jesus preaches in Nazareth and commissions the twelve disciples to proclaim God's realm.

Theme(s) of lectionary texts: Apparent weakness and abiding strength.

CALL TO WORSHIP

Great is the Lord, and greatly to be praised
    in the city of our God, atop the holy hill.
God is in the citadels,
    for God is known as our sure refuge.
O God, your praise, like your name,
    reaches to the earth's farthest end.
Your right hand is full of justice,
    and your city boasts many watchtowers.
The city of God has strong bulwarks,
    it is a stronghold in time of terror.
O Lord, you are our God forevermore;
    be our guide forever and ever. Amen.

SUGGESTED HYMNS

ENTRANCE/GATHERING HYMNS	HB	LBW	NCH	PH	RL	TFF	WOV
"All Hail to God's Anointed"	—	—	—	205	—	—	—
"Awake, My Soul"	50	269	—	456	71	—	—
HYMNS RELATED TO SCRIPTURE							
O—"O Morning Star, How Fair and Bright"	415	76	158	69	367	—	—
"This Is the Day the Lord Hath Made"	69	—	—	230	128	—	—
E—"Come, Thou Fount of Every Blessing"	379	499	459	356	449	108	—
"Jesus, Still Lead On"	—	341	446	—	586	—	—
G—"God, Whose Giving Knows No Ending"	—	408	565	422	—	—	—
"Jesus Shall Reign Where'er the Sun"	496	530	300	423	233	—	—
HYMNS OF THE TABLE							
"O Love That Wilt Not Let Me Go"	400	324	485	384	—	—	—
"One Bread, One Body"	—	—	—	—	—	122	710
SENDING FORTH							
"Fight the Good Fight"	359	461	—	307	—	—	—
"Lord, You Give the Great Commission"	—	—	—	429	—	—	756
"O God, Empower Us"	—	422	—	—	—	—	—

Fourteenth Sunday in Ordinary Time

Color: Green

PRAYER OF CONFESSION

O God our Protector,
You set us in your holy city,
where your saints have always found
security and rest amidst the toils of life.
As you have been their faithful guardian,
so you have held us fast
when all around is shaken.
Yet we turn aside from you,
worrying about meeting our own needs,
and depending upon our own strength for security.

In your mercy, forgive our failure to trust you;
remind us and strengthen us
to cast all our cares upon you.
Enable us to live by your Spirit
under the certain conviction of your abiding love,
revealed to us in the gift of your Son,
our Lord and Savior, Jesus Christ.

HYMN OF ASSURANCE

"Near to the Heart of God," *PH,* 527

PSALM 48

METRICAL—
"Great Is the Lord Our God" (SMD), *The Psalter Hymnal,* 48
"How Great Is the Lord, and Worthy of Praise," *Psalter for Christian Worship,* 61
RESPONSORIAL—
"Psalm 48," Howard Hughes, *The Psalter* (1993), 43
CHORAL/VOCAL—
"Great Is the Lord," David Ashley White (SATB), Hinshaw

ADDITIONAL SONGS

"Bless the Lord, My Soul," Jacques Berthier, *Songs and Prayers from Taizé*, GIA
"Dona Nobis Pacem," *LUYH,* 100

CHORAL/VOCAL

"Lord, Help Us Walk Your Servant Way," Randall Sansmeier (SATB), GIA G-4368
"Will You Come and Follow Me?" John Bell (SATB/solo), GIA G-4384

ORGAN

"Come, Thou Fount of Every Blessing," Gerre Hancock, in *The Bristol Connection,* vol. 1, Flammer, 5.
"Toccata on 'How Brightly Shines,'" Garth Edmundson, H. W. Gray

PIANO

"Send Me, Lord," Mark Sedio, *Dancing in the Light of God*, Augsburg-Fortress
"To God Be the Glory," John Carter, in *Hymns for Piano,* Hope, 10

HANDBELL

"Thee We Adore," Cathy Moklebust (2 octaves), Choristers Guild

STUDY CATECHISM

For today's questions and answers, see pp. 225–26.

July 13, 2003

2 Samuel 6:1–5, 12b–19 — David leads the procession and the dance following the recovery of the ark of the covenant.

Psalm 24 — A song of Zion praising God as creator and defender.

Ephesians 1:3–14 — God blesses Christians with the Holy Spirit and calls them to a vocation in Jesus Christ.

Mark 6:14–29 — The imprisonment and execution of John the Baptist.

Theme(s) of lectionary texts: Jubilation in David's court. Unity in Christ. The death of John the Baptist.

CALL TO WORSHIP

The earth is the Lord's, and all that is in it,
   the world and those who dwell in it.
**For the Lord founded it upon the waters
   and made the earth stand firm above the rivers.**
Lift up your heads, O gates;
   lift them high, O everlasting doors.
**For the Lord of hosts approaches,
   entering our midst in glory.**
Who is this glorious Sovereign?
**Our Lord, the Lord of hosts,
   is the Sovereign who rules in our midst.**

SUGGESTED HYMNS

ENTRANCE/GATHERING HYMNS	HB	LBW	NCH	PH	RL	TFF	WOV
"All People That On Earth Do Dwell"	24	245	7	220–21	120	—	—
"O God, Beyond All Praising"	—	—	—	—	—	—	797
"Rejoice, Ye Pure in Heart"	407	—	55	145–46	—	—	—
HYMNS RELATED TO SCRIPTURE							
O—"Earth and All Stars"	—	558	—	458	33	—	—
"Let All the Earth in Every Corner Sing"	22	—	—	468	11	—	—
E—"Lord, We Have Come at Your Own Invitation"	—	—	—	516	—	—	—
"There's a Wideness in God's Mercy"	110	290	23	298	349	—	—
G—"Faith of Our Fathers"	348	500	381	—	—	—	—
"God of Grace and God of Glory"	358	415	436	420	416	—	—
HYMNS OF THE TABLE							
"Blessed Assurance, Jesus Is Mine"	139	—	473	341	453	118	699
"I'll Praise My Maker While I've Breath"	—	—	—	253	140	—	—
"When in Our Music, God Is Glorified"	—	555	561	264	508	—	802
SENDING FORTH							
"Joyful, Joyful, We Adore Thee"	21	551	4	464	521	—	—
"On Our Way Rejoicing"	80	260	—	—	—	—	—

Fifteenth Sunday in Ordinary Time

Color: Green

PRAYER OF CONFESSION

God of all joy,
you have invited us
to enter your presence boldly;
yet we have turned away from you.
You have opened the way for us
to celebrate our relationship with you joyously,
but we have held back in fear.
We confess that we have resisted
your summons to intimacy.

Forgive us for turning from you;
By your gentle and firm Spirit,
bend us from our stubborn resistance.
Warm our hearts to welcome your embrace;
quicken our voices to sing your praise,
and our feet to dance with joy,
in bold assurance and glad celebration,
that we are indeed beloved by you,
and that through Christ you reign over all.

HYMN OF ASSURANCE

"Psalm 24—The King of Glory Comes," *PH,* 177

PSALM 24

METRICAL—
"Lift Up Your Heads, Ye Mighty Gates," *PH,* 8
"The Earth and All That Dwell Therein," *PH,* 176
RESPONSORIAL—
"Psalm 24," John Ferguson, *PH,* 177
CHORAL/VOCAL—
"Lift Up Your Heads," Deborah Holden-Halloway (SATB), Selah
"The Earth Is the Lord's," Don McAfee (solo), *The Solo Psalmist,* SMP

ADDITIONAL SONGS

"I Am the Light of the World," Jim Strathdee, *LUYH,* 144
"In the Bulb There Is a Flower," Natalie Sleeth, *LUYH,* 88

CHORAL/VOCAL

"Lift Up Your Heads, O Ye Gates," Peter Aston (SATB), Basil Ramsey, 1025
"My Jesus Is My Lasting Joy," Dietrich Buxtehude (unison), H. W. Gray GCMR 02727
"Your Mercy Like Rain," Rory Cooney (SATB/cantor), GIA

ORGAN

"Joyful, Joyful, We Adore Thee," Robert Powell, *Processional on "Hymn of Joy"* (2 trumpets), Flammer
"There's a Wideness in God's Mercy," Richard Purvis, *Seven Chorale Preludes,* Carl Fischer, 26

PIANO

"Lift Up Your Heads," Angela Tipps, *Keys of the Kingdom,* vol. 2, 22

HANDBELL

"When I Survey the Wondrous Cross," Hal Hopson (2 octaves), Lorenz

STUDY CATECHISM

For today's questions and answers, see pp. 226–27.

July 20, 2003

2 Samuel 7:1–14a — God establishes David as king over God's people on earth.

Psalm 89:20–37 — God's promise to sustain the descendants of David.

Ephesians 2:11–22 — Christ breaks down the dividing walls of hostility, reconciling us to our divided selves, to our neighbors, and to God.

Mark 6:30–34, 53–56 — Jesus has compassion on followers who have been wandering like sheep without a shepherd.

Theme(s) of lectionary texts: God calls men and women into community, and creates a united people.

CALL TO WORSHIP

The Lord says,
"I will establish the heirs of David forever.
His throne will endure,
as the days of heaven.
I will not take my love from him,
nor allow my faithfulness to prove false.
I will never break my covenant,
nor change the words that have passed my lips.
David's royal line shall endure forever
and his throne as the sun before me.
My promise will last forever, like the moon,
an abiding witness in the sky."

SUGGESTED HYMNS

ENTRANCE/GATHERING HYMNS	HB	LBW	NCH	PH	RL	TFF	WOV
"All Hail the Power of Jesus' Name"	132	328–29	304	142–43	593	267	—
"Christ Is Made the Sure Foundation"	433	367	400	416–17	392	—	747
HYMNS RELATED TO SCRIPTURE							
O—"I Love Thy Kingdom, Lord"	435	368	—	441	409	—	—
"The God of Abraham Praise"	89	544	24	488	595	—	—
E—"Alleluia, Sing to Jesus"	—	158	—	144	346	—	—
"O Praise the Gracious Power"	—	—	54	471	—	—	750
"Sheaves of Summer"	—	—	338	518	—	—	—
G—"Dear Lord and Father of Mankind"	416	506	502	345	—	—	—
"Live into Hope"	—	—	—	332	—	—	—
HYMNS OF THE TABLE							
"Let Us Break Bread Together"	447	212	330	513	545	123	—
"The Church of Christ in Every Age"	—	433	306	421	—	—	—
SENDING FORTH							
"God Is My Strong Salvation"	347	—	—	179	95	—	—
"Where Cross the Crowded Ways of Life"	507	429	543	408	482	—	—

Sixteenth Sunday in Ordinary Time

Color: Green

PRAYER OF CONFESSION

Living and true Word of God,
you have called us to love the Lord our God with
    all our hearts,
and to love one another as you have loved us.
You have made peace between us by your cross,
yet we have refused to live in that peace.
We have kept grudges;
we have put others down
when you have called us to build one another up.

Forgive our unwillingness to embrace your peace.
By your Spirit, help us to love each other
just as you have loved us;
empower us to be true peacemakers in a world
where peace is thought impossible,
and peacemakers are scorned;
to the glory of the God of all peace.

HYMN OF ASSURANCE

"Walk On, People of God," *PH,* 296

PSALM 89

METRICAL—
"Forever I Will Sing of Your Great Love," *Psalter
    Hymnal,* 89
RESPONSORIAL—
"Psalm 89," *The Psalter* (1993), 82
CHORAL/VOCAL—
"O Lord, My Rock of Salvation," G. F. Handel
    (SATB), Theodore Presser
"Veritas Mea," George Malcolm (SATB), Mayhew

ADDITIONAL SONGS

"Shout for Joy to God," Hal Hopson, *LUYH,* 116
"Sovereign Lord," Dave Hopkins, *LUYH,* 95

CHORAL/VOCAL

"My Shepherd Will Supply My Need," Virgil
    Thompson (SATB), H. W. Gray, 2571
"The Prophecy," Robert Powell (SAB), H. W. Gray
    GCMR 3413
"Ye Are Fellow Citizens of the Saints," Charles F.
    Waters (SATB), Novello NCM 15

ORGAN

"Adagio," from Symphony V, Charles-Marie Widor,
    various editions

PIANO

"Variations on Beautiful Savior," Curt Oliver,
    MorningStar

HANDBELL

"Fairest Lord Jesus," Charles Maggs (2–3 octaves),
    Cantabile

STUDY CATECHISM

For today's questions and answers, see p. 227.

July 27, 2003

2 Samuel 11:1–15 — David's great transgression with Bathsheba, and his murderous sin against Uriah.

Psalm 14 — Fools deny God, but the people of Zion find refuge in the Lord.

Ephesians 3:14–21 — A prayer for human comprehension of the immeasurable greatness of God's love.

John 6:1–21 — The feeding of the five thousand; thereafter, Christ walks on the water.

Theme(s) of lectionary texts: God's grace is sufficient to overcome human sin and doubt.

CALL TO WORSHIP

Fools say in their heart, "There is no God."
    There is none who does a single good thing.
The Lord looks down to see if anyone is wise,
    if there is a single person who seeks after God.
But everyone proves faithless:
    none is righteous in God's eyes; no, not one.
But the Lord is the refuge of the people of God,
    dwelling in the company of the chosen.
Israel's deliverance will come,
    proclaimed from the city of Jerusalem.
When the Lord restores the fortunes of God's people,
    Jacob will rejoice and Israel will be glad!

SUGGESTED HYMNS

ENTRANCE/GATHERING HYMNS	HB	LBW	NCH	PH	RL	TFF	WOV
"Praise, My Soul, the King of Heaven"	31	549	—	478–79	144	—	—
"Praise Ye the Lord, the Almighty"	1	543	—	482	145	—	—
HYMNS RELATED TO SCRIPTURE							
O—"Guide Me, O Thou Great Jehovah"	339	343	18–19	281	50	—	—
"Spirit of God, Descend Upon My Heart"	236	486	290	326	445	—	—
E—"Eternal God, Whose Power Upholds"	485	—	—	412	481	—	—
"Love Divine, All Loves Excelling"	399	315	43	376	464	—	—
"What a Friend We Have in Jesus"	385	439	506	403	507	—	—
G—"Lord, Speak to Me, That I May Speak"	298	403	531	426	436	—	—
"O Word of God Incarnate"	251	231	315	327	387	—	—
HYMNS OF THE TABLE							
"Come, Ye Faithful, Raise the Strain"	205	132	230	114–15	315–16	—	—
"You Satisfy the Hungry Heart"	—	—	—	521	—	—	711
SENDING FORTH							
"On What Has Now Been Sown"	—	261	—	—	—	—	—
"Ye Servants of God, Your Master Proclaim"	27	252	305	477	598	—	—

Seventeenth Sunday in Ordinary Time

Color: Green

PRAYER OF CONFESSION

Gracious Provider,
you have given us all we have needed,
just as you have promised.
Your bread has always been sufficient to sustain us,
and your gifts of faithful companions
have made our lives rich with love and security.
Yet we seek after other bread,
and break faith with friends who have been faithful
 to us.
In turning away from these, your gifts,
we have rejected you,
O Giver of all that is good in our lives.

Forgive our ingratitude and unfaithfulness.
Spirit of all comfort, soothe our seething souls.
Renew us by your love,
that we embrace with thanksgiving and singleness
 of heart
all your good gifts of love—
that our lips would declare
and our lives would display
genuine gratitude and unwavering confidence
that your love for us will never fail;
through Jesus Christ, our Lord.

HYMN OF ASSURANCE

"Guide Me, O Thou Great Jehovah," *PH,* 281

PSALM 14

METRICAL—
"The Foolish Heart Denies the Lord" (CM), *Psalter
 for Christian Worship,* 24
"The Foolish in Their Hearts Deny" (CMD), *The
 Psalter Hymnal,* 14
RESPONSORIAL—
"Psalm 14," John Ferguson, *The Psalter* (1993), 8

CHORAL—

"O That Salvation for Israel Would Come," Johann
 Geisler (SS[A]TB), Boosey & Hawkes

ADDITIONAL SONGS

"How Can I Keep from Singing?" Robert Lowry,
 LUYH, 34
"Lord, Be Glorified," Bob Kilpatrick, *LUYH,* 43

CHORAL/VOCAL

"For This Cause," Harold Friedell (SATB), H. W.
 Gray CMR 2622 (M)
"Jesus Fed the Hungry Thousands," Hal Hopson
 (unison), Hope (A)

ORGAN

"Kommst Du Nun, Jesu" (Schuebler Chorale No. 6),
 J. S. Bach, various editions
"Lobe den Herren," Johann G. Walther, *80 Chorale
 Preludes,* C. F. Peters

PIANO

"Jesus, the Very Thought of Thee," Mark Sedio, *Music
 for the Paschal Season,* Augsburg-Fortress, 63
"O Love, How Deep," Angela Tipps, *Keys of the
 Kingdom,* vol. 5, Abingdon, 32

HANDBELL

"Hosanna, Loud Hosanna," Barbara Kinyon (2–3
 octaves), Agape

STUDY CATECHISM

For today's questions and answers, see pp. 227–28.

August 3, 2003

2 Samuel 11:26–12:13a — The prophet Nathan's parable of the ewe lamb.

Psalm 51:1–12 — A psalm of confession; a prayer for mercy.

Ephesians 4:1–16 — The fundamental unity of the body of Christ.

John 6:24–35 — Jesus tells the crowd, "I am the bread of life."

Theme(s) of lectionary texts: Sin, repentance, and restitution. The bread of life.

CALL TO WORSHIP

Have mercy upon us, O God,
 according to your loving kindness.
**Wash away our wickedness,
 and cleanse us from our sin.**
Let me hear of joy and gladness,
 that my shattered being may rejoice.
**Create in me a clean heart, O God,
 and renew a right spirit within me.**
Cast me not away from your presence
 and take not your Spirit from me.
**Give me, O Lord, the joy of your salvation
 and sustain me with your bountiful Spirit.**

SUGGESTED HYMNS

ENTRANCE/GATHERING HYMNS	HB	LBW	NCH	PH	RL	TFF	WOV
"For the Fruit of All Creation"	—	563	425	553	21	—	760
"Rejoice, Ye Pure in Heart"	407	—	55	145–46	—	—	—
HYMNS RELATED TO SCRIPTURE							
O—"Just As I Am, without One Plea"	272	296	207	370	467–68	—	—
"What Does the Lord Require?"	—	—	—	405	176	—	—
E—"All Hail the Power of Jesus' Name"	132	328–29	304	142–43	593–94	267	—
"Christ, You Are the Fullness"	—	—	—	346	—	—	—
G—"Become to Us the Living Bread"	—	—	—	500	—	—	—
"Deck Yourself, My Soul, with Gladness"	—	224	—	506	536	—	—
"I Come with Joy to Meet My Lord"	—	—	349	507	534	—	—
HYMNS OF THE TABLE							
"Here, O My Lord, I See Thee Face to Face"	442	211	336	520	549	—	—
"I Am the Bread of Life"	—	—	—	—	—	—	702
"O God, Our Faithful God"	—	504	—	277	69	—	—
"Welcoming Table"	—	—	—	—	—	263	—
SENDING FORTH							
"Blessed Assurance, Jesus Is Mine"	—	—	—	341	—	118	699
"For the Bread Which You Have Broken"	449	200	—	508–509	547	—	—

Eighteenth Sunday in Ordinary Time

Color: Green

PRAYER OF CONFESSION

Have mercy on us, O God,
according to your unfailing love;
according to your great compassion blot out our
transgressions.
Wash away all our iniquity and cleanse us from sin.
Create in us a pure heart, O God,
and renew a steadfast spirit within us.
Do not cast us from your presence
or take your Holy Spirit from us.
Restore to us the joy of your salvation
and grant a willing spirit to sustain us.

HYMN OF ASSURANCE

"Amazing Grace, How Sweet the Sound," *PH,* 280

PSALM 51

METRICAL—
"Have Mercy on Us, Living Lord," *PH,* 195
RESPONSORIAL—
"Psalm 51," David Clark Isele, *PH,* 196
CHORAL—
"Create in Me a Clean Heart, O God," Dan Locklair
(SATB), Paraclete Press
"Create in Me a Clean Heart, O God," John
Mochnick (SATB), Augsburg-Fortress
"Have Mercy on Me, O God," Peter Pindar Stearns
(SATB), Paraclete Press

ADDITIONAL SONGS

"Bread, Blessed and Broken," Michael Lynch, *LUYH,*
123
"I Am the Bread of Life," S. Suzanne Toolan, *LUYH,*
128

CHORAL/VOCAL

"Bread of the World," Calvin Hampton (SATB/
soloists), Selah, 410–23
"Thee We Adore, O Hidden Savior, Thee,"
T. Frederick/H. Candlyn (SATB), Carl Fischer
CM492
"Thee We Adore, O Hidden Savior, Thee,"
A. Guilmont, K. Lee Scott, arr. (SATB),
Concordia 98-2829

ORGAN

"Deck Thyself, My Soul, with Gladness," J. S. Bach,
various editions
"Lord, Enthroned in Heavenly Splendor," Ralph
Vaughn Williams, *Three Preludes on Welsh Hymn
Tunes,* Galaxy

PIANO

"Bread of the World, in Mercy Broken," Angela
Tipps, *Keys of the Kingdom,* vol. 4, Abingdon, 7

HANDBELL

"I Am the Bread of Life," Jeffery Hall (3–5 octaves/
1–3 octaves chimes), CPH

STUDY CATECHISM

For today's questions and answers, see p. 228.

August 10, 2003

2 Samuel 18:5–9, 15, 31–33 — David mourns over the death of his rebellious son Absalom.

Psalm 130 — A song of lament; a cry from the depths of despair.

Ephesians 4:25–5:2 — A pattern for living the new life in Christ.

John 6:35, 41–51 — Jesus, the living bread, offers eternal life to those who respond in faith.

Theme(s) of lectionary texts: The reality of death; the possibilities of new life.

CALL TO WORSHIP

Out of the depths
    I have called to you, O Lord.
Lord, hear my voice
    and consider my prayers of intercession.
I wait for you, O Lord,
    my soul waits.
My soul waits for the Lord
    as sentries keep watch at dawn.
O People of God: Wait for the Lord,
    for with the Lord there is mercy;
there is a wealth of redemption with God
    who redeems the penitent from all their sins.

SUGGESTED HYMNS

ENTRANCE/GATHERING HYMNS	HB	LBW	NCH	PH	RL	TFF	WOV
"Guide Me, O Thou Great Jehovah"	339	343	18–19	281	50	—	—
"Hope of the World"	291	493	46	360	414	—	—
HYMNS RELATED TO SCRIPTURE							
O—"Abide with Me"	64	272	99	543	440	—	—
"Come, Ye Disconsolate"	373	—	—	—	—	186	—
"O Day of God, Draw Nigh"	—	—	611	452	178	—	—
E—"Forgive Our Sins As We Forgive"	—	307	—	347	—	—	—
"For the Fruit of All Creation"	—	563	425	553	21	—	760
G—"Become to Us the Living Bread"	—	—	—	500	—	—	—
"Bread of Heaven, on Thee We Feed"—	—	—	501	—	—	—	—
HYMNS OF THE TABLE							
"Blessed Jesus, at Your Word"	—	—	—	454	530	—	—
"You Satisfy the Hungry Heart"	—	—	—	521	—	—	711
SENDING FORTH							
"O God of Earth and Altar"	511	428	582	291	80	—	—
"Thine the Amen, Thine the Praise"	—	—	—	—	—	—	801

Nineteenth Sunday in Ordinary Time

Color: Green

PRAYER OF CONFESSION

Righteous and merciful Judge:
we know that the wages of sin is death,
and we acknowledge that we are sinners;
we have chosen death, rather than life.

Look upon us in mercy, and forgive us.
Reach out to us in our despair,
redeem us from our sentence of death,
and release us from our dungeon of sin,
through the life, death, and resurrection
of our Lord and Savior, Jesus Christ.
Empower us by your Spirit
to live according to your holy will,
always bearing witness to your goodness and
    grace—
that in us and through us
your boundless compassion
and reconciling love
would be proclaimed with power,
to the praise of your glorious grace.

HYMN OF ASSURANCE

"Out of the Depths," *PH,* 240

PSALM 130

METRICAL—
"Out of the Depths," *PH,* 240
RESPONSORIAL—
"Psalm 130," Hal Hopson, *The Psalter* (1993), 134
CHORAL—
"Hear My Cry, My Holy One," David Ashley White
    (SATB), Paraclete Press
SOLO—
"Out of the Depths," Eugene Butler, *The Solo*
    Psalmist, SMP

ADDITIONAL SONGS

"Eat This Bread," Daniel Charles Damon, *LUYH,*
    127
"Partakers of the Holy Food," Kevin Boyd, *LUYH,*
    131

CHORAL/VOCAL

"David's Lament," Rick Sowatch (SATB), Music 70
    M70-524
"Grieve Not the Holy Spirit," John Staines (SATB),
    Mark Foster MF2029

ORGAN

"Blessed Jesus, At Your Word," Sigrid Karg-Elert,
    Choral-Improvisations, vol. 6, Marks, 8
"Guide Me, O Thou Great Jehovah," John Ferguson,
    A New Liturgical Year, Augsburg-Fortress

PIANO

"Abide with Me," Angela Tipps, *Keys of the Kingdom,*
    vol. 3, Abingdon, 34
"Out of the Depths," Reginald Gerig, in *Piano*
    Preludes on Hymns and Chorales, Hope, 18

HANDBELL

"Guide Me, O Thou Great Jehovah," Cathy
    Moklebust (2–3 or 4–5 octaves), *Hymn Stanzas for*
    Handbells, Augsburg-Fortress

STUDY CATECHISM

For today's questions and answers, see p. 229.

August 17, 2003

1 Kings 2:10–12; 3:3–14 — Solomon succeeds his father David as king.

Psalm 111 — A song of thanksgiving for God's greatness.

Ephesians 5:15–20 — Walking as the redeemed children of God.

John 6:51–58 — Jesus challenges those who hear to find their nourishment and strength in him.

Theme(s) of lectionary texts: Transformation and rededication. Songs of rejoicing.

CALL TO WORSHIP

In the midst of the congregation
    I will give thanks to God with all my heart.
Great are the mighty works of the Lord!
    God's deeds are studied by all who delight in them.
The Lord gives food to those who fear God,
    always remembering the covenant.
God's deeds are established forever and ever,
    because they are conceived in truth and justice.
Holy and awesome is the name of the Lord
    who has commanded the covenant forever.
The fear of the Lord is the beginning of wisdom;
    the praise of the Lord endures forever!

SUGGESTED HYMNS

ENTRANCE/GATHERING HYMNS	HB	LBW	NCH	PH	RL	TFF	WOV
"Be Thou My Vision"	303	—	451	339	67	—	776
"When in Our Music God Is Glorified"	—	555	561	264	508	—	802
"When Morning Gilds the Skies"	41	545–46	86	487	365	—	—
HYMNS RELATED TO SCRIPTURE							
O—"God's Law Is Perfect and Gives Life"	—	—	—	167	—	—	—
"Take Thou Our Minds, Dear Lord"	306	—	—	392	434	—	—
E—"Spirit of God, Descend Upon My Heart"	236	486	290	326	445	—	—
"With Glad Exuberant Carolings"	—	—	—	490	—	—	—
G—"God Is Here"	—	—	70	461	—	—	719
"We Come As Guests Invited"	—	—	—	517	—	—	—
HYMNS OF THE TABLE							
"Let All Mortal Flesh Keep Silence"	148	198	345	5	188	—	—
"There's a Sweet, Sweet Spirit in the Air"	—	—	293	398	—	102	—
SENDING FORTH							
"Let All Things Now Living"	—	557	—	554	—	—	—
"O Master, Let Me Walk with Thee"	304	492	502	357	428	—	—

Twentieth Sunday in Ordinary Time

Color: Green

PRAYER OF CONFESSION

Ruler of all,
we confess that we have sought to please ourselves
instead of glorifying you.
We have set aside the fear of the Lord,
which is the beginning of wisdom,
and have relied upon our own strength
rather than upon your Spirit.

Forgive our stubborn insistence
on doing things our own way,
and serving you on our own terms;
teach us to seek your kingdom first,
and your justice before all else,
confident that your promise to care for us
is fully trustworthy,
through Jesus Christ our Lord.

HYMN OF ASSURANCE

"Seek Ye First," *PH,* 333

PSALM 111

METRICAL—
"Psalm 111," Carl Schalk, *Eight Psalms,* Augsburg-Fortress
"With My Heart I Praise My Maker," *Psalter for Christian Worship,* 128
RESPONSORIAL—
"Psalm 111," Hal Hopson, *The Psalter (1993),* 111
CHORAL/VOCAL—
"*Confitebor Tibi,*" Johann Hasse (SATB), Carl Fischer
"I Will Give Thanks to the Lord," David Cherwien (unison), CPH
"My Heart Is Full Today," Richard Proulx (2-part; children), Augsburg-Fortress

ADDITIONAL SONGS

"Great Is the Lord," Michael W. Smith, *LUYH,* 30
"I Will Call Upon the Lord," Michael O'Shields, *LUYH,* 7
"Thou Art Worthy," Pauline Michael Mills, *LUYH,* 54

CHORAL/VOCAL

"Let All the World in Every Corner Sing," Richard Proulx (SATB), Selah 418-601
"When in Our Music God Is Glorified," William Rowan (SATB), Selah 420-110

ORGAN

"I Come, O Savior, to Your Table," Carl Ziebell, Northwestern
"Partita on 'Come Let Us Eat,'" Tim Fields, MorningStar

PIANO

"Spirit of God, Descend Upon My Heart," John Carter, in *Hymns for Piano,* Hope, 6

HANDBELL

"The Church's One Foundation," Douglas Wagner (3–5 octaves/brass), AGEHR

STUDY CATECHISM

For today's questions and answers, see p. 229.

August 24, 2003

1 Kings 8:(1, 6, 10–11) 22–30, 41–43 — Solomon prays at the dedication of the Temple.

Psalm 84 — A song of the Temple rejoicing in the presence of the Lord.

Ephesians 6:10–20 — Putting on the full armor of God.

John 6:55–69 — Peter proclaims Jesus as the Holy One of God.

Theme(s) of lectionary texts: Community worship and personal commitment as responses to God's covenant love.

CALL TO WORSHIP

My soul longs for your place of worship, Lord;
my heart and being rejoice in your living presence.
**The sparrow has a dwelling, and the swallow a nest,
in the shadow of your sanctuary, my Lord and my
God.**
Happy are those who inhabit your house,
for they may ever praise you.
**Happy are the people whose strength is in God,
for their hearts are set on the pilgrim way.**
Lord God of hosts,
hear our prayers as we worship.
**For you, O Lord, are our sun and our shield;
yours alone is the grace and the glory.**

SUGGESTED HYMNS

ENTRANCE/GATHERING HYMNS	HB	LBW	NCH	PH	RL	TFF	WOV
"For the Beauty of the Earth"	2	561	28	473	5	—	—
"Glorious Things of Thee Are Spoken"	434	358	307	446	393	—	—
HYMNS RELATED TO SCRIPTURE							
O—"How Lovely, Lord"	—	—	—	207	—	—	—
"Immortal, Invisible, God Only Wise"	85	526	1	263	7	—	—
E—"Christ Is Alive!"	—	363	—	108	—	—	—
"Fight the Good Fight"	359	461	—	307	—	—	—
G—"Blessed Assurance"	139	—	473	341	453	118	699
"For the Bread Which You Have Broken"	449	200	—	508–509	547	—	—
HYMNS OF THE TABLE							
"Draw Us in the Spirit's Tether"	—	—	337	504	—	—	703
"Eat This Bread, Drink This Cup"	—	—	—	—	—	—	706
SENDING FORTH							
"Lead On, O King Eternal"	332	495	573	447–48	423	—	—
"Now Thank We All Our God"	9	533–34	419	555	61	—	—
"Stand Up, Stand Up for Jesus"	349	389	—	—	—	—	—

Twenty-First Sunday in Ordinary Time

Color: Green

PRAYER OF CONFESSION

Almighty Sovereign,
who alone dwells in light and holiness—
we come before you as a sinful people,
unworthy to stand in your awesome presence.
We confess that we have not stood firm
in resistance to the evils
that pervade within us and around us.
Our sin has led us away from you,
and our pride has kept us from returning to you.

Draw us again to your dwelling place,
and heal our backsliding.
Cleanse us, sanctify us, empower us—
that we may be your faithful ambassadors,
a people holy unto you,
for the sake of the world,
and of our holy Savior,
Jesus, your Anointed Deliverer.

HYMN OF ASSURANCE

"How Lovely, Lord," *PH,* 207

PSALM 84

METRICAL—
"How Lovely, Lord," *PH,* 207
RESPONSORIAL—
"Psalm 84," Chrysogonus Waddell, *PH,* 208
CHORAL—
"How Dear to Me Is Your Dwelling," David Hurd
(2-part), Augsburg-Fortress
"It Is to God I Shall Sing," Samuel Adler (SATB,
div.), Paraclete Press

ADDITIONAL SONGS

"Love the Lord Your God," Jean and Jim Strathdee,
LUYH, 96

"You Are Here," Martin Nystrom and Don Moen,
LUYH, 18

CHORAL/VOCAL

"Adorn Yourself, My Soul," Johann Peter (SATB),
Hinshaw HMC-1123
"Be Strong in the Lord," Sydney Nicholson (SS),
Corwen ASCM 1528
"Hear the Voice and Prayer of Thy Servants," Thomas
Tallis (SATB), Novello NECM 18

ORGAN

"Glorious Things of Thee Are Spoken," John Knowles
Paine, *Complete Works,* McAfee Music, 23
"Immortal, Invisible," Emma Lou Diemer, *With
Praise and Love,* SMP, 23

PIANO

"Jesus, the Very Thought of Thee," Fred Bock, *Bock's
Best,* vol. 4, Fred Bock Music

HANDBELL

"My Jesus, I Love Thee," David Peninger (2 octaves),
Van Ness Press

STUDY CATECHISM

For today's questions and answers, see pp. 229–30.

August 31, 2003

Song of Solomon 2:8–13 — The renewing power of love.

Psalm 45:1–2, 6–9 — An enthronement song for the crowning of a new king in Jerusalem.

James 1:17–27 — Turn from human desires, and act according to God's Word.

Mark 7:1–8, 14–15, 21–23 — The things that make a person unclean.

Theme(s) of lectionary texts: New love, new life, new insights.

CALL TO WORSHIP

God's anointed is fair and gracious,
 full of blessing and inspiration.
**You have been set upon the throne forever,
 reigning with a scepter of righteousness.**
The Lord loves righteousness
 and hates iniquity.
**Therefore, God has anointed you
 and raised you up above the people.**
**In the temple, music resounds
 and the hearts of the people are glad.**

SUGGESTED HYMNS

ENTRANCE/GATHERING HYMNS	HB	LBW	NCH	PH	RL	TFF	WOV
"All My Hope on God Is Founded"	—	—	408	—	156–57	—	782
"Come, Thou Fount of Every Blessing"	379	499	459	356	449	108	—
"O Worship the King"	26	548	—	476	2	—	—
HYMNS RELATED TO SCRIPTURE							
O—"All Things Bright and Beautiful"	456	—	31	267	15	—	767
"My Song Is Love Unknown"	—	94	222	76	284	—	661
"What Wondrous Love Is This"	—	385	223	85	—	—	—
E—"Great Is Thy Faithfulness"	—	—	423	276	155	283	771
"The Church's One Foundation"	437	369	386	442	394	—	—
G—"As a Chalice, Cast of Gold"	—	—	—	336	—	—	—
"Jesu, Jesu, Fill Us with Your Love"	—	—	498	367	—	83	765
"Lord, Whose Love through Humble Service"	—	423	—	427	—	—	—
HYMNS OF THE TABLE							
"An Upper Room Did Our Lord Prepare"	—	—	—	94	—	—	—
"Let Us with a Gladsome Mind"	28	521	—	244	136	—	—
SENDING FORTH							
"Holy God, We Praise Your Name"	—	535	276	460	619	—	—
"O That the Lord Would Guide My Ways"	—	480	—	—	—	—	—

Twenty-Second Sunday in Ordinary Time

Color: Green

PRAYER OF CONFESSION

Fountain of Love,
You lavish us with gracious welcome.
Even when we spurn your love,
you continue to reach out to us,
sending us every good and perfect gift,
calling us ever back into your embrace.
Yet we take your nearness for granted;
we are careless about the most precious treasures,
while consumed with things that are trivial.

In your tender mercy, forgive us.
Melt our coldness of heart,
and give us a new heart of abiding and passionate
**   love**
for one another, as well as for you;
that our love may flourish in grateful response
to the treasures of love you have lavished upon us
through Jesus of Nazareth,
your Son and our Lord.

HYMN OF ASSURANCE

"Love Divine, All Loves Excelling," *PH,* 376

PSALM 45

METRICAL—
"How Our Hearts with Joy Abound," *Psalter for Christian Worship,* 57
RESPONSORIAL—
"Psalm 45," *The Psalter* (1993), 39
CHORAL/VOCAL—
"Grace Is Poured Abroad," Daniel Pinkham (SATB), C. F. Peters
"How Lovely Shines the Morning Star," Harald Rohlig (SAB), CPH
"O Morning Star, So Pure, So Bright," Ludwig Lenel (unison), CPH

ADDITIONAL SONGS

"By Grace We Have Been Saved," Rusty Edwards, *Worship & Praise,* 25
"You Are Mighty," Craig Musseau, *LUYH,* 149

CHORAL/VOCAL

"Arise, My Love, My Fair One," Richard DeLong (SATB), E. C. Schirmer
"First Fruits," Ralph M. Johnson (2-part, mixed), Augsburg-Fortress 11-10205
"The Call," David Ashley White (SATB), Selah 418-606

ORGAN

"Inward Light," Margaret Sandresky, *Margaret Sandresky Organ Music,* vol. 2, Wayne Leopold Editions WL 600032

PIANO

"For the Beauty of the Earth," Angela Tipps, *Keys to the Kingdom,* vol. 1, Abingdon, 12

HANDBELL

"Hail the Day That Sees Him Rise," Hal Hopson (2 octaves), Lorenz

STUDY CATECHISM

For today's questions and answers, see pp. 230–31.

September 7, 2003

Proverbs 22:1–2, 8–9	Those who are generous are blessed.
Psalm 125	Trust in the Lord, and be true to God.
James 2:1–10 (11–13), 14–18	By your works, you demonstrate your faith.
Mark 7:24–37	Jesus heals a Gentile woman.

Theme(s) of lectionary texts: Virtues that reflect grace and faithfulness. Healing from affliction.

CALL TO WORSHIP

Those who trust in the Lord stand firm,
    like Mount Zion which cannot be moved.
As the hills surround Jerusalem,
    so the Lord encircles the people of God.
The wicked shall not long hold sway
    over a land populated by the just.
Those who are true to God
    will not soon turn their hands to evil.
Show your goodness, O Lord,
    to all who are true of heart.
Lead away evildoers into exile, O God,
    but may peace remain upon your people.

SUGGESTED HYMNS

ENTRANCE/GATHERING HYMNS	HB	LBW	NCH	PH	RL	TFF	WOV
"God of the Ages"	515	567	592	262	494	—	—
"Hail Thee, Festival Day"	—	142	262	120	—	—	—
HYMNS RELATED TO SCRIPTURE							
O—"Arise, Your Light Is Come"	497	—	164	411	418	—	652
"O Lord, Open My Eyes"	—	—	—	—	—	134	—
E—"Behold the Goodness of the Lord"	—	—	—	241	—	—	—
"O Master, Let Me Walk with Thee"	304	492	502	357	428	—	—
"Though I May Speak"	—	—	—	335	—	—	—
G—"I Come with Joy"	—	—	349	507	534	—	—
"O for a Thousand Tongues to Sing"	141	559	42	466	362–63	—	—
HYMNS OF THE TABLE							
"God, Whose Giving Knows No Ending"	—	408	565	422	—	—	—
"There Is a Balm in Gilead"	—	—	553	394	465	185	737
SENDING FORTH							
"O for a World"	—	—	575	386	—	—	—
"We All Are One in Mission"	—	—	—	435	—	—	755

Twenty-Third Sunday in Ordinary Time

Color: Green

PRAYER OF CONFESSION

Righteous God,
we confess that we have sinned against you
in thought, word, and deed.
We have professed our faith in you,
and our loyalty to you;
but our words ring hollow.
We do not live by the truth we speak.

Forgive us for seeking to serve you
merely by saying the right things.
Empower us by your Spirit
to live according to your word.
so that people may see our good works,
and glorify you as the true Savior and Redeemer.

HYMN OF ASSURANCE

"Blest Are the Uncorrupt in Heart," *PH,* 233

PSALM 125

METRICAL—
"All Who with Heart Confiding," *Psalter Hymnal,* 125
"Those Who Place on God Reliance," *Psalter for Christian Worship,* 146
RESPONSORIAL—
"Psalm 125," Hal Hopson, *The Psalter* (1993), 129
CHORAL—
"All Who with Heart Confiding," Orlando DiLasso (SATB), Elkan-Vogel
"They That Put Their Trust in the Lord," Robin Orr (SATB), Oxford
"They Who Trust in the Lord," Peter Hallock (SATB), GIA

ADDITIONAL SONGS

"Go with God," Isaiah Jones Jr., *LUYH,* 138
"Healing Grace," Gary Sadler/John Chisum, *LUYH,* 68
"Lord of All," Danny Daniels, *LUYH,* 42

CHORAL/VOCAL

"Ecce Dominus," Gerald Near (SATB), Aureole Editions AE59
"He Hath Done All Things Well," Jan Bender (SATB), Concordia 98-1067
"Soundless Were the Tossing Trees," Carol Doran/ Thomas Troeger (unison), in *New Hymns for the Lectionary,* Oxford

ORGAN

"I Sing the Mighty Power of God," Flor Peeters, *Hymn Preludes for the Liturgical Year,* vol. 12, C. F. Peters
"O for a Thousand Tongues to Sing," Emma Lou Diemer, *With Praise and Love,* vol. 1, SMP

PIANO

"O Sacred Head, Now Wounded," Fred Bock, *Bock's Best,* vol. 4, Fred Bock Music, 86

HANDBELL

"Canticle of Faith," Cynthia Dobrinski (3–5 octaves), Augsburg-Fortress

STUDY CATECHISM

For today's questions and answers, see pp. 231–32.

September 14, 2003

Proverbs 1:20–33 — Wisdom's voice cries out, but will people listen?

Psalm 19 — God is made known through the wonders of creation and the Word.

James 3:1–12 — The need to exercise control over our own speech.

Mark 8:27–38 — Jesus explains the way of suffering that lies ahead.

Theme(s) of lectionary texts: The power of God's Word and the danger in human words. How to listen and speak with care.

CALL TO WORSHIP

The heavens are telling the glory of god,
   and creation displays the work of God's hands.
One day speaks good news to another,
   and one night imparts wisdom to the next.
The fear of the Lord is clean and endures forever;
   the judgments of the Lord are true and righteous altogether.
More to be desired are they than gold,
   sweeter far than honey in the comb.
O Lord, keep your servant from presumptuous sin,
   for then I shall be whole and sound.
Let the words of my mouth and the meditation of
   my heart
   be acceptable in your sight, O Lord,
   my strength and my redeemer.

SUGGESTED HYMNS

ENTRANCE/GATHERING HYMNS	HB	LBW	NCH	PH	RL	TFF	WOV
"God of Our Life"	108	—	366	275	58–59	—	—
"O for a Thousand Tongues to Sing"	141	559	42	466	362–63	—	—
"O Splendor of God's Glory Bright"	46	271	87	474	76	—	—
HYMNS RELATED TO SCRIPTURE							
O—"Be Thou My Vision"	303	—	451	339	67	—	776
"Once He Came in Blessing"	—	312	—	—	—	—	—
E—"Jesus, Lover of My Soul"	216	—	546	303	—	—	—
"Lord, I Want to Be a Christian"	298	403	531	426	436	—	—
"O God, our Faithful God"	—	504	—	277	69	—	—
G—"Go to Dark Gethsemane"	193	109	—	97	—	—	—
"Weary of All Trumpeting"	—	—	—	—	—	—	785
HYMNS OF THE TABLE							
"God Is Here"	—	—	70	461	—	—	719
"When I Survey the Wondrous Cross"	198	482	224	101–102	292–93	79	—
SENDING FORTH							
"Lift High the Cross"	—	377	198	371	415	—	—
"Sent Forth by God's Blessing"	—	221	76	—	—	—	—

Twenty-Fourth Sunday in Ordinary Time

Color: Green

PRAYER OF CONFESSION

Eternal God,
you are the fountain of all wisdom.
Yet we have sought out other counselors,
looking to our own understanding
to determine what is right, good, and beautiful,
rather than trusting your life-giving Word.
We have blinded our eyes to your light,
and closed our ears to your voice.

Forgive us, for we have forsaken your path of life,
and have insisted on making our own way.
Humble our hearts to embrace your wisdom with
**   gladness;**
guide the words of our mouths
and the meditations of our hearts,
that we may witness more faithfully
to your goodness and mercy,
for the sake of Jesus Christ,
our Way, our Truth, and our Life.

HYMN OF ASSURANCE

"The One Is Blest," *PH,* 158

PSALM 19

METRICAL—
"God's Law Is Perfect, and Gives Life," *PH,* 167
"Psalm 19," *Psalter for Christian Worship*, 19
"The Heavens Declare God's Praise," *PH,* 166
RESPONSORIAL—
"Psalm 19," *The Psalter* (1993), 12–13
CHORAL/VOCAL
"The Heavens Declare the Glory of God," Heinrich
    Schuetz (SSATTB), G. Schirmer
"The Heavens Are Telling," Richard McKinney
    (SAB), CPH

ADDITIONAL SONGS

"Come and See," Graham Kendrick, *LUYH,* 147
"Lay It All Down," Brian Marsh, *LUYH,* 92
"There Is a Longing," Anne Quigley, *LUYH,* 141

CHORAL/VOCAL

"Take My Life, and Let It Be Consecrated," Roy
    Hopp (SATB), Selah 410-331

ORGAN

"O Gott, Du frommer Gott," Johann G. Walther,
    Church Organist's Golden Treasury, vol. 3
"Partita on 'O Gott, Du frommer Gott,'" J. S. Bach,
    various editions

PIANO

"In the Garden," Daniel Kallman, *Two Hymns for Two
    Violins and Piano*, MorningStar
"O Love, How Deep," Angela Tipps, *Keys of the
    Kingdom,* vol. 5, Abingdon, 32

HANDBELL

"Lenten Meditation," Paul McKleen (2–3 octaves),
    CPH

STUDY CATECHISM

For today's questions and answers, see p. 232.

September 21, 2003

Proverbs 31:10–31 — A celebration of faithful women.

Psalm 1 — God's blessing on the righteous.

James 3:13–4:3, 7–8a — True wisdom comes from above.

Mark 9:30–37 — The nature of "greatness" in God's eyes.

Theme(s) of lectionary texts: The qualities of lives that are precious in the sight of God.

CALL TO WORSHIP

Happy are they who do not walk the way of the wicked,
   nor sit in the seat of scoffers!
Their delight is in the law of the Lord,
   and on this law they meditate day and night.
They are like a tree that is planted by the water,
   bearing fruit in due season;
the leaves of such a tree do not wither,
   and everything such people do will prosper.
It is not so with the wicked:
   they are like chaff blown away by the wind.
The Lord knows the way of the righteous,
   but the way of the wicked offers no hope.

SUGGESTED HYMNS

ENTRANCE/GATHERING HYMNS	HB	LBW	NCH	PH	RL	TFF	WOV
"All People That on Earth Do Dwell"	24	245	7	220–21	120	—	—
"Christ Is Alive!"	—	363	—	108	—	—	—
HYMNS RELATED TO SCRIPTURE							
O—"Child of Blessing, Child of Promise"	—	—	325	498	—	—	—
"With Grateful Hearts Our Faith Professing"	—	—	—	497	—	—	—
E—"Come Down, O Love Divine"	—	508	289	313	444	—	—
"Lord Jesus, Think on Me"	270	309	—	301	248	—	—
G—"Lord, Whose Love through Humble Service"	—	423	—	427	—	—	—
"Loving Spirit"	—	—	—	323	—	—	683
HYMNS OF THE TABLE							
"O Day of Radiant Gladness"	—	—	66	470	—	—	—
"Wonder of Wonders Here Revealed"	—	—	328	499	—	—	—
SENDING FORTH							
"Savior, Again to Thy Dear Name We Raise"	77	262	80	539	517	—	—
"What a Friend We Have in Jesus"	385	439	506	403	507	—	—

Twenty-Fifth Sunday in Ordinary Time

Color: Green

PRAYER OF CONFESSION

Holy Sovereign of all,
we confess that we have been filled with self-
**   importance;**
we have sought more to be served than to serve.
We strive relentlessly for personal gain,
and care little for your glory,
or for the needs of others.
In mercy, forgive us, and renew us.

By your Spirit, help us become as little children,
so that we may receive your kingdom gladly and
**   freely,**
without regard for personal advantage.
Soften our hearts,
that we will more fully please you
and more freely serve one another,
and in so doing will know the deep joy
of being all that you have made us to be,
in the footsteps of our Master, Jesus Christ.

HYMN OF ASSURANCE

"Jesus Loves Me," *PH,* 304

PSALM 1

METRICAL—
"The One Is Blest," *PH,* 158
RESPONSORIAL—
"Psalm 1," Michael Burkhardt, *Psalms for the Church
    Year*, MorningStar
CHORAL—
"Blest Is the Man," Orlando DiLasso (SSS),
    Augsburg-Fortress
"Happy Is the Man Who Fears the Lord," Richard
    Proulx (unison), Augsburg-Fortress
"Psalm 1," Heinrich Schuetz (SATB), Mercury

ADDITIONAL SONGS

"Jesus Took a Towel," Chrysogonus Waddell, *LUYH,*
    146
"She Flies On!" Gordon Light, Daryl Nixon, arr.,
    LUYH, 86

CHORAL/VOCAL

"A Woman of Valor," Isadore Freed (SATB),
    Transcontinental
"Lord, Whose Love in Humble Service," Richard
    Wienhorst (SATB), MorningStar 50-9059
"Whoever Would Be Great Among You," Ronald A.
    Nelson (SAB), Augsburg-Fortress

ORGAN

"All People That on Earth Do Dwell," Henry Purcell,
    The Organ Works, Novello

PIANO

"Amazing Grace," John Carter, *Hymns for Piano*,
    Hope, 6

HANDBELL

"Amazing Grace," Charles Maggs (3–4 octaves),
    Genesis Press
"Lord, I Want to Be a Christian," Sallie Lloyd
    (3 octaves), Beckenhorst

STUDY CATECHISM

For today's questions and answers, see pp. 232–33.

September 28, 2003

Esther 7:1–6, 9–10; 9:20–22 — Queen Esther foils Haman's plot to destroy the Jewish people.

Psalm 124 — Our help is in the name of the Lord.

James 5:13–20 — The power of prayer.

Mark 9:38–50 — Overcoming self in the service of others.

Theme(s) of lectionary texts: Standing up to the principalities and powers that threaten the downtrodden and oppressed.

CALL TO WORSHIP

If the Lord had not been on our side,
  let the people of God now say:
**If the Lord had not been on our side
  when enemies rose up against us,
they would have swallowed us up alive
  in their fierce anger toward us.**
The water would have overwhelmed us,
  and swift torrents would have swept over us.
**Blessed be the Lord who has not made us their prey.
  Our help is in the name of God who made
  heaven and earth.**

SUGGESTED HYMNS

ENTRANCE/GATHERING HYMNS	HB	LBW	NCH	PH	RL	TFF	WOV
"Praise to the Lord, the Almighty"	1	543	—	482	145	—	—
"Sing Praise to God Who Reigns Above"	—	—	—	483	—	—	—
HYMNS RELATED TO SCRIPTURE							
O—"Lift Every Voice and Sing"	—	562	593	563	—	296	—
"Live into Hope"	—	—	—	332	—	—	—
E—"Dear Lord and Father of Mankind"	416	506	502	345	—	—	—
"God Is Here"	—	—	70	461	—	—	719
G—"Come, Labor On"	287	—	532	415	75	—	—
"How Clear Is Our Vocation, Lord"	—	—	—	419	433	—	—
"Spirit"	—	—	286	319	—	—	684
HYMNS OF THE TABLE							
"I Love the Lord Who Heard My Cry"	—	—	511	362	—	—	—
"Open Now the Gates of Beauty"	40	250	—	489	502	—	—
SENDING FORTH							
"Guide Me, O Thou Great Jehovah"	339	343	18–19	281	50	—	—
"People, Clap Your Hands"	—	—	—	194	—	—	—

Twenty-Sixth Sunday in Ordinary Time

Color: Green

PRAYER OF CONFESSION

God of salvation,
You have not left us alone in times of distress,
but have drawn near to comfort us,
bound up our wounds,
brought light into our darkness,
and made our way safe.
Yet we have turned away from you,
looking to other sources for prosperity,
to other teachers for wisdom,
and to other healers for wholeness.
Rather than keeping our hearts and eyes
firmly fixed upon you,
we have set our gaze and fastened our grasp
on things of this world.
We have claimed to be your followers,
but have lost sight and hold of you.

In mercy, forgive us.
By your Spirit, draw us again near to yourself,
that our hearts would be rekindled
to trust and proclaim the good news
of how kind you are to your children,
how merciful you are to the wayward,
and how strong you are to the weak,
and how responsive you are
to all who call upon you;
through Jesus Christ, our Lord.

HYMN OF ASSURANCE

"Your Faithfulness, O Lord, Is Sure," *PH,* 251

PSALM 124

METRICAL—
"If God the Lord Were Not Our Constant Help,"
   Psalter Hymnal, 124
"Now May Israel Say," *PH,* 236

RESPONSORIAL—
"Psalm 124," Peter Hallock, *The Psalter* (1993), 128
CHORAL/VOCAL—
"A Song of Battle," C. V. Stanford (SATB), Banks
"Psalm 124," Alice Parker and Robert Shaw (SATB),
   G. Schirmer
"Psalm 124," Leo Sowerby (TTBB), H. W. Gray

ADDITIONAL SONGS

"Everything Is Yours, Lord," Geoff Weaver, *LUYH,* 115
"Give Thanks with a Grateful Heart," Henry Smith,
   LUYH, 114

CHORAL/VOCAL

"I Love You, Lord," Laurie Klein/Jack Schrader
   (SATB), Hope
"Prayer," Lloyd Pfautsch (2-part), Lawson Gould
"Rejoice in the Lord," (SATB), Oxford
"Spirit of Gentleness" (SATB/piano/sax), Augsburg-
   Fortress

ORGAN

"Praise, My Soul, the King of Heaven," Kevin Norris,
   Reflections on Six Hymn Tunes, Art Masters
"Sing Praise to God Who Reigns Above," Norman
   Lockwood, *Eight Preludes,* Augsburg-Fortress

PIANO

"Christ for the World We Sing," Reginal Gerig, *Piano
   Preludes on Hymns and Chorales,* Hope

HANDBELL

"A Psalm of Praise," Paul McKleen (3–5 octaves), Lake
   State
"Psalm 19," Benedetto Marcello (3–5 octaves), Prism

STUDY CATECHISM

For today's questions and answers, see pp. 233–34.

October 5, 2003

Job 1:1, 2:1–10 — Job is brought to ruin, yet he remains a person of faith.

Psalm 26 — A plea to God for justice.

Hebrews 1:1–4; 2:5–12 — Jesus is God's Word for our generation and the pioneer who leads humanity to faith.

Mark 10:2–16 — Jesus teaches about marriages and the family of God.

Theme(s) of lectionary texts: The struggle to discover God's will amid complexity and aggravation.

CALL TO WORSHIP

Test me, O Lord, and try me;
and judge whether I live with integrity.
**For your love is always before my eyes,
and I try to walk faithfully with you.**
I do not reside with the worthless,
nor do I consort with the deceitful.
**Lord, I love the house of your worship
and the place where I sense your glory.**
I am determined to live with integrity;
redeem me, O Lord, and have mercy upon me.
**Place my feet on steady ground, O God,
that I may worship in your congregation.**

SUGGESTED HYMNS

ENTRANCE/GATHERING HYMNS	HB	LBW	NCH	PH	RL	TFF	WOV
"Christ, for the World We Sing"	489	—	—	—	422	—	—
"God of Grace and God of Glory"	358	415	436	420	416	—	—
"Immortal, Invisible, God Only Wise"	85	526	1	263	7	—	—
HYMNS RELATED TO SCRIPTURE							
O—"Give to the Winds Thy Fears"	364	—	—	286	149	—	—
"God Is My Strong Salvation"	347	—	—	179	95	—	—
E—"Deep in the Shadows of the Past"	—	—	320	330	—	—	—
"Of the Father's Love Begotten"	7	42	118	309	190–91	—	—
G—"Gracious Spirit, Holy Ghost"	—	—	61	318	—	—	—
"Our Father by Whose Name"	—	357	—	—	522	—	—
HYMNS OF THE TABLE							
"I Come with Joy"	—	—	349	507	534	—	—
"O Word of God Incarnate"	251	231	315	327	387	—	—
SENDING FORTH							
"This Is My Father's World"	101	554	—	293	14	—	—
"When Love Is Found"	—	—	362	—	—	—	749

Twenty-Seventh Sunday in Ordinary Time

Color: Green

PRAYER OF CONFESSION

Almighty Deliverer and Guardian—
You have always been good
to those who trust in you.
Yet when faced with distress,
we have lost confidence in your goodness;
we have complained and questioned,
rather than keeping our hope steadfast.
In seasons of uncertainty and struggle,
we have broken faith with you,
as well as with those who are near to us.

In mercy, forgive our faithlessness.
Renew in us the Spirit of devotion,
that we may steadfastly trust
in your abiding love,
keeping faith and hope
in plenty and in want,
in joy and in sorrow,
for the sake of the one who loved us to the end,
Jesus of Nazareth, our Savior and Lord.

HYMN OF ASSURANCE

"Jesus, Thy Boundless Love to Me," *PH, 366*

PSALM 26

METRICAL—
"Be Thou My Judge, O Lord, My God," *Psalter for Christian Worship*, 37
"Give Judgment for Me, O God," *A New Metrical Psalter*, 60
RESPONSORIAL—
"Psalm 26," David Clark Isele, *The Psalter* (1993), 24
CHORAL/VOCAL—
"O Lord, I Love the Habitation of Your House," Mark Bender (2-part mixed), CPH

ADDITIONAL SONGS

"Beauty for Brokenness," Graham Kendrick, *Worship & Praise*, Augsburg-Fortress
"Sanctuary," John Thompson, *Renew*, Hope

CHORAL/VOCAL

"Day by Day," Mark Hayes (SATB), Augsburg-Fortress
"The Lament of Job," Dale Jergenson (SATB), G. Schirmer
"Whoever Does Not Receive the Kingdom," Jan Bender (unison), Chantry

ORGAN

"Christ Is Made the Sure Foundation," David Johnson, *Wedding Music*, Augsburg-Fortress
"Immortal, Invisible," Robert Powell, *Eleven Chorale Preludes on Hymn Tunes*, Flammer

PIANO

"You Satisfy the Hungry Heart," Daniel Kane, in *More Selectable Delectables*, Augsburg-Fortress, 6

HANDBELL

"Children of the Heavenly Father," Jane McFadden (3–4 octaves), in *Two Swedish Melodies*, Augsburg-Fortress

STUDY CATECHISM

For today's questions and answers, see pp. 234–35.

October 12, 2003

Job 23:1–9, 16–17   Job's wishes to present his case before the Lord.

Psalm 22:1–15   A cry of desolation is followed by a song of hope.

Hebrews 4:12–16   The Word of God and our great high priest.

Mark 10:17–31   The two great commandments, and "what more is needed."

Theme(s) of lectionary texts: Even in the face of seemingly insurmountable obstacles, with God all things are possible.

CALL TO WORSHIP

My God, my God,
   why have you forsaken me?
Why are you so far from my cry
   in the hour of my distress?
Yet you are the Holy One
   in whom our ancestors put their trust.
They cried out to you and were delivered;
   they trusted, and you delivered them.
Be not far away, O Lord, for you are our strength.
Your face is not hidden from the needy,
   but when we cry out, O Lord, you hear us.

SUGGESTED HYMNS

ENTRANCE/GATHERING HYMNS	HB	LBW	NCH	PH	RL	TFF	WOV
"All My Hope on God Is Founded"	—	—	408	—	156–57	—	782
"For the Beauty of the Earth"	2	561	28	473	5	—	—
HYMNS RELATED TO SCRIPTURE							
O—"O Lord, Make Haste to Hear My Cry"	392	—	—	249	—	—	—
"We Walk by Faith and Not by Sight"	—	—	—	399	—	—	—
E—"Lord, Enthroned in Heavenly Splendor"	—	172	258	154	537	—	—
"What a Friend We Have in Jesus"	385	439	506	403	507	—	—
G—"God, Whose Giving Knows No Ending"	—	408	565	422	—	—	—
"O Jesus, I Have Promised"	307	503	493	388–89	471	—	—
HYMNS OF THE TABLE							
"Lord Jesus, Think on Me"	270	309	—	301	248	—	—
"O for a Closer Walk with God"	319	—	450	396–97	437	—	—
SENDING FORTH							
"A Hymn of Glory Let Us Sing"	—	157	259	141	332	—	—
"Blessed Assurance, Jesus Is Mine"	139	—	473	341	453	118	699

Twenty-Eighth Sunday in Ordinary Time

Color: Green

PRAYER OF CONFESSION

Light Eternal,
we confess that we have turned away from you.
We have sought the cover of darkness,
so our willful selfishness would go unexposed.
Open our eyes,
that we may see how we have fallen short of
your calling;
open our ears,
that we may clearly hear your summons anew;
pierce our hearts,
that we might be opened fully
to the work of our Spirit in and through us.
Let it be so done unto us
by your Word of healing grace and transforming
power,
given to us through Jesus Christ, our Lord.

HYMN OF ASSURANCE

"Open My Eyes That I May See," *PH,* 324

PSALM 22

METRICAL—
"Lord, Why Have You Forsaken Me?" *PH,* 168
"My God, Am I Forsaken?" *Psalter for Christian
Worship,* 32
RESPONSORIAL—
"Psalm 22," Hal Hopson, in *Eighteen Psalms for the
Church Year,* Hope
"Psalm 22," Hal Hopson, in *Ten More Psalms,* Hope
CHORAL—
"When We Are Tempted to Deny Your Son," Sally
Ann Morris (SATB), GIA

ADDITIONAL SONGS

"Baptized and Set Free," Cathy Skogen-Soldner,
Worship & Praise, Augsburg-Fortress
"Lord, You Are the Holy One," Lynn DeShazo,
LUYH, 45

CHORAL/VOCAL

"Lord, You Have Been Our Refuge," John Bell
(SATB), GIA
"Weary of All Trumpeting," Richard Proulx
(SAB/Brass), GIA

ORGAN

"Joyful, Joyful, We Adore Thee," Hal Hopson,
Processionals of Joy, Carl Fischer

PIANO

"My Faith Looks Up to Thee," Reginald Gerig, in
Piano Preludes on Hymns and Chorales, Hope

HANDBELL

"Lord, I Lift Your Name on High," Peggy Betcher
(2–3 octaves), Agape

STUDY CATECHISM

For today's questions and answers, see p. 235.

October 19, 2003

Job 38:1–7, 34–41	The Lord God replies to Job's arguments.
Psalm 104:1–9, 24, 35c	A song of praise in response to God's majesty.
Hebrews 5:1–10	God has appointed Jesus Christ as our mediator.
Mark 10:35–45	Jesus replies to the desire of James and John to sit at his right and left hand.

Theme(s) of lectionary texts: Human suffering, and God's power and steadfast love.

CALL TO WORSHIP

Bless the Lord, O my soul!
> For God has set the earth on its foundations.
You wrap yourself with light as with a cloak,
> **and you spread out the heavens like a curtain.**
O Lord, you make the winds your chariots,
> and you ride on the wings of the wind.
O God, you covered the globe with waters,
> **but at your voice they made way for land.**
O Lord, how manifold are your works!
> In wisdom you have made us all.
Bless the Lord, O my soul!
> **Hallelujah! Amen.**

SUGGESTED HYMNS

ENTRANCE/GATHERING HYMNS	HB	LBW	NCH	PH	RL	TFF	WOV
"Praise the Lord, God's Glories Show"	4	—	—	481	142	—	—
"When Morning Gilds the Skies"	41	545–46	86	487	365	—	—
HYMNS RELATED TO SCRIPTURE							
O—"Immortal, Invisible, God Only Wise"	85	526	1	263	7	—	—
"When the Morning Stars Together"	—	—	453	486	510	—	—
E—"Jesus, Thy Boundless Love to Thee"	404	336	—	366	454	—	—
"More Love to Thee, O Christ"	397	—	456	359	—	—	—
G—"Christ, Whose Glory Fills the Skies"	47	265	—	462–63	463	—	—
"Give Thanks, O Christian People"	—	—	—	552	—	—	—
HYMNS OF THE TABLE							
"Jesu, Jesu, Fill Us with Your Love"	—	—	498	367	—	83	765
"Lord, Speak to Me That I May Speak"	298	403	531	426	436	—	—
SENDING FORTH							
"The Church of Christ in Every Age"	—	433	306	421	—	—	—
"Walk On, People of God"	—	—	614	296	—	—	—

Twenty-Ninth Sunday in Ordinary Time

Color: Green

PRAYER OF CONFESSION

Compassionate God,
you have shown your great love to us
by coming to us in the form of a Servant.
You have called us to serve, even as we have been
served;
yet, we have put our own interests first,
and have turned away from the needs of others.
We are so self-absorbed that we trample over others
and elbow our way to places of honor,
scarcely noticing the violence of our ways.

Show us your mercy, and forgive us.
Strengthen us by your Spirit
that we may show our love for you
by showing tenderness and humility
in our relationship to one another.
Enable us to lay down our lives for Christ's sake,
demonstrating that we truly are faithful
disciples.

HYMN OF ASSURANCE

"Piedad/Have Mercy, Lord, on Me," *PH*, 395

PSALM 104

METRICAL—
"Bless the Lord, My Soul and Being," *PH*, 224
RESPONSORIAL—
"Psalm 104," *The Psalter* (1993), 104
"Psalm 104," Hal Hopson, *Ten Psalms*, Hope
CHORAL—
"Bless the Lord, O My Soul," Rene Clausen (SATB),
    Mark Foster
"I Will Sing to the Lord," John Hofmann (SATB),
    Selah
"Psalm of Joy," William Boyce, Jane McFadden/Janet
    Linker, arr. (2-part), Choristers Guild

ADDITIONAL SONGS

"On Eagles' Wings," Michael Joncas, *LUYH*, 87
"Sing Out, Earth and Skies," Marty Haugen, *Worship*
    & Praise, Augsburg-Fortress

CHORAL/VOCAL

"The Voice of the Whirlwind," Ralph Vaughn
    Williams (SATB), Oxford
"We Know That Christ Is Raised," C. V. Stanford
    (SATB), CPH
"Whoever Would Be Great Among You," Ronald A.
    Nelson (SAB), Augsburg-Fortress

ORGAN

"Praise the Lord, God's Glories Show," Robert Groves,
    Six Welsh Hymn Tune Preludes, Elkin
"When Morning Gilds the Skies," Stanley Saxton,
    A Galaxy of Hymn Tune Preludes, Galaxy

PIANO

"To God Be the Glory," John Carter, *Hymns for Piano*,
    Hope, 16

HANDBELL

"On Eagles' Wings," Michael Joncas, arr., Honore
    (3–5 octaves), CPH

STUDY CATECHISM

For today's questions and answers, see pp. 235–36.

October 26, 2003

Job 42:1–6, 10–17 — Job's encounter with God climaxes in doxology and repentance.

Psalm 34:1–8 (19–22) — "I sought the Lord, who answered me."

Hebrews 7:23–28 — Jesus is our great high priest.

Mark 10:46–52 — Jesus restores the sight of a blind beggar.

Theme(s) of lectionary texts: God responds to human prayer and pleading.

CALL TO WORSHIP

I sought the Lord, who answered me
  and delivered me from terror.
Look upon the Lord and be radiant,
  and let not your faces be ashamed.
At all times I will bless the Lord,
  whose praise shall be ever in my mouth.
I will glory in the Lord:
  let all who are humble hear and rejoice.
I called in my affliction, and God heard me
  and saved me from all my troubles.
Taste and see that the Lord is good;
  happy are they who trust in God!

SUGGESTED HYMNS

ENTRANCE/GATHERING HYMNS	HB	LBW	NCH	PH	RL	TFF	WOV
"Praise Ye the Lord, the Almighty"	1	543	—	482	145	—	—
"Sing Praise to God, Who Reigns Above"	15	—	—	—	146	—	—
HYMNS RELATED TO SCRIPTURE							
O—"Be Thou My Vision"	303	—	451	339	67	—	776
"Our God, to Whom We Turn"	128	—	37	278	—	—	—
E—"My Hope Is Built on Nothing Less"	368	293–94	403	379	459–60	192	—
"O Sing a Song of Bethlehem"	177	—	51	308	356	—	—
G—"O Christ the Healer"	—	360	175	380	—	—	—
"O Savior in This Quiet Place"	—	—	—	390	—	—	—
HYMNS OF THE TABLE							
"Come, Christians, Join to Sing"	131	—	—	150	357	—	—
"O Lamb of God Most Holy"	—	—	—	82	—	—	—
SENDING FORTH							
"Christ Is Alive!"	—	363	—	108	—	—	—
"Ye Servants of God, Your Master Proclaim"	27	252	305	477	598	—	—

Thirtieth Sunday in Ordinary Time

Color: Green

PRAYER OF CONFESSION

Almighty God,
we acknowledge the greatness of your majesty,
and the depth of our spiritual poverty.
We have thought too highly of ourselves,
and have failed to give due glory to you.
You call us into being by your Word,
yet we shun the counsel of that same Word.

Lord, have mercy on us.
Forgive our arrogance and selfishness.
Help us to live to your honor
by granting your Word its rightful place,
and by letting the power of that Word
transform us and equip us—
to dismantle evil and heal the broken,
according to the teaching and example
of our Lord and Savior, Jesus Christ.

HYMN OF ASSURANCE

"A Mighty Fortress," *PH,* 259–60

PSALM 34

METRICAL—
"Unto the Lord My Praise I Sing," *Psalter for Christian Worship,* 46
RESPONSORIAL—
"Psalm 34," Hal Hopson, *The Psalter* (1993), 32
CHORAL/VOCAL—
"I Will Rejoice in the Lord," G. P. Telemann (2-part), Choristers Guild
"O Taste and See," Eugene Hancock (SATB), H. W. Gray
"Taste and See," Richard Proulx (SATB/congregation), GIA

ADDITIONAL SONGS

"Love the Lord Your God," Jean and Jim Strathdee, *LUYH,* 96
"Rock of My Salvation," Teresa Muller, *Worship & Praise,* Augsburg-Fortress

CHORAL/VOCAL

"I Stand on the Rock," John Bertalot (SAB), Augsburg-Fortress
"Lord, Keep Us Steadfast in Your Word," Dietrich Buxtehude (SATB/strings), CPH
"Prayer," Lloyd Pfautsch (2-part), Lawson-Gould

ORGAN

"Praise Ye the Lord, the Almighty," J. S. Bach, various editions
"Praise Ye the Lord, the Almighty," Max Reger, *Thirty Short Chorale Preludes,* C. F. Peters

PIANO

"Every Time I Feel the Spirit," John Carter, *Spirituals for Piano,* Hope, 16

HANDBELL

"Psalm 100," Judith Hunnicutt (2 octaves), *Psalms for Bells,* Agape, 133

STUDY CATECHISM

For today's questions and answers, see p. 236.

October 31, 2003

2 Kings 23:1–3	Josiah institutes an era of religious reform.
Psalm 46	God is our rock and refuge in time of trouble.
2 Corinthians 5:16–6:2	Ambassadors of Christ and minister of reconciliation.
Matthew 3:1–12	John the Baptist preaches a baptism of repentance.

Theme(s) of Reformation Day texts: The cleansing effect of review and renewal of God's covenant with believers.

CALL TO WORSHIP

God is our refuge and our strength,
    a very present help in trouble.
Therefore, we will not fear,
    even if the earth moves beneath us.
Though the mountains be toppled,
    and the waters rage and foam:
The Lord of hosts is with us;
    the God of Jacob is our stronghold.
It is the Lord who makes war to cease,
    who breaks the bow and shatters the spear.
"Be still," says the Lord, "and know that I am God.
    I will be exalted by all nations on earth." Amen.

SUGGESTED HYMNS

ENTRANCE/GATHERING HYMNS	HB	LBW	NCH	PH	RL	TFF	WOV
"A Mighty Fortress Is Our God"	91	228–29	439–40	259–60	179	—	—
HYMNS RELATED TO SCRIPTURE							
"All People That on Earth Do Dwell"	24	245	7	220–21	120	—	—
"By Gracious Powers"	—	—	413	342	55	—	—
HYMNS OF THE TABLE							
"Christ Is Made the Sure Foundation"	433	367	400	416–17	392	—	747
"Take Thou Our Minds, Dear Lord"	306	—	—	392	434	—	—
SENDING FORTH							
"Rejoice, the Lord Is King"	140	171	303	155	596–97	—	—

Reformation Day

Color: Green

PRAYER OF CONFESSION

Eternal God, you have called us into covenant,
yet our commitment is shallow
and our love is weak.
We place lesser concerns
high on the list of our life's priorities,
and so we sacrifice our relationship with you.
Forgive our sin, O God,
and turn us again toward your purposes.

Reform our lives by renewing our dedication
to the covenant we have entered
through our baptism in Jesus Christ.
By the leading of your Holy Spirit,
give us a new sense of our calling,
a new zeal in our faithfulness,
a new compassion toward neighbors in need,
and a new appreciation for your love
in Jesus Christ our Lord. Amen.

HYMN OF ASSURANCE

"I Greet Thee, Who My Sure Redeemer Art," *PH,*
457

PSALM 46

METRICAL—
"God Is Our Refuge and Our Strength," *PH,* 191
"God, Our Help and Constant Refuge," *PH,* 192
RESPONSORIAL—
"The Lord of Hosts Is with Us," *PH,* 193
CHORAL/VOCAL—
"God Is Our Strength and Refuge," Philip Landgrove
(unison), Hope

ADDITIONAL SONGS

"Freely, Freely," Carol Owens, *LUYH,* 136
"Grace Greater Than Our Sin," J. Johnson and
D. Towner, *LUYH,* 76
"Justified Freely," Walt Harrah, *LUYH,* 77

CHORAL/VOCAL

"A Mighty Fortress," Carl Mueller (SATB or
SSAATTBB), G. Schirmer

ORGAN

"Ein' Feste Burg," J. S. Bach, *Miscellaneous Chorale*
Preludes.
"Partita on 'Ein' Feste Burg,'" Charles Callahan,
MorningStar

Saturday, November 1, 2003

Isaiah 25:6–9 — The great feast in the presence of the Lord.

Psalm 24 — A psalm for entry into worship at the Temple.

Revelation 21:1–6a — A vision of a new heaven and a new earth.

John 11:32–44 — Jesus raises Lazarus from the tomb.

Theme(s) of lectionary texts: The communion of the saints through time and eternity.

CALL TO WORSHIP

The earth is the Lord's, and everything in it,
    the world and all who dwell therein.
**For God founded the world upon the seas
    and made it firm upon the deep rivers.**
Who can ascend the hill of the Lord?
    Who can stand in God's holy place?
**Those who have clean hands and pure hearts,
    who have not pledged themselves to falsehood.**
Such is the generation of those who seek the Lord,
    for the Lord of hosts is a glorious Sovereign.
**Lift up your heads, O mighty doors and gates,
    that the Lord of glory may enter in.**

SUGGESTED HYMNS

ENTRANCE/GATHERING HYMNS	HB	LBW	NCH	PH	RL	TFF	WOV
"Alleluia, Sing to Jesus"	—	158	—	144	346	—	—
"Holy God, We Praise Your Name"	—	535	276	460	619	—	—
HYMNS RELATED TO SCRIPTURE							
"How Firm a Foundation"	369	507	407	361	172	—	—
"Prayer Is the Soul's Sincere Desire"	391	—	508	—	—	—	—
HYMNS OF THE TABLE							
"The Church's One Foundation"	437	369	386	442	394	—	—
"You Are the Seed"	—	—	528	—	—	—	753
SENDING FORTH							
"For All the Saints"	425	174	299	526	397	—	—
"I Love Thy Kingdom, Lord"	435	368	—	441	409	—	—

All Saints' Day

PRAYER OF CONFESSION

Hope of all the saints,
You have called and sanctified us to be your holy
people
part of that great company that has lived and died
in faith.
But we have not always kept the faith:
we have been silent when we should have
proclaimed your love,
and we have been idle when we should be working
for peace and justice.
Our lives have been shaped more by fear than by
faith.
Have mercy on us, and forgive us.

Give us the courage to follow the path of that great
company of saints,
who throughout the ages have served you
with robust faith, confident hope, and steadfast
love,
that with them we may inherit the kingdom
promised, given, and ruled in majesty by the Son
of David,
our Lord and Savior, Jesus the Christ.

HYMN OF ASSURANCE

"O God of Love, O God of Peace," *PH,* 295

PSALM 24

METRICAL—
"The Earth and All That Dwell Therein," *PH,* 176
RESPONSORIAL—
"Psalm 24 (1–6)," Hal Hopson, *The Psalter* (1993), 22
"Psalm 24," Willard Jabusch and Arlo Duba, *PH,* 177
CHORAL—
"Lift Up Your Heads," Jane Marshall (unison treble
voices/optional handbells), Hinshaw

ADDITIONAL SONGS

"Make Me a Channel of Your Peace," St. Francis/
Sebastian Temple, *LUYH,* 109
"We Are the Family of God," Jon Byron, *LUYH,* 16

CHORAL/VOCAL

"And I Saw a New Heaven," Edgar Bainton (SATB),
Novello
"Day of Rejoicing," Walter Pelz (SATB/trumpet),
Augsburg
"The Raising of Lazarus," Adrian Willaert (SATB),
Ricordi

ORGAN

"Prelude on SINE NOMINE," Flor Peeters, *Hymn*
Preludes for the Liturgical Year, vol. 5, C. F. Peters
6405

PIANO

"Lord of the Dance," John Carter, *Folk Hymns for*
Piano, Hope

HANDBELL

"Near the Cross," Douglas Wagner (2–3 octaves),
Lorenz

November 2, 2003

Ruth 1:1–18 — Ruth pledges faithfully to accompany Naomi.

Psalm 146 — A song of praise and trust in the Lord.

Hebrews 9:11–14 — Christ is both our high priest and the ultimate sacrifice offered once for all.

Mark 12:28–34 — The two greatest commandments.

Theme(s) of lectionary texts: Offering oneself for others, and to God.

CALL TO WORSHIP

I will praise the Lord as long as I live;
　I will sing praise to God while I have being.
**Put not your trust in rulers, nor in any mortal,
　for there is no help in them.**
When they breathe their last, they return to earth,
　and in that day their good intentions perish.
**Happy are those whose help is the Lord!
　And whose hope is in the Lord their God!**
For God sets prisoners free
　and opens the eyes of the blind.
**The Lord shall reign forever,
　our God, throughout all generations!**

SUGGESTED HYMNS

ENTRANCE/GATHERING HYMNS	HB	LBW	NCH	PH	RL	TFF	WOV
"Guide Me, O Thou Great Jehovah"	339	343	18–19	281	50	—	—
"The God of Abraham Praise"	89	544	24	488	595	—	—
HYMNS RELATED TO SCRIPTURE							
O—"Give to the Winds Thy Fears"	364	—	—	286	149	—	—
"Wherever I May Wander"	—	—	—	294	163	—	—
E—"Alleluia, Sing to Jesus"	—	158	144	346	—	—	—
"Beneath the Cross of Jesus"	190	107	190	92	310–11	—	—
G—"Alas, and Did My Savior Bleed?"	199	98	200	78	—	—	—
"When I Survey the Wondrous Cross"	198	482	224	100–101	292–93	79	—
HYMNS OF THE TABLE							
"Fill My Cup"	—	—	—	350	—	124	—
"I Greet Thee, Who My Sure Redeemer Art"	144	—	251	457	366	—	—
SENDING FORTH							
"The Church of God in Every Age"	—	433	306	421	—	—	—
"Walk On, People of God"	—	—	614	296	—	—	—

Thirty-First Sunday in Ordinary Time

Color: Green

PRAYER OF CONFESSION

Compassionate God,
we have strayed from your fold,
pursuing the desires of our own hearts,
rather than listening to your voice.
When you have called us home,
we have run away instead.

In your mercy, forgive us.
Draw us back unto yourself by your Spirit,
that we may love you with undivided heart,
and our neighbors as ourselves,
to the glory of the one who loves perfectly,
our Master and Teacher, Jesus Christ.

HYMN OF ASSURANCE

"O for a Closer Walk with God," *PH,* 396–97

PSALM 146

METRICAL—
"I'll Praise My Maker While I've Breath," *PH,* 253
RESPONSORIAL—
"Psalm 146," John Schiavone, *PH,* 254
CHORAL/VOCAL—
"A Joyful Psalm," Jane Marshall (SATB), GIA
"Lauda anima mea dominum," Orlando DiLasso
    (SATB, English text included), G. Schirmer
"Psalm 146," Robert Powell (SB), GIA

ADDITIONAL SONGS

"Halle, Halle, Hallelujah," Geoff Weaver, arr., *LUYH,*
    28
"There Is a Redeemer," Melody Green, *LUYH,* 78

CHORAL/VOCAL

"Fill Us with Your Love," Tom Colvin (SATB), Agape
"The Promise of Eternal Inheritance," Rudolf Moser
    (unison), CPH
"You Shall Love the Lord," Eugene Englert (SATB),
    World Library

ORGAN

"The God of Abraham Praise," C. S. Lang, *Three
    Chorale Preludes*, Oxford

PIANO

"Our God, Our Help in Ages Past," Reginald Gerig,
    Piano Preludes on Hymns and Chorales, Hope, 34

HANDBELL

"Praise to Our Creator," Howard Starks (3–5 octaves),
    Augsburg-Fortress

STUDY CATECHISM

For today's questions and answers, see pp. 236–37.

November 9, 2003

Ruth 3:1–5; 4:13–17	Ruth is married to Boaz, and they become ancestors of Jesse, David, and Jesus.
Psalm 127	The blessing of family and the nurture of the young.
Hebrews 9:24–28	A new age has begun in Christ.
Mark 12:38–44	Jesus contrasts religious hypocrisy with the faith of a generous widow.

Theme(s) of lectionary texts: The mysterious ways of God are made plain in the revelation of Jesus Christ.

CALL TO WORSHIP

Unless the Lord builds the house,
    those who build it labor in vain.
**Unless the Lord watches over the city,
    the sentries keep their vigil in vain.**
Children are a heritage from the Lord,
    the coming generation is a gift.
**Like arrows in the hand of a warrior
    are the children entrusted to us.**
Happy is the warrior
    with a quiver full of them!
**The people who nurture a new generation
    shall not be put to shame in times of trouble.**

SUGGESTED HYMNS

ENTRANCE/GATHERING HYMNS	HB	LBW	NCH	PH	RL	TFF	WOV
"Eternal God, Whose Power Upholds"	485	—	—	412	481	—	—
"Let All Things Now Living"	—	557	—	554	—	—	—
"O for a Thousand Tongues to Sing"	141	559	42	466	362–63	—	—
HYMNS RELATED TO SCRIPTURE							
O—"God, Whose Giving Knows No Ending"	—	408	565	422	—	—	—
"When a Poor One"	—	—	—	407	—	—	—
E—"Blessed Assurance, Jesus Is Mine"	139	—	473	341	453	118	699
"Jesus, Thy Boundless Love to Me"	404	336	—	366	454	—	—
"O Lord, How Shall I Meet You?"	—	23	—	11	368	—	—
G—"Day by Day"	—	—	—	—	—	—	746
"I'd Rather Have Jesus"	—	—	—	—	—	233	—
"Lord of Light, Your Name Outshining"	—	405	—	425	484	—	—
HYMNS OF THE TABLE							
"Sheaves of Summer"	—	—	338	518	—	—	—
"We Come As Guests Invited"	—	—	—	517	—	—	—
SENDING FORTH							
"Love Divine, All Loves Excelling"	399	315	43	376	464	—	—
"Now Thank We All Our God"	9	533–34	419	555	61	—	—

Thirty-Second Sunday in Ordinary Time

Color: Green

PRAYER OF CONFESSION

Redeeming God,
we receive with joy your free gift of redemption,
through the offering of your Son as our sacrifice
**   for sin.**
Yet we dishonor your saving gift;
we are more concerned to be approved by others
than to honor you as our only source of hope.
We have sought esteem,
rather than embracing humility.

Forgive our stubborn pride.
Fill us with your humble Spirit,
that we may be glad servants,
demonstrating with every step, action, and word
our gratitude that you have accepted us without
**   condition,**
through the gift of your wisdom, righteousness,
**   and redemption**
through Jesus Christ, our Lord.

HYMN OF ASSURANCE

"God Whose Giving Knows No Ending," *PH*, 422

PSALM 127

METRICAL—
"Except the House Is Built by God," *Psalter for Christian Worship*, 148
"Unless the Lord the House Shall Build," *PH*, 238
RESPONSORIAL—
"Psalm 127," Hal Hopson, *The Psalter* (1993), 132

CHORAL/VOCAL

"Except the Lord Build the House," Leo Sowerby (SATB), H. W. Gray
"*Nisi dominum*," Giacomo Carissimi (SSATB), Novello

ADDITIONAL SONGS

"Freely, Freely," Carol Owens, *LUYH*, 136
"Give Thanks with a Grateful Heart," Henry Smith, *LUYH*, 114

CHORAL/VOCAL

"God's Loving Call," Wayne Wold (unison), Choristers Guild
"We Will Lay Our Burdens Down," John Bell (SATB/congregation), GIA
"We Would Offer Thee This Day," Jane Marshall (SATB), SMP

ORGAN

"Autumn Nocturne," Peter Matthews, MorningStar
"Now Thank We All Our God," Flor Peeters, *Hymn Preludes for the Liturgical Year,* vol. 12, C. F. Peters

PIANO

"How Great Thou Art," John Carter, *Today's Hymns and Songs for Piano*, Hope, 10

HANDBELL

"Offertory," Theodore Beck (4–5 octaves), Beckenhorst

STUDY CATECHISM

For today's questions and answers, see pp. 237–38.

November 16, 2003

1 Samuel 1:4–20 — Hannah's prayers are answered as she prepares to give birth to the prophet Samuel.

1 Samuel 2:1–10 — The canticle of Hannah.

Hebrews 10:11–18 — The fulfillment of the promise of a new covenant.

Mark 13:1–8 — Jesus foretells the end of the present age.

Theme(s) of lectionary texts: The transformation of human lives, and of the life of the world.

CALL TO WORSHIP

My heart exults in the Lord,
> for I rejoice in the power of God's salvation.

There is none as holy as the Lord;
> **there is no rock as strong as our God.**

The Lord is the author of life and death;
> it is God who humbles, yet God also exalts.

God raises the poor from the dust,
> **lifting the needy from the refuse heap.**

God gives them a place with princes,
> and assigns them seats of honor.

The Lord judges the ends of the earth;
> **to God be the power and the glory!**

SUGGESTED HYMNS

ENTRANCE/GATHERING HYMNS	HB	LBW	NCH	PH	RL	TFF	WOV
"A Mighty Fortress"	91	228–29	439–40	259–60	179	133	—
"God of Grace and God of Glory"	358	415	436	420	416	—	—
HYMNS RELATED TO SCRIPTURE							
O—"By Gracious Powers"	—	—	413	342	55	—	736
"I Love the Lord Who Heard My Cry"	—	—	511	362	—	—	—
"O Lord, Make Haste to Hear My Cry"	392	—	—	249	—	—	—
E—"How Clear Is Our Vocation, Lord"	—	—	—	419	433	—	—
"Take Up Your Cross, the Savior Said"	293	398	204	393	268	—	—
G—"O Jesus, I Have Promised"	307	503	493	388–389	471	—	—
"Soon and Very Soon"	—	—	—	—	—	38	744
"Spirit of God, Descend Upon My Heart"	236	486	290	326	445	—	—
HYMNS OF THE TABLE							
"Jesus, Lover of My Soul"	216	—	546	303	—	—	—
"O Wondrous Sight, O Vision Fair"	182	80	184	75	256	—	—
SENDING FORTH							
"Come, Thou Fount of Every Blessing"	379	499	459	356	449	108	—
"Lead On, O King Eternal"	332	495	573	447–48	423	—	—

Thirty-Third Sunday in Ordinary Time

Color: Green

PRAYER OF CONFESSION

God of Covenant,
through the ministry of Jesus, our High Priest,
we have been made sure heirs
of all your gracious promises.
You have made through him a new and living way
into the fullness of your fellowship and blessing.
But we have treated that fellowship as though it
  were a light thing.
We have neglected the assembly of the saints,
and the closet of personal communion with you.

By your tender mercies,
make us more tender to your Spirit.
Grant us a heart that yearns deeply for your presence,
and approaches your throne with the confidence of
  children;
that with singleness of heart we may join hands
  and voices,
in glad celebration and grateful witness
of all you have done. Restore us to fellowship
with yourself and with one another,
through the reconciling work of your anointed One,
our Lord and Savior, Jesus Christ.

HYMN OF ASSURANCE

"Alleluia! Sing to Jesus!" *PH*, 144

1 SAMUEL 2:1–10

METRICAL—
"Song of Hannah," *The Psalter Hymnal*, 158
RESPONSORIAL—
"Canticle of Hannah," *The Psalter* (1993), 172
CHORAL—
"Praise the Lord, Ye Servants," Richard Peek (unison),
  H. W. Gray (M)

ADDITIONAL SONGS

"I Will Sing of the Mercies," James H. Fillmore,
  LUYH, 75
"Soon and Very Soon," Andraé Crouch, *LUYH*, 142

CHORAL/VOCAL

"He Shall Endure," from *Elijah*, Felix Mendelssohn
  (SATB), G. Schirmer
"My Heart Rejoices in the Lord," John Horman
  (2-part treble), Augsburg-Fortress
"Those Who Are Wise," Carl Schalk (SATB),
  MorningStar
"You Are Worthy," Daniel Meyer (SAB), GIA

ORGAN

"Lord Jesus, Think on Me," W. T. Best, *Twelve
  Preludes on Old English Psalm Tunes*, Kalmus
"O God, Our Help in Ages Past," C. Hubert H.
  Parry, *Seven Chorale Preludes*, vol. 1, Novello

PIANO

"Christ Is Alive, Let Christians Sing," Angela Tipps,
  Keys of the Kingdom, vol. 6, Abingdon, 22

HANDBELL

"Hope Eternal," Cynthia Dobrinski (3–5 octaves/
  flute), Agape

STUDY CATECHISM

For today's questions and answers, see pp. 238–39.

November 23, 2003

2 Samuel 23:1–7   The final psalm of David.
Psalm 132:1–12   A psalm of the Davidic royal
(13–18)   line.
Revelation 1:4b–8   John sends greeting in Christ
to seven churches.
John 18:33–37   Christ's kingdom transcends
this world.
Theme(s) of lectionary texts: Jesus Christ rules as King
of Kings and Lord of Lords.

CALL TO WORSHIP

Lord, remember David your anointed king,
     and recall the hardships he endured:
How he vowed to bring the ark
     and set it up in your house of prayer.
For your servant David's sake,
     do not turn away from the face of your anointed.
Remember your oath that a Son of David
     will sit upon your throne forever.
For the Lord has chosen Jerusalem
     and desired it for a holy habitation.
There those who worship will be clothed in
     salvation,
     and the faithful people will rejoice and sing.

SUGGESTED HYMNS

ENTRANCE/GATHERING HYMNS	HB	LBW	NCH	PH	RL	TFF	WOV
"Crown Him with Many Crowns"	213	170	—	151	596–97	—	—
"Rejoice, the Lord Is King" (vv. 1–2)	140	171	—	155	596–97	—	—
HYMNS RELATED TO SCRIPTURE							
O—"Now Praise the Lord"	—	—	—	255 —	—	—	—
"Your Faithfulness, O Lord"	—	—	—	251	—	—	—
E—"At the Name of Jesus"	143	179	—	148	336	—	—
"Lo, He Comes with Clouds Descending"	234	27	—	6	605	—	—
"Lord, Enthroned in Heavenly Splendor"	—	172	258	154	537	—	—
G—"A Hymn of Glory Let Us Sing"	—	157	259	141	332	—	—
"Hail Thee, Festival Day"	—	142	262	120	—	—	—
"Our King and Our Sovereign, Lord Jesus"	—	—	—	157	—	—	—
HYMNS OF THE TABLE							
"Blessing and Honor and Glory and Power"	137	525	—	147	602	—	—
"Come, Thou Long Expected Jesus"	151	30	122	1–2	183	—	—
"Glory to God, We Give Thanks"	—	—	—	—	—	—	787
SENDING FORTH							
"All Hail the Power of Jesus' Name"	132	328–29	304	142–43	583–34	267	—
"God Our Lord, A King Remaining"	—	—	—	213	—	—	—
"Jesus Shall Reign"	496	530	300	423	233	—	—

Reign of Christ/ Christ the King

Color: White or gold

PRAYER OF CONFESSION

God of Covenant promise,
you anointed Jesus of Nazareth as Christ and Lord
    of all.
Yet we confess we are slow to acknowledge his sov-
    ereign rule.
We have shown allegiance to the powers of this world,
and have failed to be governed by our Lord's justice
    and love.

In your mercy, forgive us.
By your Spirit help us to acknowledge in word and
    deed
the rightful reign of Jesus,
that we may abundantly display in our manner of
    life
the life-changing wonder of his love and justice,
declaring with joyous wonder
the dazzling glory of his majesty,
and the liberating freedom of his truth.

HYMN OF ASSURANCE

"He is King of Kings," *PH,* 153

PSALM 132

METRICAL—
"Call to Mind, O Lord, the Pain," *Psalter for Christian
    Worship,* 153
"God of Jacob, Please Remember," *The Psalter
    Hymnal,* 132
"Rise to Your Resting Place, O Lord," *A New Metrical
    Psalter,* 213
RESPONSORIAL—
"Psalm 132," *The Psalter* (1993), 136
CHORAL/VOCAL—
"Antiphon on Psalm 132," Peter Hallock (SATB), GIA
"O Lord Arise," Thomas Weelkes (SSAATBB),
    Oxford

"Who Shall Ascend the Hill of the Lord," John
    Bertalot (SATB), Augsburg-Fortress

ADDITIONAL SONGS

"He Is Lord," *LUYH,* 150
"Lord, Glorify Your Name," Robert Hartmann,
    LUYH, 44
"Shine, Jesus, Shine," Graham Kendrick, *LUYH,* 50

CHORAL/VOCAL

"Lo, He Comes with Clouds Descending," Paul
    Boehnke (SATB), MorningStar
"The Last Words of David," Randall Thompson
    (SATB), E. C. Schirmer
"Unto Him That Loved Us," Ralph Vaughn Williams
    (unison), *MorningStar Choir Book 1,* CPH

ORGAN

"Lo, He Comes with Clouds Descending," Wilbur
    Held, *Four Advent Hymn Preludes, Set 1,*
    MorningStar

PIANO

"To God Be the Glory," John Carter, *Today's Hymns
    and Songs for Piano*, Hope, 16

HANDBELL

"All Hail the Power of Jesus' Name," Douglas Wagner
    (3–4 octaves), *Festival Piece on CORONATION,*
    Beckenhorst
"Crown Him with Many Crowns," Vicki Smith (3–5
    octaves), Choristers Guild
"Shine, Jesus, Shine," Peggy Betcher (2–3 octaves), Agape

STUDY CATECHISM

For today's questions and answers, see pp. 239–40.

November 27, 2003

October 13, 2003 (Canada)

Joel 2:21–27 — Creation and new creation in a world without fear.

Psalm 126 — A hymn of thanksgiving for God's deliverance of the people.

1 Timothy 2:1–7 — A model for prayers of intercession and thanksgiving.

Matthew 6:25–33 — Creation lives by the grace of God.

Theme(s) of lectionary texts: Giving thanks to God as Creator, Redeemer, and Sustainer.

CALL TO WORSHIP

When the Lord restored our good fortunes,
  we were like those who dream.
**Then our mouths were filled with laughter,
  and our tongues with shouts of joy.**
Then they said among the nations,
  "The Lord has done great things for them."
**The Lord has done great things for us,
  and we are glad indeed!**
Those who sowed in tears
  will reap with songs of joy.
**Those who go out weeping, carrying seed,
  will come again, joyfully shouldering their
  sheaves.**

SUGGESTED HYMNS

	HB	LBW	NCH	PH	RL	TFF	WOV
ENTRANCE/GATHERING HYMNS							
"Come, Ye Thankful People, Come"	525	407	422	551	18	—	—
HYMNS RELATED TO SCRIPTURE							
"Many and Great, O God, Are Thy Things"	—	—	3	271	—	—	794
"We Gather Together"	18	—	421	559	63	—	—
HYMNS OF THE TABLE							
"Come Sing a Song of Harvest"	—	—	—	558	—	—	—
"I Will Give Thanks"	—	—	—	247	—	—	—
SENDING FORTH							
"Now Thank We All Our God"	9	533–44	419	559	63	—	—

Thanksgiving

Color: Green

PRAYER OF CONFESSION

God of all bounty,
you have lavished us with good things
richly and freely to enjoy.
Yet we have failed to honor you
as the source of all these blessings;
we speak and act as though
our blessing were rooted in our own wise efforts.

In mercy, forgive our shameful pride and
ingratitude.
Fill us with the Spirit of thanksgiving,
that all we do and say would demonstrate
our full and glad acknowledgment
that our abundance comes fully from you.
Quicken us to give to others freely and gladly,
even as you have given to us so plentifully,
through Jesus Christ, our Lord.

HYMN OF ASSURANCE

"O What Shall I Render?" *PH,* 557

PSALM 126

METRICAL—
"When God Delivered Israel," *PH,* 237
RESPONSORIAL—
"Psalm 126," Hal Hopson, *The Psalter* (1993), 130
CHORAL/VOCAL—
"When the Lord Turned Again," William Billings
(SATB), Concordia

ADDITIONAL SONGS

"We Will Glorify," Twila Paris, *LUYH,* 55
"What Does the Lord Require?" Jim Strathdee/Linda
White, *LUYH,* 97

CHORAL/VOCAL

"A Song of Praise and Thanksgiving," Allen Pote
(2-part), Hinshaw
"Fear Not, O Land," John Goss (SATB), G. Schirmer
"Sometimes a Light Surprises," Jane Marshall (unison), *Ecumenical Praise,* Agape, 42

ORGAN

"Prelude on KREMSER," Gordon Young, *Hymn
Voluntaries,* Theodore Presser
"Prelude on ROYAL OAK," E. L. Diemer, *Folk Hymn
Sketches,* SMP

PIANO

"For the Beauty of the Earth," Angela Tipps, *Keys of
the Kingdom,* Abingdon, 12

HANDBELL

"Rejoice, Ye Pure in Heart," Karen Buckwalter (3–5
octaves/optional organ or brass and congregational
participation), Flammer

The Study Catechism

DECEMBER 1, 2002   FIRST SUNDAY OF ADVENT

Q. 1.   *What is God's purpose for your life?*

A.   God wills that I should live by the grace of the Lord Jesus Christ, for the love of God, and in the communion of the Holy Spirit.

DECEMBER 8, 2002   SECOND SUNDAY OF ADVENT

Q. 2.   *How do you live by the grace of the Lord Jesus Christ?*

A.   I am not my own. I have been bought with a price. The Lord Jesus Christ loved me and gave himself for me. I entrust myself completely to his care, giving thanks each day for his wonderful goodness.

DECEMBER 15, 2002   THIRD SUNDAY OF ADVENT

Q. 3.   *How do you live for the love of God?*

A.   I love because God first loved me. God loves me in Christ with a love that never ends. Amazed by grace, I no longer live for myself. I live for the Lord who died and rose again, triumphant over death, for my sake. Therefore, I take those around me to heart, especially those in particular need, knowing that Christ died for them no less than for me.

DECEMBER 22, 2002   FOURTH SUNDAY OF ADVENT

Q. 4.   *How do you live in the communion of the Holy Spirit?*

A.   By the Holy Spirit, I am made one with the Lord Jesus Christ. I am baptized into Christ's body, the church, along with all others who confess him by faith. As a member of this community, I trust in God's Word, share in the Lord's Supper, and turn to God constantly in prayer. As I grow in grace and knowledge, I am led to do the good works that God intends for my life.

DECEMBER 29, 2002   FIRST SUNDAY AFTER CHRISTMAS

Q. 5.   *What does a Christian believe?*

A.   All that is promised in the gospel. A summary is found in the Apostles' Creed, which affirms the main content of the Christian faith.

Q. 6.   *What is the first article of the Apostles' Creed?*

A.   "I believe in God the Father Almighty, Maker of heaven and earth."

Q. 7.   *What do you believe when you confess your faith in "God the Father Almighty"?*

A.   That God is a God of love, and that God's love is powerful beyond measure.

JANUARY 5, 2003   SECOND SUNDAY AFTER CHRISTMAS

Q. 8.   *How do you understand the love and power of God?*

A.   Through Jesus Christ. In his life of compassion, his death on the cross, and his resurrection from the dead, I see how vast is God's love for the world—a love that is ready to suffer for our sakes, yet so strong that nothing will prevail against it.

Q. 9.   *What comfort do you receive from this truth?*

A.   This powerful and loving God is the one whose promises I may trust in all the circumstances of my life, and to whom I belong in life and in death.

Q. 10.   *Do you make this confession only as an individual?*

A.   No. With the apostles, prophets, and martyrs, and all those through the ages who have loved the Lord Jesus Christ, and with all who strive to serve him on earth here and now, I confess my faith in the God of loving power and powerful love.

JANUARY 12, 2003   BAPTISM OF OUR LORD

Q. 11.   *When the creed speaks of "God the Father," does it mean that God is male?*

A.   No. Only creatures having bodies can be either male or female. But God has no body, since by nature God is Spirit. Holy Scripture reveals God as a living God beyond all sexual distinctions. Scripture uses diverse images for God, female as well as male. We read, for example, that God will no more forget us than a woman can forget her nursing child (Isa. 49:15). "'As a mother comforts her child, so will I comfort you,' says the Lord" (Isa. 66:13).

Q. 12.   *Why then does the creed speak of God the Father?*

A.   First, because God is identified in the New Testament as the Father of our Lord Jesus Christ. Second, because Jesus Christ is the eternal Son of the Father. Third, because when we are joined to Christ through faith, we are adopted as sons and daughters into the relationship he enjoys with his Father.

JANUARY 19, 2003   SECOND SUNDAY IN ORDINARY TIME

Q. 13.   *When you confess the God and Father of our Lord Jesus Christ, are you elevating men over women and endorsing male domination?*

A.   No. Human power and authority are trustworthy only as they reflect God's mercy and kindness, not abusive patterns of domination. As Jesus taught his disciples, "The greatest among you will be my servant" (Matt. 23:11). God the Father sets the standard by which all misuses of power are exposed and condemned. "Call no one your father on earth," said Jesus, "for you have one Father—the one in heaven" (Matt. 23:9). In fact, God calls women and men to all ministries of the church.

JANUARY 26, 2003   THIRD SUNDAY IN ORDINARY TIME

Q. 14.   *If God's love is powerful beyond measure, why is there so much evil in the world?*

A.   No one can say why, for evil is a terrible abyss beyond all rational explanation. Its ultimate origin is obscure. Its enormity perplexes us. Nevertheless, we boldly affirm that God's triumph over evil is certain. In Jesus Christ, God suffers with us, knowing all our sorrows. In raising him from the dead, God gives new hope to the world. Our Lord Jesus Christ, crucified and risen, is himself God's promise that suffering will come to an end, that death shall be no more, and that all things will be made new.

FEBRUARY 2, 2003   FOURTH SUNDAY IN ORDINARY TIME

Q. 15.   *What do you believe when you say that God is "Maker of heaven and earth"?*

A.   First, that God called heaven and earth, with all that is in them, into being out of nothing simply by the power of God's Word. Second, that by that same power all things are upheld and governed in perfect wisdom, according to God's eternal purpose.

Q. 16.   *What does it mean to say that we human beings are created in the image of God?*

A.   That God created us to live together in love and freedom—with God, with one another, and with the world. Our distinctive capacities—reason, imagination, volition, and so on—are given primarily for this purpose. We are created to be loving companions of others so that something of God's goodness may be reflected in our lives.

FEBRUARY 9, 2003   FIFTH SUNDAY IN ORDINARY TIME

Q. 17.   *What does our creation in God's image reflect about God's reality?*

A.   Our being created in and for relationship is a reflection of the Holy Trinity. In the mystery of the one God, the three divine persons—Father, Son, and Holy Spirit—live in, with, and for one another eternally in perfect love and freedom.

FEBRUARY 16, 2003   SIXTH SUNDAY IN ORDINARY TIME

Q. 18.   *What does our creation in God's image reflect about God's love for us?*

A.   We are created to live wholeheartedly for God. When we honor our Creator as the source of all good things, we are like mirrors reflecting back the great beam of love that God shines on us. We are also created to honor God by showing love toward other human beings.

Q. 19.   *As creatures made in God's image, what responsibility do we have for the earth?*

A.   God commands us to care for the earth in ways that reflect God's loving care for us. We are responsible for ensuring that earth's gifts be used fairly and wisely, that no creature suffers from the abuse of what we are given, and that future generations may continue to enjoy the abundance and goodness of the earth in praise to God.

FEBRUARY 23, 2003   SEVENTH SUNDAY IN ORDINARY TIME

Q. 20.   *Was the image of God lost when we turned from God by falling into sin?*

A.   Yes and no. Sin means that all our relations with others have become distorted and confused. Although we did not cease to be *with* God, our fellow human beings, and other creatures, we did cease to be *for* them; and although we did not lose our distinctive human capacities *completely*, we did lose the ability to use them *rightly*, especially in relation to God. Having ruined our connection with God by disobeying God's will, we are persons with hearts curved in upon ourselves. We have become slaves to the sin of which we are guilty, helpless to save ourselves, and are free, so far as freedom remains, only within the bounds of sin.

MARCH 2, 2003   TRANSFIGURATION OF THE LORD

Q. 21.   *What does it mean to say that Jesus Christ is the image of God?*

A.   Despite our turning from God, God did not turn from us, but instead sent Jesus Christ in the fullness of time to restore our broken humanity. Jesus lived completely for God, by giving himself completely for us, even to the point of dying for us. By living so completely for others, he manifested what he was—the perfect image of God. When by grace we are conformed to him through faith, our humanity is renewed according to the divine image that we lost.

MARCH 9, 2003   FIRST SUNDAY IN LENT

Q. 22.   *What do you understand by God's providence?*

A.   That God not only preserves the world, but also continually attends to it, ruling and sustaining it with wise and benevolent care. God is concerned for every creature: "The eyes of all look to you, and you give them their food in due season. You open your hand, you satisfy the desire of every living thing" (Ps. 145:15). In particular, God provides for the world by bringing good out of evil, so that nothing evil is permitted to occur that God does not bend finally to the good. Scripture tells us, for example, how Joseph said to his brothers, "As for you, you meant evil against me; but God meant it for good, to bring it about that many people should be kept alive, as they are today" (Gen. 50:20).

Q. 23.   *What comfort do you receive by trusting in God's providence?*

A.   The eternal Father of our Lord Jesus Christ watches over me each day of my life, blessing and guiding me wherever I may be. God strengthens me when I am faithful, comforts me when discouraged or sorrowful, raises me up if I fall, and brings me at last to eternal life. Entrusting myself wholly to God's care, I receive the grace to be patient in adversity, thankful in the midst of blessing, courageous against injustice, and confident that no evil afflicts me that God will not turn to my good.

MARCH 16, 2003   SECOND SUNDAY IN LENT

Q. 24.   *What difference does your faith in God's providence make when you struggle against bitterness and despair?*

A.   When I suffer harm or adversity, my faith in God's providence upholds me against bitterness and despair. It reminds me when hope disappears that my heartache and pain are contained by a larger purpose and a higher power than I can presently discern. Even in grief, shame, and loss, I can still cry out to God in lament, waiting on God to supply my needs, and to bring me healing and comfort.

MARCH 23, 2003   THIRD SUNDAY IN LENT

Q. 25.   *Did God need the world in order to be God?*

A.   No. God would still be God, eternally perfect and inexhaustibly rich, even if no creatures had ever been made. Yet without God, all created beings would simply fail to exist. Creatures can neither come into existence, nor continue, nor find fulfillment apart from God. God, however, is self-existent and self-sufficient.

Q. 26.   *Why then did God create the world?*

A.   God's decision to create the world was an act of grace. In this decision, God chose to grant existence to the world simply in order to bless it. God created the world to reveal God's glory, to share the love and freedom at the heart of God's triune being, and to give us eternal life in fellowship with God.

MARCH 30, 2003   FOURTH SUNDAY IN LENT

Q. 27.   *Does your confession of God as Creator contradict the findings of modern science?*

A.   No. My confession of God as Creator answers three questions: Who?, How?, and Why? It affirms that (a) the triune God, who is self-sufficient, (b) called the world into being out of nothing by the creative power of God's Word (c) for the sake of sharing love and freedom. Natural science has much to teach us about the particular mechanisms and processes of nature, but it is not in a position to answer these questions about ultimate reality, which point to mysteries that science as such is not equipped to explore. Nothing basic to the Christian faith contradicts the findings of modern science, nor does anything essential to modern science contradict the Christian faith.

APRIL 6, 2003   FIFTH SUNDAY IN LENT

Q. 28.   *What is the second article of the Apostles' Creed?*

A.   "And I believe in Jesus Christ, his only Son, our Lord. He was conceived by the Holy Spirit, born of the Virgin Mary, suffered under Pontius Pilate, was crucified, dead, and buried. He descended into hell. On the third day he rose again from the dead. He ascended into heaven and is seated at the right hand of the Father. He will come again to judge the living and the dead."

Q. 29.   *What do you believe when you confess your faith in Jesus Christ as "God's only Son"?*

A.   That Jesus Christ is a unique person who was sent to do a unique work.

Q. 30.   *How do you understand the uniqueness of Jesus Christ?*

A.   No one else will ever be God incarnate. No one else will ever die for the sins of the world. Only Jesus Christ is such a person, only he could do such a work, and he in fact has done it.

APRIL 13, 2003   PASSION/PALM SUNDAY

Q. 31.   *What do you affirm when you confess your faith in Jesus Christ as "our Lord"?*

A.   That having been raised from the dead, he reigns with compassion and justice over all things in heaven and on earth, especially those who confess him by faith; and that by loving and serving him above all else, I give glory and honor to God.

Q. 32.   *What do you affirm when you say he was "conceived by the Holy Spirit and born of the Virgin Mary"?*

A.   First, that being born of a woman, Jesus was truly a human being. Second, that our Lord's incarnation was a holy and mysterious event, brought about solely by free divine grace surpassing any human possibilities. Third, that from the very beginning of life on earth, he was set apart by his unique origin for the sake of accomplishing our salvation.

APRIL 20, 2003   EASTER DAY: RESURRECTION OF THE LORD

Q. 33.   *What is the significance of affirming that Jesus is truly God?*

A.   Only God can properly deserve worship. Only God can reveal to us who God is. And only God can save us from our sins. Being truly God, Jesus meets these conditions. He is the proper object of our worship, the self-revelation of God, and the Savior of the world.

Q. 34.   *What is the significance of affirming that Jesus is also truly a human being?*

A.   Being truly human, Jesus entered fully into our fallen situation and overcame it from within. By his pure obedience, he lived a life of unbroken unity with God, even to the point of accepting a violent death. As sinners at war with grace, this is precisely the kind of life we fail to live. When we accept him by faith, he removes our disobedience and clothes us with his perfect righteousness.

Q. 35.   *How can Jesus be truly God and yet also truly human at the same time?*

A.   The mystery of Jesus Christ's divine-human unity passes our understanding; only faith given by the Holy Spirit enables us to affirm it. When Holy Scripture depicts Jesus as someone with divine power, status, and authority, it presupposes his humanity. And when it depicts him as someone with human weakness, neediness, and mortality, it presupposes his deity. We cannot understand how this should be, but we can trust that the God who made heaven and earth is free to become God incarnate and thus to be God with us in this wonderful and awe-inspiring way.

APRIL 27, 2003 SECOND SUNDAY OF EASTER

Q. 36.   *How did God use the people of Israel to prepare the way for the coming of Jesus?*

A.   God made a covenant with Israel, promising that God would be their light and their salvation, that they would be God's people, and that through them all the peoples of the earth would be blessed. Therefore, no matter how often Israel turned away from God, God still cared for them and acted on their behalf. In particular, God sent them prophets, priests, and kings. Each of these was "anointed" by God's Spirit— prophets, to declare God's word; priests, to make sacrifice for the people's sins; and kings, to rule justly in the fear of God, upholding the poor and needy, and defending the people from their enemies.

Q. 37.   *Was the covenant with Israel an everlasting covenant?*

A.   Yes. With the coming of Jesus the covenant with Israel was expanded and confirmed. By faith in him Gentiles were welcomed into the covenant. This throwing open of the gates confirmed the promise that through Israel God's blessing would come to all peoples. Although for the most part Israel has not accepted Jesus as the Messiah, God has not rejected Israel. God still loves Israel, and God is their hope, "for the gifts and the calling of God are irrevocable" (Rom. 11:29). The God who has reached out to unbelieving Gentiles will not fail to show mercy to Israel as the people of the everlasting covenant.

MAY 4, 2003 THIRD SUNDAY OF EASTER

Q. 38.   *Why was the title "Christ," which means "anointed one," applied to Jesus?*

A.   Jesus was the definitive prophet, priest, and king. All of the Lord's anointed in Israel anticipated and led finally to him. In assuming these offices Jesus not only transformed them, but also realized the purpose of Israel's election for the sake of the world.

Q. 39.   *How did Jesus fulfill the office of prophet?*

A.   He was God's Word to a dying and sinful world; he embodied the love he proclaimed. His life, death, and resurrection became the great Yes that continues to be spoken despite how often we have said No. When we receive this Word by faith, Christ himself enters our hearts, that he may dwell in us forever, and we in him.

Q. 40.   *How did Jesus Christ fulfill the office of priest?*

A.   He was the Lamb of God that took away the sin of the world; he became our priest and sacrifice in one. Confronted by our hopelessness in sin and death, Christ interceded by offering himself—his entire person and work—to reconcile us to God.

Q. 41.   *How did Jesus Christ fulfill the office of king?*

A.   He was the Lord who took the form of a servant; he perfected royal power in weakness. With no sword but the sword of righteousness, and no power but the power of love, Christ defeated sin, evil, and death by reigning from the cross.

MAY 11, 2003   **FOURTH SUNDAY OF EASTER**

Q. 42.   *What do you affirm when you say that he "suffered under Pontius Pilate"?*

A.   First, that our Lord was humiliated, rejected, and abused by the temporal authorities of his day, both religious and political. Christ thus aligned himself with all human beings who are oppressed, tortured, or otherwise shamefully treated by those with worldly power. Second, and even more importantly, that our Lord, though innocent, submitted himself to condemnation by an earthly judge so that through him we ourselves, though guilty, might be acquitted before our heavenly Judge.

Q. 43.   *What do you affirm when you say that he was "crucified, dead, and buried"?*

A.   That when our Lord passed through the door of real human death, he showed us that there is no sorrow he has not known, no grief he has not borne, and no price he was unwilling to pay in order to reconcile us to God.

Q. 44.   *What do you affirm when you say that he "descended into hell"?*

A.   That our Lord took upon himself the full consequences of our sinfulness, even the agony of abandonment by God, in order that we might be spared.

Q. 45.   *Why did Jesus have to suffer as he did?*

A.   Because grace is more abundant—and sin more serious—than we suppose. However cruelly we may treat one another, all sin is primarily against God. God condemns sin, yet never judges apart from grace. In giving Jesus Christ to die for us, God took the burden of our sin into God's own self to remove it once and for all. The cross in all its severity reveals an abyss of sin swallowed up by the suffering of divine love.

Q. 46.   *What do you affirm when you say that "on the third day he rose again from the dead"?*

A.   That our Lord could not be held by the power of death. Having died on the cross, he appeared to his followers, triumphant from the grave, in a new, exalted kind of life. In showing them his hands and feet, the one who was crucified revealed himself to them as the Lord and Savior of the world.

Q. 47.   *What do you affirm when you say that "he ascended into heaven and is seated at the right hand of the Father"?*

A.   First, that Christ has gone to be with the Father, hidden except to the eyes of faith. Second, however, that Christ is not cut off from us in the remote past, or in some place from which he cannot reach us, but is present to us here and now by grace. He reigns with divine authority, protecting us, guiding us, and interceding for us until he returns in glory.

Q. 48.   *How do you understand the words that "he will come again to judge the living and the dead"?*

A.   Like everyone else, I too must stand in fear and trembling before the judgment seat of Christ. But the Judge is the one who submitted to judgment for my sake. Nothing will be able to separate me from the love of God in Christ Jesus my Lord. All the sinful failures that cause me shame will perish as through fire, while any good I may have done will be received with gladness by God.

Q. 49.   *Will all human beings be saved?*

A.   No one will be lost who can be saved. The limits to salvation, whatever they may be, are known only to God. Three truths above all are certain. God is a holy God who is not to be trifled with. No one will be saved except by grace alone. And no judge could possibly be more gracious than our Lord and Savior, Jesus Christ.

Q. 50.   *Is Christianity the only true religion?*

A.   Religion is a complex matter. When used as a means to promote self-justification, war-mongering, or prejudice, it is a form of sin. Too often all religions—and not least Christianity—have been twisted in this way. Nevertheless, by grace, despite all disobedience, Christianity offers the truth of the gospel. Although other religions may enshrine various truths, no other can or does affirm the name of Jesus Christ as the hope of the world.

JUNE 15, 2003   TRINITY SUNDAY

Q. 51.   *How will God deal with the followers of other religions?*

A.   God has made salvation available to all human beings through Jesus Christ, crucified and risen. How God will deal with those who do not know or follow Christ, but who follow another tradition, we cannot finally say. We can say, however, that God is gracious and merciful, and that God will not deal with people in any other way than we see in Jesus Christ, who came as the Savior of the world.

Q. 52.   *How should I treat non-Christians and people of other religions?*

A.   As much as I can, I should meet friendship with friendship, hostility with kindness, generosity with gratitude, persecution with forbearance, truth with agreement, and error with truth. I should express my faith with humility and devotion as the occasion requires, whether silently or openly, boldly or meekly, by word or by deed. I should avoid compromising the truth on the one hand and being narrow-minded on the other. In short, I should always welcome and accept these others in a way that honors and reflects the Lord's welcome and acceptance of me.

JUNE 22, 2003   TWELFTH SUNDAY IN ORDINARY TIME

Q. 53.   *What is the third article of the Apostles' Creed?*

A.   "I believe in the Holy Spirit, the holy catholic church, the communion of saints, the forgiveness of sins, the resurrection of the body, and the life everlasting. Amen."

Q. 54.   *What do you believe when you confess your faith in the Holy Spirit?*

A.   Apart from the Holy Spirit, our Lord can neither be loved, nor known, nor served. The Holy Spirit is the personal bond by which Jesus Christ unites us to himself, the teacher who opens our hearts to Christ, and the comforter who leads us to repentance, empowering us to live in Christ's service. As the work of the one Holy Spirit, our love, knowledge, and service of Christ are all inseparably linked.

Q. 55.   *How do we receive the Holy Spirit?*

A.   By receiving the Word of God. As the midwife of the new creation, the Spirit arrives with the Word, brings us to rebirth, and assures us of eternal life. The Spirit nurtures, corrects, and strengthens us with the pure spiritual milk of the Word (1 Pet. 2:2).

JUNE 29, 2003   THIRTEENTH SUNDAY IN ORDINARY TIME

Q. 56.   *What do you mean when you speak of "the Word of God"?*

A.   "Jesus Christ as he is attested for us in Holy Scripture, is the one Word of God which we have to hear and which we have to trust and obey in life and in death" (Barmen Declaration, Article I).

Q. 57.   *Isn't Holy Scripture also the Word of God?*

A.   Yes. Holy Scripture is also God's Word because of its content, its function, and its origin. Its central content is Jesus Christ, the living Word. Its basic function is to deepen our love, knowledge, and service of him as our Savior and Lord. And its ultimate origin is in the Holy Spirit, who spoke through the prophets and apostles, and who inspires us with eager desire for the truths that Scripture contains.

Q. 58.   *Isn't preaching also the Word of God?*

A.   Yes. Preaching and other forms of Christian witness are also God's Word when they are faithful to the witness of Holy Scripture. By the power of the Spirit, preaching actually gives to us what it proclaims—the real presence of our Lord Jesus Christ. Faith comes by hearing God's Word in the form of faithful proclamation.

JULY 6, 2003   FOURTEENTH SUNDAY IN ORDINARY TIME

Q. 59.   *Does the Holy Spirit ever speak apart from God's Word in its written and proclaimed forms?*

A.   Since the Spirit is not given to the church without the Word, true proclamation depends on Scripture. Since the Word cannot be grasped without the Spirit, true interpretation depends on prayer. However, as the wind blows where it will, so may the Spirit speak or work in people's lives in unexpected or indirect ways, yet always according to the Word, never contradicting or diluting it.

Q. 60.   *Aren't people without faith sometimes wiser than those who have faith?*

A.   Yes. The important question for the church is not so much where an insight may come from as the norm by which to test it. Truth is where one finds it, whether inside or outside the church, and whether supporting or contradicting one's own most cherished opinions. Our faithful discernment of what is true, however, depends finally on God's Word as conveyed in Holy Scripture. The church is therefore reformed and always being reformed according to the Word of God.

Q. 61.   *Doesn't modern critical scholarship undermine your belief that Holy Scripture is a form of God's Word?*

A.   No. The methods of modern scholarship are a good servant but a bad master. They are neither to be accepted nor rejected uncritically. Properly used they help us rightly and richly interpret Scripture; improperly used they can usurp the place of faith (or establish an alternative faith). Wise interpreters use these methods in the service of faithful witness and understanding. The methods of modern scholarship remain a useful tool, while Holy Scripture remains reliable in all essential matters of faith and practice.

JULY 13, 2003   FIFTEENTH SUNDAY IN ORDINARY TIME

Q. 62.   *What do you affirm when you speak of "the holy catholic church"?*

A.   The church is the company of all faithful people who have given their lives to Jesus Christ, as he has given and gives himself to them. Since Christ cannot be separated from his people, the church is holy because he is holy, and universal (or "catholic") in significance because his is universal in significance. Despite all its remaining imperfections here and now, the church is called to become ever more holy and catholic, for that is what it already is in Christ.

Q. 63.   *What is the mission of the church?*

A.   The mission of the church is to bear witness to God's love for the world in Jesus Christ.

Q. 64.   *What forms does this mission take?*

A.   The forms are as various as the forms of God's love, yet the center is always Jesus Christ. The church is faithful to its mission when it extends mercy and forgiveness to the needy in ways that point finally to him. For in the end it is always by Christ's mercy that the needs of the needy are met.

Q. 65. *Who are the needy?*

A. The hungry need bread, the homeless need a roof, the oppressed need justice, and the lonely need fellowship. At the same time—on another and deeper level—the hopeless need hope, sinners need forgiveness, and the world needs the gospel. On this level no one is excluded, and all the needy are one. Our mission as the church is to bring hope to a desperate world by declaring God's undying love—as one beggar tells another where to find bread.

JULY 20, 2003   SIXTEENTH SUNDAY IN ORDINARY TIME

Q. 66. *What do you affirm when you speak of the "communion of saints"?*

A. All those who live in union with Christ, whether on earth or with God in heaven, are "saints." Our communion with Christ makes us members one of another. As by his death he removed our separation from God, so by his Spirit he removes all that divides us from each other. Breaking down every wall of hostility, he makes us, who are many, one body in himself. The ties that bind us in Christ are deeper than any other human relationship.

Q. 67. *How do you enter into communion with Christ and so with one another?*

A. By the power of the Holy Spirit as it works through Word and sacrament. Because the Spirit uses them for our salvation, Word and sacrament are called "means of grace." The Scriptures acknowledge two sacraments as instituted by our Lord Jesus Christ—baptism and the Lord's Supper.

JULY 27, 2003   SEVENTEENTH SUNDAY IN ORDINARY TIME

Q. 68. *What is a sacrament?*

A. A sacrament is a special act of Christian worship, instituted by Christ, which uses a visible sign to proclaim the promise of the gospel for the forgiveness of sins and eternal life. The sacramental sign seals this promise to believers by grace and brings them what is promised. In baptism the sign is that of water; in the Lord's Supper, that of bread and wine.

Q. 69. *How do you understand the relationship between the word of promise and the sacramental sign?*

A.   Take away the word of promise, and the water is merely water, or the bread and wine, merely bread and wine. But add water, or bread and wine, to the word of promise, and it becomes a visible word. In this form it does what by grace the word always does: it brings the salvation it promises, and conveys to faith the real presence of our Lord Jesus Christ. The sacraments are visible words which uniquely assure and confirm that no matter how greatly I may have sinned, Christ died also for me and comes to live in me and with me.

Q. 70. *What is the main difference between baptism and the Lord's Supper?*
A.   While I receive baptism only once, I receive the Lord's Supper again and again. Being unrepeatable, baptism indicates not only that Christ died for our sins once and for all, but that by grace we are also united with him once and for all through faith. Being repeatable, the Lord's Supper indicates that as we turn unfilled to him again and again, our Lord continually meets us in the power of the Holy Spirit to renew and deepen our faith.

AUGUST 3, 2003   EIGHTEENTH SUNDAY
                                  IN ORDINARY TIME

Q. 71. *What is baptism?*
A.   Baptism is the sign and seal through which we are joined to Christ.

Q. 72. *What does it mean to be baptized?*
A.   My baptism means that I am joined to Jesus Christ forever. I am baptized into his death and resurrection, along with all who have received him by faith. As I am baptized with water, he baptizes me with his Spirit, washing away all my sins and freeing me from their control. My baptism is a sign that one day I will rise with him in glory, and may walk with him even now in newness of life.

Q. 73. *Are infants also to be baptized?*
A.   Yes. Along with their believing parents, they are included in the great hope of the gospel and belong to the people of God. Forgiveness and faith are both promised to them as gifts through Christ's covenant with his people. These children are therefore to be received into the community by baptism, nurtured in the Word of God, and confirmed at an appropriate time by their own profession of faith.

Q. 74. *Should infants be baptized if their parents or guardians have no relation to the church?*
A.   No. It would be irresponsible to baptize an infant without at least one Christian parent or guardian who promises to nurture the infant in the life of the community and to instruct it in the Christian faith.

Q. 75. *In what name are you baptized?*

A. In the name of the Trinity. After he was raised from the dead, our Lord appeared to his disciples and said to them, "Go and make disciples of all nations, baptizing them in the name of the Father and of the Son and of the Holy Spirit" (Matt. 28:19).

Q. 76. *What is the meaning of this name?*

A. It is the name of the Holy Trinity. The Father is God, the Son is God, and the Holy Spirit is God. And yet they are not three gods, but one God in three persons. We worship God in this mystery.

Q. 77. *What is the Lord's Supper?*

A. The Lord's Supper is the sign and seal by which our communion with Christ is renewed.

Q. 78. *What does it mean to share in the Lord's Supper?*

A. When we celebrate the Lord's Supper, the Lord Jesus Christ is truly present, pouring out his Spirit upon us. By his Spirit, the bread that we break and the cup that we bless share in our Lord's own body and blood. Through them he once offered our life to God; through them he now offers his life to us. As I receive the bread and the cup, remembering that Christ died even for me, I feed on him in my heart by faith with thanksgiving, and enter his risen life, so that his life becomes mine, and my life becomes his, to all eternity.

Q. 79. *Who may receive the Lord's Supper?*

A. All baptized Christians who rejoice in so great a gift, who confess their sins, and who draw near with faith intending to lead a new life, may receive the Lord's Supper. This includes baptized children who have expressed a desire to participate and who have been instructed in the meaning of the sacrament in a way they can understand.

Q. 80. *What do you mean when you speak of "the forgiveness of sins"?*

A. That because of Jesus Christ, God no longer holds my sins against me. Christ alone is my righteousness and my life; Christ alone is my hope.

Grace alone, not my merits, is the basis on which God has forgiven me in him. Faith alone, not my works, is the means by which I receive Christ into my heart, and with him the forgiveness that makes me whole. Christ alone, grace alone, and faith alone bring the forgiveness I receive through the gospel.

Q. 81.   *Does forgiveness mean that God condones sin?*

A.   No. God does not cease to be God. Although God is merciful, God does not condone what God forgives. In the death and resurrection of Christ, God judges what God abhors—everything hostile to love—by abolishing it at the very roots. In this judgment the unexpected occurs: good is brought out of evil, hope out of hopelessness, and life out of death. God spares sinners and turns them from enemies into friends. The uncompromising judgment of God is revealed in the suffering love of the cross.

Q. 82.   *Does your forgiveness of those who have harmed you depend on their repentance?*

A.   No. I am to forgive as I have been forgiven. The gospel is the astonishing good news that while we were yet sinners Christ died for us. Just as God's forgiveness of me is unconditional, and so precedes my confession of sin and repentance, so my forgiveness of those who have harmed me does not depend on their confessing and repenting of their sins. However, when I forgive the person who has done me harm, giving up any resentment or desire to retaliate, I do not condone the harm that was done or excuse the evil of the sin.

Q. 83.   *How can you forgive those who have really hurt you?*

A.   I cannot love my enemies, I cannot pray for those who persecute me, I cannot even be ready to forgive those who have really hurt me, without the grace that comes from above. I cannot be conformed to the image of God's Son, apart from the power of God's Word and Spirit. Yet I am promised that I can do all things through Christ who strengthens me.

AUGUST 31, 2003   **TWENTY-SECOND SUNDAY IN ORDINARY TIME**

Q. 84.   *What do you mean when you speak of "the resurrection of the body"?*

A.   Because Christ lives, we will live also. The resurrection of the body celebrates our eternal value to God as living persons, each one with a unique and distinctive identity. Indeed, the living Savior who goes before us was once heard, seen, and touched in person, after the discovery of his empty tomb. The resurrection of the body means hope for the whole person, because it is in the unity of body and soul, not in soul alone, that I belong in life and in death to my faithful Savior Jesus Christ.

Q. 85.   *What is the nature of resurrection hope?*

A.   Resurrection hope is a hope for the transformation of this world, not a hope for escape from it. It is the hope that evil in all its forms will be utterly eradicated, that past history will be redeemed, and that all things that ever were will be made new. It is the hope of a new creation, a new heaven, and a new earth, in which God is really honored as God, human beings are truly loving, and peace and justice reign on earth.

SEPTEMBER 7, 2003   **TWENTY-THIRD SUNDAY IN ORDINARY TIME**

Q. 86.   *Does resurrection hope mean that we don't have to take action to relieve the suffering of this world?*

A.   No. When the great hope is truly alive, small hopes arise even now for alleviating the sufferings of the present time. Reconciliation—with God, with one another, and with oneself—is the great hope God has given to the world. While we commit to God the needs of the whole world in our prayers, we also know that we are commissioned to be instruments of God's peace. When hostility, injustice, and suffering are overcome here and now, we anticipate the end of all things—the life that God brings out of death, which is the meaning of resurrection hope.

Q. 87.   *What do you affirm when you speak of "the life everlasting"?*

A.   That God does not will to be God without us, but instead grants to us creatures—fallen and mortal as we are—eternal life. Communion with Jesus Christ is eternal life itself. In him we were chosen before the foundation of the world. By him the eternal covenant with Israel was taken up, embodied, and fulfilled. To him we are joined by the Holy Spirit through faith and adopted as children, the sons and daughters of God. Through him we are raised from death to new life. For him we shall live to all eternity.

Q. 88.   *Won't heaven be a boring place?*

A.   No. Heaven is our true home, a world of love. There the Spirit shall be poured out into every heart in perfect love. There the Father and the Son are united in the loving bond of Spirit. There we shall be united with them and one another. There we shall at last see face to face what we now only glimpse as through a distant mirror. Our deepest, truest delights in this life are only a dim foreshadowing of the delights that await us in heaven. "You show me the path of life. In your presence there is fullness of joy; in your right hand are pleasures forevermore" (Ps. 16:11).

| SEPTEMBER 14, 2003 | TWENTY-FOURTH SUNDAY IN ORDINARY TIME |

Q. 89. *What are the Ten Commandments?*

A. The Ten Commandments give a summary of God's law for our lives. They teach us how to live rightly with God and one another.

Q. 90. *Why did God give this law?*

A. After rescuing the people of Israel from their slavery in Egypt, God led them to Mount Sinai, where they received the law through Moses. It was the great charter of liberty for Israel, a people chosen to live in covenant with God and to serve as a light to the nations. It remains the charter of liberty for all who would love, know, and serve the Lord today.

Q. 91. *Why should you obey this law?*

A. Not to win God's love, for God already loves me. Not to earn my salvation, for Christ has earned it for me. Not to avoid being punished, for then I would obey out of fear. With gladness in my heart I should obey God's law out of gratitude, for God has blessed me by it and given it for my well-being.

Q. 92. *What are the uses of God's law?*

A. God's law has three uses. First, it shows me how grievously I fail to live according to God's will, driving me to pray for God's mercy. Second, it functions to restrain even the worst of sinners through the fear of punishment. Finally, it teaches me how to live a life which bears witness to the gospel, and spurs me on to do so.

| SEPTEMBER 21, 2003 | TWENTY-FIFTH SUNDAY IN ORDINARY TIME |

Q. 93. *What is the first commandment?*

A. "You shall have no other gods before me" (Exod. 20:3; Deut. 5:7).

Q. 94. *What do you learn from this commandment?*

A.   No loyalty comes before my loyalty to God. I should worship and serve only God, expect all good from God alone, and love, fear, and honor God with all my heart.

Q. 95.   *What is the second commandment?*
A.   "You shall not make for yourself an idol" (Exod. 20:4; Deut. 5:8).

Q. 96.   *What do you learn from this commandment?*
A.   First, when I treat anything other than God as though it were God, I practice idolatry. Second, when I assume that my own interests are more important than anything else, I make them into idols, and in effect make an idol of myself.

Q. 97.   *What is the third commandment?*
A.   "You shall not make wrongful use of the name of the Lord your God" (Exod. 20:7; Deut. 5:11).

Q. 98.   *What do you learn from this commandment?*
A.   I should use God's name with reverence and awe. God's name is taken in vain when used to support wrong. It is insulted when used carelessly, as in a curse or pious cliche.

SEPTEMBER 28, 2003   TWENTY-SIXTH SUNDAY IN ORDINARY TIME

Q. 99.   *What is the fourth commandment?*
A.   "Remember the Sabbath day, and keep it holy" (Exod. 20:8; Deut. 5:12).

Q. 100.   *What do you learn from this commandment?*
A.   God requires a special day to be set apart so that worship can be at the center of my life. It is right to honor God with thanks and praise, and to hear and receive God's Word, so that I may have it in my heart and on my lips, and put it into practice in my life.

Q. 101.   *Why set aside one day a week as a day of rest?*
A.   First, working people should not be taken advantage of by their employers (Deut. 5:14). My job should not be my tyrant, for my life is more than my work. Second, God requires me to put time aside for the regular study of Holy Scripture and for prayer, not only by myself but also with others, not least those in my own household.

Q. 102.   *Why do we Christians usually gather on the first day of the week?*
A.   In worshiping together on the first day of the week, we celebrate our

Lord's resurrection, so that the new life Christ brought us might begin to fill our whole lives.

Q. 103. What is the best summary of the first four commandments?

A. These teach me how to live rightly with God. Jesus summed them up with the commandment he called the first and greatest: "You shall love the Lord your God with all your heart, and with all your soul, and with all your mind" (Matt. 22:37; Deut. 6:5).

OCTOBER 5, 2003 — TWENTY-SEVENTH SUNDAY IN ORDINARY TIME

Q. 104. What is the fifth commandment?

A. "Honor your father and your mother" (Exod. 20:12; Deut. 5:16).

Q. 105. What do you learn from this commandment?

A. Though I owe reverence to God alone, I owe genuine respect to my parents, both my mother and father. God wills me to listen to them, be thankful for the benefits I receive from them, and be considerate of their needs, especially in old age.

Q. 106. Are there limits to your obligation to obey them?

A. Yes. No mere human being is God. Blind obedience is not required, for everything should be tested by loyalty and obedience to God. When it seems as though I should not obey, I should always be alert to possible self-deception on my part and should pray that we may all walk in the truth of God's will.

Q. 107. What is the sixth commandment?

A. "You shall not murder" (Exod. 20:13; Deut. 5:17).

Q. 108. What do you learn from this commandment?

A. God forbids anything that harms my neighbor unfairly. Murder or injury can be done not only by direct violence but also by an angry word or a clever plan, and not only by an individual but also by unjust social institutions. I should honor every human being, including my enemy, as a person made in God's image.

Q. 109. What is the seventh commandment?

A. "You shall not commit adultery" (Exod. 20:14; Deut. 5:18).

Q. 110. What do you learn from this commandment?

A. God requires fidelity and purity in sexual relations. Since love is God's great gift, God expects me not to corrupt it, or confuse it with momentary desire or the selfish fulfillment of my own pleasures. God forbids all sexual immorality, whether in married or single life.

<table>
<tr><td>OCTOBER 12, 2003</td><td>TWENTY-EIGHTH SUNDAY
IN ORDINARY TIME</td></tr>
</table>

Q. 111. What is the eighth commandment?

A. "You shall not steal" (Exod. 20:15; Deut. 5:19).

Q. 112. What do you learn from this commandment?

A. God forbids all theft and robbery, including schemes, tricks, or systems that unjustly take what belongs to someone else. God requires me not to be driven by greed, not to misuse or waste the gifts I have been given, and not to distrust the promise that God will supply my needs.

Q. 113. What is the ninth commandment?

A. "You shall not bear false witness against your neighbor" (Exod. 20:16; Deut. 5:20).

Q. 114. What do you learn from this commandment?

A. God forbids me to damage the honor or reputation of my neighbor. I should not say false things against anyone for the sake of money, favor, or friendship, for the sake of revenge, or for any other reason. God requires me to speak the truth, to speak well of my neighbor when I can, and to view the faults of my neighbor with tolerance when I cannot.

<table>
<tr><td>OCTOBER 19, 2003</td><td>TWENTY-NINTH SUNDAY
IN ORDINARY TIME</td></tr>
</table>

Q. 115. Does this [ninth] commandment forbid racism and other forms of negative stereotyping?

A. Yes. In forbidding false witness against my neighbor, God forbids me to be prejudiced against people who belong to any vulnerable, different, or disfavored social group. Jews, women, homosexuals, racial and ethnic minorities, national enemies are among those who have suffered terribly from being subjected to the slurs of social prejudice. Negative stereotyping is a form of falsehood that invites actions of humiliation, abuse, and violence as forbidden by the commandment against murder.

Q. 116. What is the tenth commandment?

A.   "You shall not covet what is your neighbor's" (Exod. 20:17; Deut. 5:21).

Q. 117. *What do you learn from this commandment?*

A.   My whole heart should belong to God alone, not to money or the things of this world. "Coveting" means desiring something wrongfully. I should not resent the good fortune or success of my neighbor or allow envy to corrupt my heart.

OCTOBER 26, 2003	THIRTIETH SUNDAY IN ORDINARY TIME

Q. 118. *What is the best summary of the last six commandments?*

A.   These teach me to live rightly with my neighbor. Jesus summed them up with the commandment which is like the greatest one about loving God: "You shall love your neighbor as yourself" (Matt. 22:39; Lev. 19:18).

Q. 119. *Can you obey these commandments perfectly?*

A.   No. I am at once a *forgiven* sinner and a forgiven *sinner*. As a sinner without excuse, I fail to obey these commandments as God requires. "For whoever keeps the whole law but fails in one point has become accountable for all of it" (James 2:10). I should not adjust the law to my failures, nor reduce my failures before God. Yet there is more grace in God than sin in me. While I should not cease to pray to God for mercy, I can be confident that God is forgiving and that I will be set free from all my sins. By grace I can confess my sins, repent of them, and grow in love and knowledge day by day.

NOVEMBER 2, 2003	THIRTY-FIRST SUNDAY IN ORDINARY TIME

Q. 120. *What is prayer?*

A.   Prayer means calling upon God whose Spirit is always present with us. In prayer we approach God with reverence, confidence, and humility. Prayer involves both addressing God in praise, confession, thanksgiving, and supplication, and listening for God's Word within our hearts. When we adore God, we are filled with wonder, love, and praise before God's heavenly glory, not least when we find it hidden in the cross of Golgotha. When confessing our guilt to God, we ask for forgiveness with humble and sorry hearts, remembering that God is gracious as well as holy. When giving thanks to God, we acknowledge God's great goodness, rejoicing in God for all that is so wonderfully provided for us. Finally, when calling upon God to hear our requests, we affirm that God draws near in every need and sorrow of life, and ask God to do so again.

Q. 121. *What is the purpose of prayer?*

A.   Prayer brings us into communion with God. The more our lives are rooted in prayer, the more we sense how wonderful God is in grace, purity, majesty, and love. Prayer means offering our lives completely to God, submitting ourselves to God's will, and waiting faithfully for God's grace. Through prayer God frees us from anxiety, equips us for service, and deepens our faith.

Q. 122. *How does God respond to our prayers?*

A.   God takes all our prayers into account, weighing them with divine wisdom, and responding to them by a perfect will. Although for the time being God's answers may seem beyond our understanding, or sometimes even bitter, we know nonetheless that they are always determined by the grace of our Lord Jesus Christ. God answers our prayers, particularly for temporal blessings, only in ways that are compatible with the larger purposes of God's glory and our salvation. Communion with God is finally the answer within the answers to all our prayers.

Q. 123. *What encourages us to pray each day?*

A.   The God who has adopted us as children is the God who encourages and commands us to pray. When we pray, we respond with love to that greater love which meets us from above. Before we enter into prayer, God is ready to grant all that we need. We may turn to God with confidence each day, not because we are worthy, but simply because of God's grace. By praying we acknowledge that we depend on grace for all that is good, beautiful, life-giving, and true.

NOVEMBER 9, 2003   THIRTY-SECOND SUNDAY IN ORDINARY TIME

Q. 124. *What prayer serves as our rule or pattern?*

A.   Our rule or pattern is found in the Lord's Prayer, which Jesus taught to his disciples:
>   Our Father in heaven,
>   hallowed be your name,
>   your kingdom come,
>   your will be done,
>   on earth as in heaven.
>   Give us today our daily bread.

> Forgive us our sins
> as we forgive those who sin against us.
> Save us from the time of trial
> and deliver us from evil.
> For the kingdom, the power, and the
> glory are yours
> now and for ever. Amen.

These words express everything that we may desire and expect from God.

Q. 125. What is the design of the Lord's Prayer?

A.   The Lord's Prayer falls into two parts, preceded by an opening address, and concluded by a "doxology" or word of praise. Each part consists of three petitions. The first part concerns God's glory; the second part, our salvation. The first part involves our love for God; the second part, God's love for us. The petitions in part one will not be fulfilled perfectly until the life to come; those in part two relate more directly to our present needs here and now.

Q. 126. What is meant by addressing God as "Our Father in heaven"?

A.   By addressing God as "our Father," we draw near with childlike reverence and place ourselves securely in God's hands. Although God is certainly everywhere, God is said to exist and dwell "in heaven." For while God is free to enter into the closest relationship with the creature, God does not belong to the order of created beings. "Heaven" is the seat of divine authority, the place from which God reigns in glory and brings salvation to earth. Our opening address expresses our confidence that we rest securely in God's intimate care and that nothing on earth lies beyond the reach of God's grace.

NOVEMBER 16, 2003

THIRTY-THIRD SUNDAY IN ORDINARY TIME

Q. 127. What is meant by the first petition, "Hallowed be your name"?

A.   This petition is placed first, because it comprehends the goal and purpose of the whole prayer. The glory of God's name is the highest concern in all that we pray and do. God's "name" stands for God's being as well as for God's attributes and works. When we pray for this name to be "hallowed," we ask that we and all others will know and glorify God as God really is and that all things will be so ordered that they serve God truly for God's sake.

Q. 128. What is meant by the second petition, "Your kingdom come"?

A.   We are asking God to come and rule among us through faith, love, and justice—and not through any one of them without the others. We pray for both the church and the world, that God will rule in our hearts through faith, in our personal relationships through love, and in our institutional affairs through justice. We ask especially that the gospel will not be withheld from us, but rightly preached and received. We pray that the church will be upheld and increase, particularly when in distress; and that all the world will more and more submit to God's reign, until that day when crying and pain are no more, and we live forever with God in perfect peace.

Q. 129. *What is meant by the third petition, "Your will be done, on earth as in heaven"?*

A. Of course, God's will is always done and will surely come to pass, whether we desire it or not. But the phrase "on earth as in heaven" means that we ask for the grace to do God's will on earth in the way that it is done in heaven—gladly and from the heart. We thus ask that all opposition to God's will might be removed from the earth, and especially from our own hearts. We ask for the freedom to conform our desires and deeds more fully to God's, so that we might be completely delivered from our sin. We yield ourselves, in life and in death, to God's will.

Q. 130. *What is meant by the fourth petition, "Give us today our daily bread"?*

A. We ask God to provide for all our needs, for we know that God, who cares for us in every area of our life, has promised us temporal as well as spiritual blessings. God commands us to pray each day for all that we need and no more, so that we will learn to rely completely on God. We pray that we will use what we are given wisely, remembering especially the poor and the needy. Along with every living creature we look to God, the source of all generosity, to bless us and nourish us, according to the divine good pleasure.

NOVEMBER 23, 2003   **REIGN OF CHRIST/
                                           CHRIST THE KING**

Q. 131. *What is meant by the fifth petition, "Forgive us our sins as we forgive those who sin against us"?*

A. We pray that a new and right spirit will be put within us. We ask for the grace to treat others, especially those who harm us, with the same mercy that we have received from God. We remember that not one day goes by when we do not need to turn humbly to God for our own forgiveness. We know that our reception of this forgiveness can be blocked by our unwillingness to forgive others. We ask that we will not delight in doing evil, nor in avenging any wrong, but that we will survive all cruelty without bitterness and overcome evil with good, so that our hearts will be knit together with the mercy and forgiveness of God.

Q. 132. *What is meant by the final petition, "Save us from the time of trial and deliver us from evil"?*

A. We ask God to protect us from our own worst impulses and from all external powers of destruction in the world. We ask that we might not yield to despair in the face of seemingly hopeless circumstances. We pray for the grace to remember and believe, despite our unbelief, that no matter how bleak the world may sometimes seem, there is nonetheless a depth of love which is deeper than our despair, and that this love—which delivered Israel from slavery in Egypt and raised our Lord Jesus from the dead—will finally swallow up forever all that would now seem to defeat it.

Q. 133. *What is meant by the closing doxology, "For the kingdom, the power, and the glory are yours now and for ever"?*

A. We give God thanks and praise for the kingdom more powerful than all enemies, for the power perfected in the weakness of love, and for the glory that includes our well-being and that of the whole creation, both now and to all eternity. We give thanks and praise to God as made known through Christ our Lord.

Q. 134. *What is meant by the word "Amen"?*

A. "Amen" means "so be it" or "let it be so." It expresses our complete confidence in the triune God, the God of the covenant with Israel as fulfilled through our Lord Jesus Christ, who make no promise that will not be kept, and whose steadfast love and mercy endures forever.